Waltzing a Two-Step

Reckoning
Family, Faith, and Self

DAN JUDAY

 Calling Card Books

www.CallingCardBooks.com

Cover design, interior design, and editing
by Calling Card Books.
www.CallingCardBooks.com
Sacramento, California

Copyright © 2021 Dan Juday

First Edition
Paperback ISBN: 978-1-7354845-3-2
E-book ISBN: 978-1-7354845-4-9

Library of Congress Control Number: 2021936674

Printed in the United States of America

for
Woodrow

Acknowledgments

I ASK FOR THE FORBEARANCE OF MY SIBLINGS, WHOSE NAMES appear in this book. I found it impossible to tell my story without including you. Nevertheless, I have tried to keep the focus on me, not you. I hope I haven't discomfited you.

I have changed the names of several true-to-life characters out of that same concern: this is my story, not theirs. The thin veil of anonymity that name-change provides is meant to honor that distinction.

I would never have completed this manuscript without the animating encouragement of Barbara Taylor, who told me to go on—more than once. It was essential to my effort.

I also owe my gratitude to Marta Zarrella and Kate Zarrella, the publisher and creative director at Calling Card Books. They responded to my initial query with warmth, and they have provided excellent insight, expert advice, and remarkable patience throughout.

PART I

Family

I think you have to acknowledge
that the story that makes the most honorable effort
is still not going to get at everybody's truth.
But the effort is worthy.

—*Author, Alice Munro*

'An Interview With Alice Munro,'
Virginia Quarterly Review Spring 2013

One

THE FIRST IMAGES OF THE WORLD SUFFICIENTLY CLEAR TO CITE as my earliest memories contain furniture legs and linoleum. It was crawling before walking, looking at things while on all fours that frames these memories. I was told I spoke in complete sentences before learning to balance myself on two feet. That is not my sense of things. I remember a reticence to speak, a happiness with the quiet, a caution in the face of all the adaptations being demanded.

When I was a toddler old enough to observe things from the proper vantage point of *homo erectus*, those images formed a broad and varied plane stitched together from dark floor boards, flowered carpets held down by brass tacks, and a doorsill piled with muddy boots. The world flowed seamlessly through that doorway and across a front porch, down cold cement steps to a red toy wagon, fresh-mown grass, and grey and flinty driveway gravel that hurt the hands and knees and feet. Everything was under the influence of gravity, and gravity demanded all of my attention if I was to move about. Downward was the strongest and surest contact with the world whose unraveling was my task. Even when I mastered the art of walking, what I recall are the things I saw looking between my feet.

The center of that flat and unchartered world was the threshold between the kitchen linoleum and the wooden floor of the parlor, where I was put to rest in the afternoon. There was quiet peace in the parlor. I loved its idleness and gloom. My sister Lee Ann was a year older than me. She begrudged that I should have come along to siphon off so much attention. My playpen was shoved into a protective corner to shield me on at least two sides from her efforts to avenge my presence.

In one of our peaceful moments, both of us seated inside a large tractor tire filled with sand, I looked down onto the lovely, variegated granules falling from my shovel onto my bare knees and hers. I was mesmerized by their smooth flow through my short, splayed fingers. Attached to this memory is the feel of warm sun deliciously heating my head and shoulders. My vision tilts upward, perhaps in gratitude for the warmth, and I can see even now the bright and searing sunlight reflected off the clapboard, whitewashed barn beyond the drive. My sister is looking at it, too. We are both aware of the whiteness of its wall and aware that each other sees it. It is my first moment of self-awareness, reflected in my sister's eyes.

The barn that so dazzled me that summer afternoon was part of the Jessie Miller Farm in Tipton County, Indiana. It was there I was brought home after being delivered of my mother in Mercy Hospital in nearby Elwood. Her mother, my grandmother, was a nurse on staff there, and she had pride of place in the delivery room, as she had with my sister before me. Elwood was my mother's territory. Tipton County was my father's.

I was born in 1948, one small cipher in the post-war baby boom. Three years earlier, the Army Air Force had returned my father, trained as a "ninety-day wonder" pilot and now deemed surfeit with the war winding down, to his family farm in Tipton County where they determined he would be needed to jump-start the country's post-war revival. Within a few months, he married his high school sweetheart, an Irish-Catholic and an Elwood girl, over the protestations of his Calvinist father. After the wedding, my mother attempted a stint at cohabitation with her in-laws in the family farmhouse. It proved unworkable. Within six months, the young couple relocated their "mixed marriage" to the nearby Jessie Miller Farm to take up the work of tenant-farming. Within less than four months, my sister joined them. Almost exactly a year later, I came along.

Tipton County, like Elwood – that other country two miles east on Highway 28 – was a place of white wooden houses, each set among a remarkably similar collection of multiple outbuildings in proper rectangular relation to the four points of the compass. A grid of gravel crossroads delineated their square-cornered properties. In late summer, these ran between fields laden with green-leaved crops. In winter, post-harvest, they simply stretched out across dun-colored, abandoned fields shorn of their yields. Deadly dangerous highways interlaced small, thriving market towns like Elwood and Tipton, each with a downtown core of ornately decorated storefronts shouldered together around imposing town halls capped with glimmering domes. Women were stockinged and girdled. Men, whether in suits or bibbed overalls, wore hats. Among the era's unheralded strengths were its captive media markets and a since-lost comfort with unstructured time.

All this was beyond my ken, of course. I was limited to what I observed, mostly in silence: the sounds and smells of a Hoosier farmstead. I made careful study of the opening creak and closing slam of the screen-door, eager to see my father walk through. I listened from the parlor to my mother's kitchen noises, my sister following her dutifully, imitating her earnestness. I listened to the feeder lid banging shut when a sated sow pulled out her snout and to the squeals of distressed and feuding gilts. I smelled the pungent tang of fresh hog shit. I heard the whir and clip of the push-mower blades engaging with the drive chain, and I learned to love the Edenic aroma of new-mown grass. There was the Doppler rise and fall of cars whooshing by in high gear and the gritty cloud of gravel dust thrown left and right in their wake, rolling across the front lawn like a powdery, passing plague.

All this played out in no particular sequence, with no real urgency, and for no discernible objective. Or so it seemed. Still anxiously reading the clues surrounding me, lacking the proper words to control what befell me, I was enwrapped in a languorous waiting, only to be startled now and then by the world's immediacy. The gaps between the bars of my playpen were wide enough that one day my sister finally managed a one-armed intrusion, potato peeler in hand, to exact her revenge for my existence. She made glancing contact with my skull and set me wailing. My mother dropped her dishtowel to lift her infant son, convulsed and bloody-faced, from the playpen. Washing me down, she discovered a small ogee-curved cut high on my forehead, font of so much bleeding. I was too young to recognize the momentary moral advantage over my sister, caught up as I was in looking down into the terror of my own blood.

Across the county line, my Grandma Boyle's house in Elwood sat in a denser, darker place. Elwood emerged out of a 19th Century natural gas boom, built along a railroad line and atop a street plan formed by the intersection of two state highways running true north-south and true east-west. As with the gravel roads of Tipton County, everything in Elwood was square with the world. Above and below Main Street were two mirrored sets of lettered streets: South A, B, C, and so on down the alphabet; and North A, B, C, and so on up the alphabet. Across this axis lay a single set of numbered streets running from First Street on the west end of town to 28th Street on the east end, reading left to right on a properly held map. It was a place of modest, front-gabled clapboard houses, their porches trimmed in wooden jigsaw flourishes, nearly all of which bore "north" or "south" addresses: 148 South A and 148 North A; 520 South 19th and 520 North 19th. The only exceptions sat on Highway 28, named Main Street, in honor of its aspirations. Grandma lived on East Main, where two-story brick homes, snug behind deep lawns and hydrangea bushes, housed the town's doctors, lawyers, and merchants.

Everyone seemed content with this pragmatic — if featureless — streetnaming system. It was serviceable and self-obvious. It suggested a general consensus that there was no one from the town worth memorializing. And it offered a kind of ahistorical absolution for the eradication of an earlier, indigenous population.

When my grandmother's marriage fell apart in the 1930s, she moved herself and her daughter Jane, my mother, from their now-broken Chicago home to her parents' house on Main Street. Grandma's father, youngest of an Irish immigrant family, was an architect and engineer, and he numbered among the town's quasi-elite. They had moved to Elwood from Chicago in search of commissioned work soon after the stock-market crash of

1929. Mom was 12 when she moved down. Once she moved in, Grandma effectively ceded responsibility for her only child to her parents. For all three generations, Elwood was a kind of fall from grace. Nevertheless, they somehow maintained an air of "citiness" about them.

Visits to Grandma Boyle usually centered around the mid-day meal. She put real butter on her table. I loved to slather it on the potatoes and the white bread and, if I could persuade her, on her sweet and crumbly homemade desserts. Her table was a happy place in spite of all the admonitions about not leaning on our elbows and waiting to speak until we were spoken to. My mother seemed amused by Grandmas' attempts to put manners on us, and we understood these were to be borne with outward grace and inner amusement.

Grandma had copies of *Life* and *Look* magazines to pore over and a box of pencils and drawing paper to distract us. My great grandfather had the most marvelous utensils – calipers with wickedly dangerous points, clear plastic rulers scored to measure the smallest increments, and wooden folding yardsticks with dull brass hinges. His pencils were like those my mother used throughout her life, hard-leaded and sharply pointed. They left a thin, delicate, nearly illegible script. I would design bridges and rooftops, and other contraptions for Grandma to critique. She would laugh and shake her head without ever actually commenting on much of anything.

My brother Glenn now made for three of us, and Grandma Boyle feared each was liable to death from wandering into the traffic on Main Street, jumping from her front porch onto her shrubbery, or falling through the open coal bin doors at the back of the house. In truth, we had more than once pried those doors open to thrill at the pungent, black-sooted coal chute that led to who knew what inferno. An alley ran along one side of the house, and on the other side, there was a narrow walkway between her house and Frieda's, a retired lady who tatted lace on her front porch in the summer and who forbore our frequent visits with grace. There was an intriguing attic on the second floor, but we were not allowed to go up there because the stairway steps made a right-angle turn, and Grandma said she worried we would fall to our deaths. Many years later, I discovered her brother, my great-uncle Jim, leaving behind his own failed marriage and bringing with him his out-of-control thirst for gin, had secreted hundreds of empty liquor bottles behind the lathe-work of the attic walls. These, I'm certain, worried my grandmother more than the bend in the stairs.

These were the limits on our wandering when my mother left us alone with Grandma. We often stayed inside where my great grandfather Louis Diamond, when he was still alive, smoked his pipe and stared at us, bemused and unsure what to say. In the foyer off the sitting room, the west window was diamond-shaped, in honor of the family name, with panes of colored glass: a purple diamond set in its center surrounded by smaller squares running diagonal borders in amber, ruby, emerald, and cobalt. With the front window sheers and Venetian blinds nearly always drawn, this deep-hued totem dominated the afternoon mood. There was the heady odor of the humidor with Great Grandpa's tobacco. The haze of pipe smoke added to the gloom.

When Mom and my siblings were there, Grandma was on hostess footing, cooking a meal for us on her day off. But when I was older, stronger, and of more use, I would sometimes be taken to Elwood to spend the night alone with her so I could help with chores too demanding for an older, obese woman with fallen arches and a two-pack-a-day habit. On those visits, I cherished our shared intimacy. On the last day of the visit, she usually had to prepare for an evening hospital shift while I waited for Mom to collect me.

I would watch her, dressed in her slip in the dark parlor under the round Rafael reproduction over the mantel, standing in front of an ironing board. In her cheery moments, she recited for me the names that had accrued to her over her lifetime: Mary Marvel Magdalene Diamond Boyle. She always wore a rough penitential scapular. It would be tossed around to her back, the coarse fabric dangling just below the laced top of her slip. She was ambidextrous, able to have either hand work the iron back and forth, pressing starch into a clean uniform, while the other moved a cigarette in and out of her pursed lips. Between smoky exhalations, she recited what she called her "ejaculations." These were short spiritual exhortations that she believed were earning her a reduced stay in purgatory. *O, Lord Jesus, Son of God, have mercy on me, a sinner.* By accumulating these special indulgences while she was still alive, her plan was to reach heaven on a much shorter trajectory than otherwise.

That in her poor health and solitary state she was still going to the hospital night after night for a minimum wage, to tend to the sick and dying, sharing with them her optimism about the compensations of life after death—this surely had already earned her a direct path to that heaven she so ardently sought.

I have a few photographs taken on my parents' wedding day. They were married on April 29, 1946, at a time when the Catholic Church would not allow weddings inside the sanctuary if one in the couple wasn't Catholic. They were married by the priest in his rectory. The wedding couple in the black-and-white photos dressed in what we would call business-formal today. Mom wearing a light-colored, fitted suit, white gloves, and a tallish, black cocked hat with a trace of netting that suggests a veil. Dad, in a double-breasted grey suit, sports a boutonnière looking stunningly young and almost impishly happy.

In a separate photo taken that same day, from that same angle in the alley looking onto Great Grandpa Diamond's porch in Elwood, Dad's parents, Mom's mother, and Mom's grandparents pose as the rest of the wedding party. Grandma Juday stands tall and, aware of the camera, tries a faint smile. At her side is my dark-browed, square-jawed Grandpa Juday. Both are well-dressed and have an impatient air that seems to say, "we should be doing something useful."

Grandma Boyle, short, round, and oval-faced, is in the center. She pulls her in-laws closer toward her, crooking Grandpa and Grandma Juday's elbows with each hand. She smiles, as if happy to disappear between them. It looks as though she is trying to create a bond between her parents and her in-laws while she slips away. My great grandparents, the Diamonds, look unfazed by the moment, and indeed, Great Grandpa's composed and inscrutable face is looking away from the camera that everyone else is smiling for. The only enthusiasm in the photos is that shared by the newlyweds.

The other sphere of extended family life centered on my paternal grandparents' kitchen table on their farm in Tipton County. I have only a few early memories of sitting there. I remember dairy-rich and broth-heavy meals served on a patterned oilcloth. I remember my grandfather taking up the pitcher of non-homogenized milk brought in fresh that morning from the dairy barn. He stands up to finish it off, chugging the heavy cream that has risen, unfiltered, to the neck of the jar. The image was frequently recalled by my mother, too. It became a familiar trope in her portfolio of stories about the hard adjustments she had to make to rural life. Dad would later cite the image as he slowly came to appreciate the price his wife had paid in her metamorphosis during those early days.

In the 1920s, about the time my grandparents married, the Ku Klux Klan, resurgent in an era of heavy post-war immigration, established its national headquarters in Elwood. I once asked my father what he knew about that. We were standing in one of the fields behind his boyhood home. He recounted how his father told him that he was visited one day by Klansmen recruiting the better citizenry of Madison County to stand up against the influx of foreigners and colored people. Dad looked down to the furrows at his feet as he recalled that conversation. A small, pursed smile settled on his face, one that sought to diminish the vileness of what was being proposed – that my grandfather suit up and march with them in a campaign to drive the Negroes and the Catholics out. Dad told me Grandpa demurred, told me he said as little as possible. Was that talk he had with Grandpa after Dad met Mom? Or did they talk before he met Mom, and did he start seeing her anyway? He tried to sound mildly amused. "Just a bunch of 'good ole boys,' your Grandpa called them. They meant no harm."

Grandpa Juday made his initial opposition to the marriage clear, but as time passed, the relationship between the two generations grew even colder. I suspect it was triggered by Dad's conversion to Catholicism, somewhere about the time I was getting ready for my First Holy Communion. The breach, whatever its cause and however intense its depth, never healed. In her last years, my mother alluded once to her final conversation with this man, her father-in-law. She said he asked her for forgiveness as he lay on his deathbed, for his years of disapproval. I didn't ask what she said in response. She didn't volunteer it in her recounting. She lived by the belief that one never has to eat words that were never uttered. Perhaps her silence in that moment at Grandpa's bedside was all the compensation she needed.

There were occasional gatherings with the Juday aunts, uncles, and cousins. At a minimum, there was a summer baseball game in the farm lot each year, the annual rally for manly tenacity. When they were our age, we were reminded, Dad and my uncles wore no shoes all summer. "We walked in our bare feet on the gravel roads," Dad would say as he threw his best hardball at me. My cousins always rose to the bait, running as fast, throwing as hard, and leaping as high for a fly-ball as they could. Details of a Spartan childhood piled up in a running dialogue. They chuckled over deprivations and miseries, carefully enumerating them like so many earned merit badges. My efforts were focused on surreptitiously avoiding embarrassment, in a state of utter dread in the far outfield, fervently hoping no one hit a fly-ball in my direction.

And there was the infrequent, stiff distribution of Christmas gifts to the cousins on New Year's Day. We'd sit looking out at the Sears and Roebuck trim on Grandma's and Grandpa's wrap-around porch, each of us holding our present – sometimes one gift to be shared among all siblings – until we were instructed to open it. Their tree never looked like a real Christmas tree. The flow of events was more like pageant than party. The awkward afternoons were preceded by my mother's admonishing us not to ask for food and my grandmother's receiving us with, "Oh, dear, I hope you've eaten."

My cousins spoke in the same laconic tones as did my Grandpa, jaws slightly clenched and voices subdued for minimal inflection. The onus fell on the listener to make out what was being said. They were naturally close to each other and were their own frequent playmates. They were uncertain of what to make of our branch of the family tree. They often instructed us how to act. Their advice made no space for invention or chance, tending toward reprimand, even at their tender ages.

I remember one afternoon in my Aunt Marge's living room, sitting among them, embarrassed by the smell of my wet wool pullover. I was on her large sofa. The furniture was widely spaced for adult conversation and left me awkwardly shuffling back and forth across the wall-to-wall carpet, alternately creating distance from, then proximity to, those present as I searched for a conversational thread. Adults entered the room in conversing pairs, and I moved down one pillow cushion at a time to make room until I ran out of space. I sat on the armrest until Aunt Marge admonished me against it. The talk meandered about for a fresh topic and was cut short by another well-intentioned aunt singling me out for a summation of my school year thus far. Relief came with the announcement that food was on the kitchen table, and we were to serve ourselves. Once the pie and cakes were eaten, a sugar high kicked in. For several gleeful minutes, we cousins took turns dashing up and sliding down the basement stairs, and a kind of fellowship settled around the house. Those are the moments I remember now, more than the wary scrutiny.

Grandpa set the bar for scrutiny. He was suspicious of everyone around him. Suspicion permeated nearly every sphere of his life. He brought it to church on Sunday morning, listening carefully to the preacher for any unorthodoxy. When he found any, he removed himself, his family, and his generous tithing to a new congregation where he would monitor the new preacher for his particular anathema. He brought the same wariness to family relations. He fell out with his sister – the mysterious Aunt Ruby – over some obscure dispute. In her dotage, penniless, she was forced to move into the house where Dad was born, part of extended family holdings. It was less than a quarter-mile from where my grandparents were then living. Consequently the house, like Aunt Ruby herself, was off-limits. I never met the woman. Dad and Mom retired to that very house and lived out their later years there. When I came as an adult to visit them, Dad would tell stories about growing up in the house. He always seemed surprised that I didn't remember it from my childhood.

The falling out between Dad and his father was a deep wound for the clan. The damage never really healed. My grandfather's final services were in a funeral parlor; he had run out of churches. After his casket closed, after the slow cortege across town to the Protestant graveyard on South 13ᵗʰ Street, after we lowered him into the ground, we gathered at what was suddenly now just Grandma's house. Grandpa had built the comfortable ranch on North 9ᵗʰ Street, near friends and a corner store, as a concession to Grandma on their retirement from farming. In the pastel green living room, a large and formal party sat around tables attended by caterers. The company was composed of older, distant relatives I would hardly have known. I sat in the kitchen with the rest of my cousins, most of us in our 30s or 40s. The usual awkwardness obtained, but it was diminished by the novelty of gathering together for the first time in years. I went into the living room to greet my Grandmother.

She seemed surprised to see me and said, "Danny. I haven't seen you all day."

"Grandma, that's because you still have me sitting at the kiddie table."

My cousins broke into loud and sustained laughter. I suspect it came from the same niggling sense of belittlement I felt and from our shared relief over the end of the tyranny of righteousness that was my Grandfather's sword and shield. They wouldn't have said it. They were raised within the sphere of his heavy influence.

They would have felt closer to him than I did. But when the first guffaw broke out, I knew they shared my sense of release. I saw the day's funeral as lifting the disapproval in which we all moved about. Me. Mom. And Dad, Grandpa's oldest son.

Reading my father's memoirs, it's clear his childhood was shaped by parental sternness and unspoken grievance over the few comforts, physical and emotional, he would have been allowed. His accounts of games and friendships are retold as playing out under the shadow of an impatient, industrious, and unschooled father. In one entry, he writes of seeing his father asleep with a book on agricultural methodology lying open across his chest. My father observes, "No dime novels for him!" For all of the professed admiration for his father in that remark, I am left wanting to comfort the boy who wrote it, who no doubt loved dime novels as much as any other bright child.

Strangely I have no presence in my father's memoirs. I am mentioned only once in a passing reference to me as a small child with an apparently bottomless capacity at feeding time. His focus instead is on his forbearers. He links together an unbroken line of ancestors demonstrating that each and every man or woman in the genetic chain he lifts up bore offspring, of which he is the living proof. His emphasis on this selective genealogy omits me. I am now a childless old man. Perhaps that is why I write my own memoir.

Two

THE COMMERCIAL JINGLES OF AMERICA IN THE 1950S, AS THEY had for decades and continue to do, emphasized innovation. Opportunities appeared that hadn't been there a year earlier. Exhortations to new, more modern ways of living purred from everyone's radio vacuum tubes. Advertisements "from coast to coast" promoted faster automobiles, waterproof watches, and sexier cigarettes, beguiling even the illiterate. Most large cities had a few flickering black-and-white television broadcasts offering more and better merchandise to a growing consumer base. The GI Bill, passed by a grateful nation, guaranteed veterans home loans and educational grants, a chance to improve their lot as they settled back into civilian life.

My father seized his moment and took training courses as a livestock appraiser with Stark & Wetzel, a meat-packing company in Indianapolis. And so it was, one day, after living life thus far in a mission-style farmhouse on the flat plains of Tipton County, I woke up in a small mass-produced National Home, a Levittown house on a narrow, newly seeded lot on Indianola Avenue, on the near north side of Indianapolis.

I don't remember moving in, but I do remember the initial excitement of new rooms and a new path through a new house. There was a fenced-in backyard, and there were neighbors on the other side of the fence. There was mud and machinery for new construction down the road, where a fast-disappearing woodland was rapidly turning into the mirror-image of our street, lot by lot, new and tidy houses set cheek by jowl. There was the white-lined, cross-hatched asphalt of Indianola Avenue, strictly off-limits. There were neighbor kids, some of them wild and also off-limits.

In the long summer evenings, after bedtime, there was the slow death of the day as backdrop against adult conversations held over fences or on back patios, sometimes drowned out by a power mower. The outside world was framed by windows with sills just above my line of vision as I lay in bed and listened. My cropped views held sky and cloud and the tops of newly planted saplings, and on those late, warm summer nights, the stars, undimmed yet by streetlights.

The house was small. A fourth child had come home from Mercy Hospital. Maureen was born the day before my fourth birthday, and I welcomed her as a personal birthday gift. I ran into her room to monitor her first thing every morning to ensure she was still there, still growing. She was soon bouncing in her crib. My heart leaped to see her jumping up and down. I marveled at the beauty of her auburn hair and her pale, freckled face. I would sing to her: "You're no bigger than my thumb. Thumbelina, dance, Thumbelina sing." She would smile at me, and we would bask in a kind of shared generosity of spirit.

Now there were six of us moving about, recklessly romping or seriously navigating with adult intent. There was an all-pervasive physical intimacy throughout the day. I kept up a vigilant campaign to keep my older sister placated, alert for any signs of sudden aggression. Our mother orchestrated daily life and doled out permission or denial to an endless chorus of "Mommy, can I?" Only when Dad was home did an air of deferent calm descend on the household.

I sought boundaries. I shared a room with my brother. He was quiet and quick to fall asleep at nap-time and evening bedtime. I was attuned to his presence across the room but felt no need to converse with him. We co-existed with minimal interaction, as if each of us were responding to a different set of imperatives. He lay there asleep with his shallow, rhythmic breathing, his face turned from me, the back of his skull showing downy blond hair. His small, sharp shoulder blades were exposed as if he were some wingless cherub fallen from another place. Meanwhile, in my own bed, my mind disentangled the day's insufficiently examined events. I speculated on the disjointed sounds wafting through the room. I stared at the electric outlets, awed by their power to shock when prodded with bobby pins. I fought back the terrors of darkness as bravely as I could. I became adept at what I thought of as "floating away."

I struggled for control of my persona, for something that distinguished me from the others with whom I shared the daily jostle. From an open bathroom door, I silently watched my father shave, studying the ritual carefully. I determined I would not grow a beard, would not be bothered by such a tiresome daily chore. I surprised myself when I said it aloud to him, not knowing from where the notion had come, this reluctance to grow a beard like my father. He seemed amused; I could tell by his voice, the one that adults use when egging on a child. Even then, I could hear that tone.

Where before I splashed in the tub for an evening bath shared with my sister or brother, always distractedly aware of body differences, this now seemed too consequential. I no longer wanted any part of communal bathing or public nakedness. This was accepted without comment or further ado and honored by all involved. It was a new boundary. I was determined to defend it.

The dinner table sat in an area separated from the living room by an archway. I don't remember our family meals there. This strikes me as strange. We were well fed, the family dinner hour was sacrosanct, and I was a formidable eater. My only clear memory at that table, however, is of a hot bowl of navy bean soup set before me by a baby-sitter. I am adding to it a sizeable dollop of ketchup and a few fistfuls of crushed saltine crackers. I am thrilled with my creation, with its pungent, salty, toothy taste and texture. The memory even now brings back an odd tingle of discovery and contentment. I don't know why it stands out so clearly against all the solid, three-course meals my mother so dependably put in front of us on that table, evening after evening.

Off the kitchen was a utility area leading to the back door and the backyard that was our daily world except in bitter cold and heavy rain. We had a clothes washer in that room and a rack for drying clothes when they couldn't be hung outside on the line. There was a tall stool on which my father sat my brother, and me in turn, every other Saturday morning for our haircuts. He used what we called the electric clippers to administer a traditional buzz cut, close-cropped. "Clean and manly," he called it. I resented the phrase as if it were an admonishment. There was a hearty briskness to those Saturday haircuts, a cheery, boys-only aura, a mood that disturbed me. I resented having something so personally mine – my own hair, which I had grown myself – taken from me. I felt as if my father and I were traveling in different directions, that it didn't bode well. I loved my father's attentions but not this eagerness for biweekly shearing.

The first day of school ripped in two my delicately constructed understanding of life. One half of that torn fabric was the era when there was no school; the other half was when school was here and now and looming ahead into the foreseeable future. Suddenly I had to learn to execute a repetitive performance: wake up on time, finish my breakfast, board a bus, settle into my desk, behave all morning, and stay awake. This momentous partition of time took place on the first day of kindergarten, at Christ the King Parochial School, in the autumn of 1954.

There would have been some warning. My sister was only a year older. I must have seen her leave for school, tearfully, if she were true to form. I must have known that my day would come. Whatever the case, when it did, I took the whole thing quite stoically. I stood sentry-like on the sidewalk of Indianola Avenue, waiting for the bus. Any minimalist parting scenes were played out in the privacy of the house. I memorized all the new names and numbers that were my clues to navigating the half-days of that first year. I simply stopped thinking about the things that once kept me occupied around the house, pre-school.

Mrs. Grisham was our teacher. She treated us, she often said, like grown-ups, because, she reminded us, that's what we were becoming. The basement classroom had windows that sat high over even Mrs. Grisham's head. They framed the anklets of girls at play in the schoolyard outside and the navy-blue trouser legs of the boys' uniforms. In that basement room with the piano against the wall and the cursive alphabet above the chalkboard, there must have been many six-year-olds who couldn't sit still, who didn't want to be treated as an adult, whose need to run and play and scream and chase would have got the better of them from time to time. I wasn't one of them. I relished the moments of calm, of obedience, of scrutinizing the alphabet and its clever way of making words. I loved the books, the clean pages, the smell of crayons and pencil shavings and chalk dust. I was enchanted with what Mrs. Grisham had to say in her between-us-adults patter. There was myself, the general stir around me, and Mrs. Grisham with her expressive face and animated pleasure over new words and new ideas. Best of all, there was her approval, which could be earned by a kind of monastic calm, and by close, rapt attention to what she was saying. Unless we were asked a question. In which case, the prize went to the first of us to answer.

Everything about school was serious. I adored seriousness. I enjoyed structure. I was partial to reason and explanation, to assurances that chaos could be kept at bay through proper comportment. I earned excellent report cards. I brought them home like a herald returned from triumphant battle. My mother wordlessly received the card and returned it to me the next day with her perfect Palmer penmanship signature on the back. I remember no conversations about them.

I still have those cards encased in an album my mother sent me. Reading them over, it seems my weakest subject was religion, with which the nuns infused everything in those formative days. The comportment categories bear a check-mark where improvement is needed. The full list includes: obedience, courtesy, truthfulness, justice and charity, cooperation, punctuality, health and safety habits, and respect for school property. We were to internalize these virtues and measure our daily performance by them. Mrs. Grisham noted that I needed to work on staying silent while others were speaking. This seems to have been a consistent problem throughout each grading period. And yet, still, I remember myself as mute.

The wordless exchange of the report card with my mother was of a piece with so much else between us. She was both central to the awareness of myself and as tangential as the rest of the world. She doled out food and wisdom, discipline, and comfort. She defined justice in sibling disputes and explained the function of mechanical things. She cleaned and undressed me, and calmed me at night before bedtime. She was busy, and she was certain about things. She put on makeup and dressed up for Dad, to be pretty when they went to play cards or eat in restaurants. She was always there. Maybe because she was so many-sided, it was difficult to bring her fully into focus.

I did not see in her the 12-year-old girl living with her defeated mother in her grandparents' house in a small, depression-era Indiana town. She would have dreamt about the Chicago she left behind, about her aunts and uncles who still spoke with a brogue. She would have missed the streetcars, the El, the lakeshore, and the department stores on Michigan Avenue. And she would have missed her father, who wrote her infrequent letters that began "Dear Bugsy" and were filled with homely poems copied from weekly magazines. She would have read these again, and again, willing the borrowed sentimentality to be his own assurances to her. Perhaps they were; perhaps they resonated with his true feelings for the daughter growing up without him.

In December of my first-grade year, with Sister Mary Theresine, OSB, as the new focus of my life, we moved house again, this time to Vera Drive, off Keystone Boulevard on Indianapolis' farther north side. There were more half-finished streets running between more construction sites. Behind the house was a small stand of trees across a backyard of newly-sodded lawn.

I know it was December because there was a nagging, worrisome threat that, without a miracle, we might not have a Christmas tree. It might have been that we were waiting for the electricity to be connected. Maybe it was just the challenge of getting ourselves and a decorated tree moved in by the deadline of Christmas Eve. There were backroom whispers with my older sister Lee Ann about the plausibility of there being a Santa Claus and our need to protect "the little kids" from any whiff of doubt. A sense of the miraculous may have come from Mom and Dad to keep Lee Ann and me in the fold of believers. Whatever the rumors, we reveled in our good fortune on Christmas morning, the tree lit, toys heaped beneath, and all of us snug in a new house in a new suburban development, nestled among neighbors with their own young and growing families.

Before the following spring, I contracted a severe case of chickenpox. Large scabs blossomed on my face and scalp. I ran high temperatures. On at least two separate occasions, I was visited at night by a floating, disembodied face in the far upper corner of the ceiling in my bedroom. Our twin beds were stacked now, and I slept in the top bunk, which meant the face was close to mine. It bore down on me with a fiendish grin and a mocking voice, laughing at my sweaty misery. Half frozen with fear, I felt compelled to speak back to the demon. He answered aggressively. He described lurid scenes of hell and laughed that I would learn about it soon enough. My end of the conversation was to tell him to go away, that he was wrong about me, that I was a good boy, that I didn't want him in my room. My mother woke once to the sound of our arguing, or at least to my end of the argument. She came into the room, waking my brother in his lower bunk with the sudden rudeness of the overhead light. Still half-mad with spiking temperatures, I could see genuine concern on her face. I was pleased to see her worry as she checked the thermometer and patted my pocked brow with a damp cloth.

Those satanic exchanges lost none of their clarity after the fever passed. I remained unnerved by them. Worse, I was upset that no one else took them seriously. I argued their reality for weeks. Banshees and wee folk were a residual tradition in my maternal lineage, which ensured that my fears were never fully dismissed. Rather, my grandmother and my mother averted their eyes when I recounted the dark conversations, gently guiding the talk elsewhere. The effect of their indirection was to confirm for me the existence of evil, and to convince me that I was in a struggle against it. This was not the struggle Sr. Theresine meant when she told us to tell the truth and obey our parents. This was a larger, darker battle, one that threatened my soul. I had been exposed to the possibility of damnation. My vulnerability had been laid bare.

That spring, the four of us siblings, eager to reclaim the outdoors after a long, wet, grey winter, wandered out on the first Saturday morning in which navigation was once again possible. We set out to explore the construction sites further down Vera Drive. It had been raining and sleeting for weeks. All work pouring cement footings was halted, rendered impossible by the mud. The empty, dark brown lots had planks thrown down from streetside to the troughs that were dug for the foundations. The mud was thick and pasty. As we cut a short path across it, it sucked our boots down into its depths. Within minutes it was impossible for any of us to pull either boot-shod foot up from the muck.

A steady diet of television shows with luckless cowboys caught in quicksand fueled panic in me. I was convinced we were doomed. My natural recourse, honed by weekly mass and morning and bedtime prayers, was to call God for help. I led off a chorus of Hail Mary's, with Glenn and Lee Ann in fervent response. We implored the heavens, voices tinged with fear but steeled against our doom. "Holy Mary, Mother of God, pray for us sinners now and at the hour of our death. Amen." It was frightening, but oddly thrilling that we should perish so dramatically.

Somewhere in the second decade of the rosary, Maureen slipped out of her little yellow plastic boots and trotted back up the street to the house in her stocking feet. By the third decade, our voices were in full lamentation, just like the early Christian martyrs we studied in school. The bubble burst when we saw Maureen had returned with Mom, who stood at the edge of the street, hands on hips. She shouted at us to stop praying and just step out of our boots, "like your baby sister had the sense to do." There was the cut of annoyance in her voice. I felt a wrenching shift from the warm uplift of fervent prayer for divine salvation to the chill of her stern and serious scold. It was deflating. Clear in Mom's disapproving voice was the message that I had made a fool of myself.

The three of us slipped out of our boots, squished painstakingly across the brown, slurping goop in our socks, and followed her up Vera Drive back to the house in a parade of public humiliation. I don't know that anyone was out looking at us on that freshly asphalted street without sidewalks, but the shame felt quite public nonetheless.

Later I was sent out by myself to collect the abandoned boots. Now in a practical frame of mind, I managed to pry the boots out with a stick while kneeling on the construction planks. My earlier proximity to eternity was a mere awkward memory.

The fear I felt in my fevered talks with the devil was real and intense. The pleading and supplication that accompanied the rosary in the muddy construction site were heartfelt as well.

They were a natural extension of the piety in which I had been raised and schooled. But the belittling at my mother's hand on Vera Drive told me that I could not give free expression to the emotions roiling within me. I determined that, from there on in, I would need to maintain a calm and confident demeanor. This would be the wall between my interior self and the others. A new geography was mapped. I lived in a place of personal turmoil. I was surrounded by the vast sea of an uncaring world. My defense against its churlishness and ridicule would be an air of carefully groomed indifference.

Seven Months Old

With Siblings

Three Years Old

Father's Childhood Home

Three

WITHIN A YEAR, WE MOVED HOUSE ONCE MORE, LEAVING BEHIND yet again familiar certainties. My father was born into the same farmhouse from which he left to join the Army when nearly 18, the same house to which he returned, however briefly, with his bride. Yet by 1956, he had relocated his own young family to their fifth house, and it would not be the last move before I left home.

The new house was a modern ranch, an hour's drive north of Indianapolis, in rural Clinton County. Its prize feature was a "picture" window in the living room that looked across State Highway 28 to wire-fenced fields running off to the horizon. That window nearly filled the room's south wall, its lower ledge no more than a foot above the floor. In winter, it offered an unimpeded view of flat and empty land, dotted here and there with a few still-copsed acres. The house itself stood among oak and hickory trees on land once owned by our neighbor across the highway, the wonderfully named Mr. Fudge. To support his wife and two girls, Sarah and Sue, Mr. Fudge sold off tracts of his inherited land for building sites. He had already sold two that lay to the east of us. They were inhabited by people who had no children, and they failed to attract our attention. To the west was a State rest park, a tree-covered few acres with a gravel parking lot where weary motorists could avail of a water pump, a shelter house, and picnic tables. Most of its visitors were truckers who stopped to park and sleep off the exhaustion of a long-distance haul.

Behind the house and its deeply shaded backyard was a thick stand of native hardwood forest. This, too, was owned by Mr. Fudge. The woods ran across nearly ten acres, heavy with undergrowth. A small spring in wet weather gave seasonal rise to a stream flowing to the gravel road connecting Highway 28 with the notional town of Avery to the north. Avery was nothing more than a few scattered houses that lay a straight and level mile away. The railroad ran through it, the same one that ran east to Tipton County and Elwood and west to Illinois. It was called the Nickel Plate Road. Its shining steel rails and coarse, splintery cross-ties reeking of creosote lay on an elevated gravel bed in an uninterrupted course from New York to Chicago and St. Louis. It was the northernmost edge of our world, and it beckoned us in all kinds of weather. We knew every tree, every ditch, and every farmhouse that stood between our house and those tracks. We learned to place the soft metal staves that worked loose from the ends of the cross-ties onto the steel tracks, then shelter ourselves in the ditch as the freight trains roared through. When the coast was clear, we would run back up to the tracks to claim these newly flattened metal sculptures. When staves could not be found, pennies worked as well. But pennies had their commercial value lost in the squashing.

The railroad system was fast losing much of its transport business to the truck traffic bearing down the parallel Highway 28. Even by 1956, before the completion of Eisenhower's national freeway system, Avery had become isolated. Its only relevance for us was its appearance in our telephone number: Avery 456.

The first few summers after the move, I had virtually no limits on my time or territory. Fess Parker was Davey Crockett on television's Disneyland, and I was Davey Crockett in Mr. Fudge's woods. We were overtly discouraged from playing in the woods, but there was tacit permission as long as we didn't damage anything, or upset Mr. Fudge, who monitored our construction projects with a begrudging tolerance. Lee Ann had little interest in outdoor activities, but Glenn and Maureen were quite pliable and keen to be part of the frontier scene. The three of us built a fort – a few small huts composed of fallen branches laid across each other like the Lincoln Log™ cabins we built indoors in the winter. We roofed them with crossbeams made of more branches and covered them with chunks of fallen bark. The scarcity of building material meant that they were quite low to the ground. The fort's protective fencing was a patchy wall of dried horseweed stalks. As we lay face down cramped inside dank quarters, drama was supplied by narrating a fictional war against imagined Indian invaders, inventing threats, and ever-successful counterstrategies. The suspension of disbelief depended on all three of us agreeing that, yeah, that's what happened. We almost always agreed and so passed many afternoons absorbed in historic battles whose epic deeds have gone unrecorded. The same building pattern served us well in winter, after the heavy snows that seemed to fall so often and linger so long in those days. We built igloos with frozen blocks of snow and carved out trenches through the snowbanks. As with our summer fort, each of us had his or her own quarters in an interconnected settlement we knew to be besieged by outside forces.

The fields surrounding our oak and hickory grove were of a deep, black loam, the alluvial plains of the last ice age, deforested over centuries by both native and invading European populations. Time-honored crop rotations controlled soil depletion and provided ground-cover after harvest to minimize erosion; root and stalk decay replenished nutrients. The lucrative cash crops that took advantage of these conditions in the 1950s were corn and tomatoes.

The corn came into its glory in late summer, when the stalks were tall and bore ripening ears. We made forays through straight and seemingly endless furrows. We knocked down a few stalks to allow passage between the otherwise impenetrable rows. Farmers would have been furious to discover the remnants of our path-building, but the high-tasseled corn itself was our cover. Our pathways turned and doubled back on themselves in meandering routes, meant to disorient ourselves amid all the featureless leaves and cobs, thrilling us with the threat that we might get lost entirely: a kind of maze in the maize.

When the tomato crops ripened, Mexican and Mexican American migrant workers were trucked in as if out of nowhere, filling the fields with their stooped labor, working from early morning until early evening. They appeared on flatbed trucks and left just as surreptitiously. They were quartered in migrant camps; small clusters of portable, one-room shacks set up around water pumps on quiet country back roads. We were forbidden contact with them but got an occasional wave of hello from a distance. When we boldly made a rare approach, we were proffered vine-ripened field tomatoes, a friendly token bearing the essential, eternal flavor of Indiana.

My best afternoons were spent alone. Outdoors, in the slight and constant wind off the open plains that pleasantly filled the ears and dampened ambient noise, I was free to ponder things or simply daydream. Staring far away at a stand of trees across the fields, or squatting to peer closely at a patch of parkland grass between my legs, searching for bug life, I would consider my problems. What pleased me was the vagueness of my thoughts, the unstructured flow of images, ideas, and random words. Being alone meant I didn't have to answer to anyone, or amuse anyone. I could shed my assigned household identity. It was a time to carve out a sense of myself, to test the several theories I had of me. New personae could be donned wordlessly, without anyone's by-your-leave, without any explanations. These could then be cast aside without apology. They could be molded and modified as required. I switched among them without a second thought.

Here was a way of thinking about things that differed from the dualism of my Christ-the-King world, where virtues were clear and pressing: obedience, truthfulness, cooperation. Failure in any of those categories would invoke the very devil who taunted me throughout the days and nights of the chickenpox. Glory or damnation was the choice. The nuns insisted I strive for goodness daily - indeed, moment by moment - since any act, carefully examined, could be the ultimate test. Who knew when Jesus might come knocking at my cottage door, a lamp held high, asking me if I were ready?

In my alternative unfocussed, contemplative moments, looking away from unresolved particulars, my options flowed without favor. I could be angry. I could forgive. I could say something to hurt back. I could hold my breath and die. I could tell no one. Each response, among ample other choices, floated in front of me in due course. Watching each one pass by contented me. The right response, the proper framing of any problem, might just appear on its own in the process. It might ripen like an egg that is ready to hatch and – *voila* - the perfect answer. And until then, there were other options, other ways of reading things. I could not have drawn such clear distinctions between those two different approaches at that young age. But I did feel myself move back and forth between two ways of being, sometimes willingly. I knew they were there.

We moved to Clinton County so my father could manage the former Stark & Wetzel stockyards that he and his business partner bought, part of a small business network holding that included leased pens in the central Indianapolis yards. Clinton County was just west of Dad's native Tipton County and Mom's adopted Elwood, but this was a pioneering move for them all the same. It was one thing to lose close proximity to their respective families, roots, and histories. The move to suburban Indianapolis certainly required leaving those things behind. But in exchange, they had gained a busy north-side suburb, growing within an expanding economy. New shopping malls, churches, and residential developments were mushrooming there in Indianapolis, and all comers were welcome. Clinton County, on the other hand, was still moored to its foundation as a Protestant fortress. Frankfort, the county seat, was settled by burghers who came from German Reformation stock, bringing a bit of Frankfurt-am-Main and the old country with them. They were joined, after municipal incorporation in the 1830s, by evangelicals from more newly minted schisms. The small, leafy town was the domain of Lutherans and Methodists, amplified by the Gospel Light Baptist Church, First Church of the Nazarene, Evangelical

Presbyterian Church, and dozens more. In its more recent past, it had also harbored a local chapter of the Ku Klux Klan, a satellite of the Elwood headquarters.

Frankfort's sole Catholic church, St. Mary's, was built at the turn of the 20th century out of the missionary zeal of the Franciscan Fathers in Lafayette, an independent diocese since the First World War, and was assigned its own parish priest. St. Mary's was a refuge for the few Irish, Italian, and Polish families infiltrating the town. In harvest season, its pews also held scores of migrant Mexican families. On the down-scale, western edge of town, the parish was an odds-and-ends collection of committed faithful submissively mumbling Latin phrases in the heart of the Hoosier Bible Belt.

Its primary school on Second Street was just behind the old brick church on Walnut Avenue. My mother went to the Board of Education to arrange to have the school bus collect us. She was told the county's final bus discharge point was Frankfort High School. The buses went no farther. It was clear we weren't welcome on board. Mom insisted. We paid state and county taxes equal to everyone else, and we would use the bus. The eventual compromise was that Lee Ann and I, at nine- and eight-years of age, would ride the bus to Frankfort High School on the east side of town, then walk nearly a mile to St. Mary's elementary on the west side every morning. No one raised any concern about our vulnerability. We walked the main street of a small midwest town in a comparatively innocent age. Even less fuss was made over our exposure to the elements for nine months of the year. I was given a bright yellow raincoat with a visor hood for my birthday. This, alternating with a thick woolen coat and a series of soon-lost mittens and scarves, was intended to keep me safe from inclement weather.

The presence of adult supervision filters out the immediacy of the moment for a child. It keeps the present at a remove. Our walk across town without that filter leant an intensity to everything we saw. We knew what to do and where to go, but we had a choice in the process. In the winter, sharp western winds kept my gaze downward, my head wrapped tightly in all that wool. On rainy days, water gathered into puddles in the crevices between the off-kilter sidewalk slabs. These begged to be stomped on or trenched with a stick into canals and drained away, slowing our progress toward school. But warm, dry spring and autumn days brought wonders. The sidewalk took us past the front doors of two different Protestant churches, which we fixedly ignored, and past the medical building downtown so tall it had an elevator inside. Nearer St. Mary's, there were a few blocks of townhouses that regularly changed seasonal decorations in their windows and on their doors, each change ratcheting up our anticipation for the coming holiday.

With some regularity, we crossed paths with a middle-aged man in a topcoat, hair combed back with pomade, smoking a cigar, and taking his morning constitutional at the same hour we were heading to school. He walked Walnut Street in a deliberate, observant manner, head topped by a fedora and chin held high, holding his hands together behind his back in a wide-shouldered posture that showed his approval of the town that lay before him. He never spoke to us, or even nodded his fedora our way. Yet his particular bearing still walks through my dreams on occasion. He was the kind of man I supposed I would become. In my dreams, he is sometimes enigmatic and faceless, like the man in a Magritte canvas. He is sometimes a head of state in a solemn, televised ceremony. He still strides among the other ghosts alive in my memories.

The first few days of my mother's commuting plan passed quietly. We were all finding our way through the anonymity of the back-to-school hubbub. The bus stopped near the entrance to the rest park. We piled into it, where students ranging in age from six to 18 rode together. But word soon got out that when the bus pulled up to James Whitcomb Riley Elementary, my sister and I stayed on board, all the way to the High School. When we stepped off with the high schoolers we walked across town to St. Mary's. This put us beyond the pale.

One morning, after a few weeks, with no warning of what was coming, Lee Ann and I boarded the bus and took our seats near the front. Within the first few minutes, from the rear, there began a sing-song chorus to which I was at first oblivious. As it grew, I could hear "cat-lickers," prompting images of kittens grooming themselves. I turned in my seat to see what the fun was. It was then I realized some older kids at the back of the bus were aiming their taunts at us. They were saying, "Look at the cat-lickers. Look at the cat-lickers," as a slur on our religion.

When I understood what was happening, I turned around and faced forward. I could feel the force of their contempt hurled against my back. Facing forward meant I didn't have to dissemble the shame I felt. I looked into the rear-view mirror centered above the windshield and saw the bus driver smirking. Beside me, my sister's face squeezed into a grimace and turned beet red. She began crying. I was powerless to stop any of it. It was seeing her so disconsolate that shamed me most. I could only hunker down and bear it until it passed.

The cat-licker moniker soon shifted to "mackerel snapper," an allusion that escaped me entirely at the time. The phrase would have meant nothing to midwestern farm kids a thousand miles from the nearest ocean, kids who ate meat and potatoes in those days, not mackerel or seafood of any kind. Clearly, adults were arming the taunters. The campaign continued for a few days until they tired of it. We weathered it stoically and said nothing about it at home. I knew if I did, my father would urge me to "fight them, fight back, fight harder." It was his standard advice for any adversity. My shame would be made even more intense for not taking on 10 or 15 kids in a slugfest. In the end, it was instructive. It let me know where I stood. There would be no making friends with these kids. I had solid proof that I was set apart.

The route home from school required another special arrangement. Fred and Catherine Ruth lived down Highway 28 from us, even further out of town. We knew them, as we knew virtually all friends of our family, through church. Fred was an insurance agent. He was a small, wiry, and somewhat distracted man with a physical disability who walked unsteadily, bent over, and always with a cane. One of his arms seemed nearly useless to him. Catherine was a large, pale, and freckled woman with strawberry blonde hair done up in long braids crowned atop her head. Her hearty laugh and beaming smile emitted warmth and encouraged familiarity. Everyone called her Babe. Babe worked the day-shift at Frankfort Hospital. She got off work at 3 PM. My mother arranged to have her collect us at St. Mary's at 3:15 every afternoon. We were excused early to leave with her. The stir in the room this caused was another mark of being set apart from the others. It was a consequence of our rural existence, which needed an accommodation the townies didn't.

St. Mary's school was a tidy little one-story glass and stone building with large-windowed classrooms jutting off a central hall in four annexes forming an "H." It stood in modern contrast to its large, solid brown-brick church topped with a pitched slate roof. There were only three classrooms in the school and three teaching nuns for the eight grades. First and second graders shared one classroom, third and fourth graders shared another. Grades five through eight shared the third classroom. We shared teachers, too. Each grade group had its section of the room, sometimes a single row of desks. Sister would teach one class its lessons for the period, then assign seatwork while she attended to the next row. This alternated throughout the day.

School days began with morning Mass. Communion was forbidden to anyone who had eaten anything since the prior midnight or drunk anything but water less than an hour before Mass, so Mom packed us each a breakfast and a lunch in one brown-paper bag and sent us off early in the morning unfed. After the hurried Low Mass in the cold, dark church, we walked into our warm and well-lit school and were given a few minutes at our desks to eat breakfast. By that point, I was so hungry I often ate through the cold fried-egg sandwich or boiled-egg-and-toast that was designated as breakfast and proceeded on to the bologna or peanut-butter-and-jelly sandwich that was meant to be lunch. It should have been an early lesson in self-restraint. Instead, I suspect it was foundational to my life-long voracious appetite.

In my second year at St. Mary's, a young Mexican boy joined the class. He was introduced as Junior Montalvo. His real name was Geronimo, but the nuns decided it was either too frightening or too open to ridicule. He came from a family of twenty-one children, the nuns were thrilled to point out. I thought that was astounding. He was going to stay in school for a while, we were told, while the rest of his family moved on, presumably to the next harvest in another state. This was part of the endless cycle of work that kept the migrants in their below-poverty state and kept the country well fed. I tried to strike up a friendship with Junior, but our lack of a common language was an impediment.

He sat at a desk shoved against the blackboard, apart from the rest of us, where he leafed through books and drew pictures with colored crayons. He had long, thick, jet-black hair and dark brown skin. His eyes were nearly black. He was shy and always smiling. The backs of his hands were a rich walnut color and his palms as pale as mine. I found that a beautiful thing, as did Sr. Theresa Ann. She held them up and told the class they were so beautiful he should be a priest so he could lift up the sacred host with them. I never got Junior to engage with me. He continued leafing through his books, not reading them. He left after a few months, no doubt inconsolably homesick for his constantly homeless family.

Because my schoolmates lived in town, we spent little time together outside the classroom or playground. One exception was Maurice. He was what is now called a nerd. He wore thick glasses, always did well in spelling, and was a stickler for accuracy, which was the quality in him I most admired. He was earnest and insisted on getting his facts straight. His mother was eager to encourage our friendship, and I was invited to spend the occasional Friday night at his house. I remember a few Saturday mornings painting ceramic-cast figurines in his kitchen and dodging the swallows that tried to keep us away from his neighbor's barn.

At lunch one school day, while I was out back in the playground, a few of our classmates rushed out to tell us Maurice had been hit by a truck on Second Street in front of the school. They were beside themselves, describing the scene, how Maurice rolled over and over underneath the truck, barely escaping a crushing between the tires as he lay in the center of the street. "You should have seen it," someone said. I took that as literal judgment. Yes, I should have seen it. I should have been there like the faithful disciple John beneath the cross. Maurice was my friend, and I wasn't there. I was relieved when I heard he had only broken a rib and would return to school in a couple of weeks. The nuns had us say a special prayer at Mass in gratitude for the obvious miracle. But after that, I felt a kind of shame around Maurice, as if I had let him down, as if his accident required my witness, as if my presence might have forestalled it. The awkwardness put a distance between us.

Terry was another special friend. He was as absorbed by science fiction as I was. We traded books we had read and liked, and by the fourth-grade, we decided to write our own book. Our technique was to alternate chapters, each, in turn, bringing his latest text to the other as a spur toward completion. We had differing ideas about the plot, no doubt in response to our differing anxieties. Each of us was soon spending most of his energy pulling the lead character – about whom he also had a different understanding – back onto his own singular, determined path.

The nuns shared living quarters in a two-story house two blocks from school. This was a decade before the reforms of the Second Vatican Council. They still wore habits as medieval as any worn by the most veiled of Muslim women. Rather than a *burqa*, their head was covered by a *coronet*, beneath which they were tightly wrapped in a starched linen *coif* and *bandeau* covering the forehead, temples, and throat. To this was pinned a long black veil that fell to below waist level, adding to the considerable weight they were already supporting with their neck. The veil could be unpinned and rearranged to cover the entire top half of their body, including their face. The contour of their breasts was dissembled beneath a neutering, starched white *wimple*. Their overall physical shape was further obscured by a long, loose-sleeved, floor-length outer *tunic*, fronted by another muffling body-length panel of black serge. They cut a remarkable figure walking along Frankfort's leafy sidewalks, closely observed by their sensible, conformist, and suspicious Baptist neighbors.

I hadn't an adult's curiosity about who those women were, where they came from, or what had led them to their lives of self-abnegation. I can only wonder, now that it is too late to ask. The number of men and women who joined in religious community living reached its peak in America that decade, the last stand of a certitude that wouldn't be sustained. Secular modernity lapped constantly against the bulwark of the vowed life, and its ancient solidity began to crumble. Before that crumbling and in my innocence, I was seduced by its aura. Everything we were told about the moral life suggested those who lived in religious orders had more value and would ultimately be paid higher rewards. Black serge and roman collars seemed to swathe a higher, purer, more admirable caste than that of the moms and dads who sent us to St. Mary's for instruction.

One defense the nuns employed to steel themselves against the lures of a sexualized culture was their focus on chastity. They exuded chastity. They were virginal Brides of Christ. They harangued us children about chastity. Girls were to be always monitored, especially at play, where a spinning merry-go-round might reveal too much under a flared-out skirt. They warned us boys not to stand with our feet too far apart, lest we have impure thoughts. Constant reference was made to the purity of our souls. A vigorous weekly examination of conscience was urged on each of us.

I tried to take these instructions to heart, but given their unrelenting constancy and lack of specificity, I soon developed the ability to nod to their wisdom while totally disregarding them. At an almost pre-sexual stage in life, the exact meaning of chastity was a bit fuzzy. It seemed more like an abstemious attitude toward cleanliness, a carefulness that should inform your homework and your fingernails. It was clear there was more to it than that, especially since there was a constant delineation between boys and girls, that yawning gap always running right down the center of the known world.

I accepted the basic moral bearings, but I also saw they were re-interpreted on an as-needed basis when circumstances required. The Ten Commandments were fairly clear and self-evident, although there was some vagueness about false gods and coveting. I knew that I wasn't allowed to hit girls, no matter how provocative my sister could be. I listened carefully to Mom and Dad's talk with each other and adopted much of their attitudes toward Christian love and forgiveness. These seemed to tolerate a fair amount of sarcasm and self-justification when talking about guiding principles. There was always plenty of room to argue about who should have done what in the first place.

I was an average child with an above-average desire to do the right thing. I found myself in an education system that emphasized perfection, obedience, and martyrdom. The notions of purity and abstinence, the idea of God's being pleased when I offered Him up my suffering – all of this overburdened my ability to make sense of the core values being inculcated. From time to time, my good intentions collapsed under the weight of so much moral admonition.

It was a weight that eventually brought everyone down, including the nuns. Sr. Eulalia's nerves had been worn so thin over so many years of purity and chastity that she had no tolerance left for the slightest deviation. The year my brother Glenn was in her class, she discovered him with a *Scrooge McDuck* comic book during his lunch-hour. In a snit, she summoned my mother for a conference over this lascivious choice of reading material. Even if no one else could see what the problem was, she clearly saw that the ducks were walking about with no trousers, their bare bottoms showing.

I LOVED ST. MARY'S CHURCH EVEN MORE THAN I LOVED THE
school. The cramped little schoolhouse was full of small, unfocussed
children struggling to comprehend what was being asked of them.
Everything was scaled down to fit us: small desks and chairs,
low-mounted urinals in the boy's room, short lunch-room tables
at which our parents looked ridiculously out of scale during music
recitals. The mirror in the hallway was hung so that we would see
ourselves in it and correct any grooming errors. Once, when I saw
the priest walk by it, I realized it was hung so low he couldn't see
his own face.

But the church was for adults. It had high, vaulted ceilings
with distant, shadowy corners. That it made plain its efforts at
physical beauty excited me. With pilastered apses and faux-marble

communion rails, patterned tile floors, luridly painted Stations of the Cross, and stained-glass windows depicting Pre-Raphaelite virgins and beggars, it was big, broad, and enthralling. Its dignity and purpose felt authoritative.

Boys served on the altar at Mass; girls were not allowed. Mass was in Latin, and altar boys were expected, by dint of rote, to manage the Latin responses. Boys and girls sang together in the choir. As in most Catholic churches, the adult singing was timid, almost sub-audible. Occasionally the recessional hymn enticed a few adults into awkwardly mumbling the words, *soto voce*, under the safe cover of the organ's loud hum. Choir duties were seasonal. We sang ancient musical forms in a mix of English and Latin. I thrilled to *Regina ceoli* on high Marian feast days, to the *Asperges me* before Holy Week ceremonies and to the tricky *Vidi aquam* during Easter season. On those occasions, the nuns displayed us proudly as a sign of their personal accomplishment by seating us in folding chairs on the steps at the communion rail. I didn't understand the Latin words we sang, but the setting in which we sang them, the emotional heft of the music itself, and the reliable turning of the seasons in which each was invoked were all I needed to understand.

We were also the choir for funeral masses and sang the *Requiem*. We sat up in the choir loft, next to Sister Lillian, as she played the rumbling pipe organ and vigorously nodded her head to keep us in tempo. Distance protected us some from what was going on down around the coffin at the foot of the altar, where the sniffling friends and family of the deceased milled around. We sang several pensioners and cardiac victims off to their greater glory during those years. I was still in childhood's fog and didn't often make the connection between the coffin one morning and an empty pew the next Sunday.

Part of the arrangement with Babe Ruth's taking us home from school was my helping her husband, Fred, at lunchtime. His office was on the second floor of the building that housed F.W. Woolworth's, what Dad called the "five and dime." The building was part of a continuous row of Victorian facades fronting the town square. The exaggerated ceiling height of the ground floor made for a steep stairwell up to Fred's second-story office, a navigational challenge for him. I was paid the splendid sum of fifty cents a day to come to his office on my lunch-hour. He laid out a series of tasks for me on arrival: go to the bank with a deposit purse, bring his lunch tray up from the Woolworth counter (without spilling the soup in its shallow bowl), go to the Post Office, and other odd errands. Most weeks, I had three days of this highly remunerative employment. Always anxious for approval, I executed my instructions with focused attention under the watchful eye of the town's tellers and merchants. I wrote down key words I would have to repeat. I stood in line at the Farmer's Bank with the zippered purse of deposit slips and endorsed checks muttering "for deposit only." I queued at the Post Office with a note that reminded me to order "two block planes of three-cent stamps."

With the lunch tray delivered and the deposit slips reviewed, Fred would hand me a fifty-cent coin and commend my "dependability." He once confided I had just handled a transaction worth over ten thousand dollars. That seemed a marvelous amount of money, none of which I actually saw in cash, but the fifty-cent piece was tangible. I walked back to school on my own recognizance, increasingly clear about how things worked: finances, the labor market, traffic flow, and personal time management. The autonomy I enjoyed in this arrangement was exceptional even then, in that much less monitored world.

The other beloved institution was the public library. Frankfort had a Carnegie Endowment *Beaux-Arts* library with wide marble steps, high-coffered ceilings, and stacks and stacks of musty books. I presume my mother left all or most of us at the library while she did her Saturday shopping. I presume, too, that my brother or sisters enjoyed themselves in it. I only remember soaking up its sights and smells on my own, relishing every Saturday morning spent there. I loved the pockets inside the back covers and their removable cards stamped with return dates, little tokens of civic duty. I usually began in the children's section, but the illustrated, over-sized, brightly covered children's literature wasn't as thrilling as the real books. The real books were silent on the outside, somber in their dark hardback covers, unapologetically text-laden. I wandered through the fiction stacks, then into history. Part of the library's spell was silence, a mute throb sent up by all those closed and unread books. I was late to discover the card catalogs and never paid any attention to the Dewey decimal system. It was easy to see books were grouped by subject, and I relied on the serendipitous, wandering until some title caught my eye. I would inspect my random choice, then dip into the books surrounding it to see if any looked equally or more interesting. I sampled a few pages of each, interpolating which might be the best read. I was after no specific knowledge. I was content with the serendipitous.

The "Ur" book, the ultimate bridge between the "picture books" for children and more serious reading, wasn't from the library. *Redcap Runs Away* was a Christmas gift. It was serious enough at more than 300 pages, a lightly illustrated tale of England in the middle ages. Red Cap, a rural peasant boy, haunted by rumors of an uncle traveling the world as a minstrel, sets out in pursuit of him. Red Cap becomes a minstrel himself, roaming from hamlet to village to royal court in a picaresque filled with minstrel songs and riddles. Searching for the illusive uncle draws him out into the world beyond his own village. It was my book, and there was no hurry to finish it. I would take it to bed with me and read it under the blankets with a flashlight or on long summer evenings when late sunsets gave me time to savor it. I would then drift off to sleep while the passing auto headlights from Highway 28 played across the bedroom walls. As I floated away, I rooted for the young hero and yearned to meet the minstrel uncle. Both characters are lodged within me yet. Both still sing of the cuckoo, the jolly juggler, and the squire and his lady. I have never been more transported, and I have left behind the age at which I could be.

Such sweet reverie. Besides broadening and populating an otherwise quiet existence, reading helped me ignore a world in which I didn't seem to have a natural perch. I would occasionally hear my parents remark on how much time I spent with my "nose in a book." My mother took to comparing me to Ferdinand the Bull, a popular children's book character. He was a Charles Atlas of a bull who ignored the taunts of those trying to goad him into the bull ring, preferring instead to pick flowers and sit in a meadow. I inferred, through her tone and gesture, that she considered me to be falling short of some larger, other purpose. It wasn't clear if she did this for amusement, as a corrective, or simply out of disappointment.

My parents tried to make their peace with my passive nature and love of reading. I had cover as long as I kept up with my chores. But it was wrenching to emerge from some gripping, exotic world to have to attend to chores left undone, or worse, half done. It was a struggle to focus on their agenda. I was torn between the adventures of a new planet with new forms of intelligent life on the one hand, and the ultimatum to get the garbage put into the garbage can "right now." I went through distracted motions, failing at the effort until brought round to reality. What they sought was an end to my mental wandering, for me to get focused on how they saw things. What they used to bring me round was physical confrontation. After insisting I acknowledge what I had failed to do, Mom administered a series of sharp slaps to the seat of my pants with a wooden paddle or yardstick. When she found the infraction particularly maddening, I was forced to pull my pants down, adding shame to the terror. Protecting my buttocks with my hands simply meant absorbing the pain with my knuckles, a more acute pain. The nuns often told us it hurt our parents dearly to punish us, and I tried to understand my mother's plight. I once blurted out between strokes that I knew she was doing this because she loved me. It sent her off into a spasm of enraged spanking. The nuns clearly misunderstood what motivated my mother.

One of my biweekly chores was to help my father haul our household refuse to the county dump. On trash-hauling Saturdays, he and I hitched a two-wheeled trailer to the tow-knob on the back of the car, filled the trailer bed with what wouldn't burn in the backyard fire barrel, and towed it to the dump. This was exciting because, in addition to providing me time with Dad, it meant running the gauntlet of the dump. There were always fires smoldering inside its refuse pile, lit in the theory that at least some of it would combust. The stench of the massive heap was overwhelming, lending a further sense of danger to things. Suddenly, and with some frequency, an aerosol can would explode out of the fire, and everyone would duck and cover his head. The can would shoot out into its trajectory with such force that anyone in its path was in danger of serious injury. When the moment passed, people would look up with sheepish grins, chuckling that they had once again avoided bodily harm, a standard risk of our environmental nonchalance.

It was in the camaraderie of one of those trash-hauling days that my father first brought up the subject of sex. I had unfocussed thoughts and theories on the subject. I knew I had some kind of problem in that department, but I couldn't have put into words what was wrong. I just knew my urges and reactions were not like those of other boys. People let me know that I found the wrong things beautiful and the wrong things distasteful. I had no clear thoughts about it, only a sense of dread of some future disaster.

So when I heard my father talking about where babies come from, some core part of me left the front seat of the Chevy and mentally hovered above it, looking down on my small self and my self-conscious father, both of us staring intently over the high metal dashboard, out through the windshield at the gravel road flowing beneath us. I heard something about "daddy's peanuts" and "mommy's jeans" and conjured an image of my father putting snacks into my mother's pants pockets, as if feeding some strange animal in a weird zoological ritual.

He was taking his first few steps out onto thin ice that was the issue of his son's sexuality. He had named the unspoken thing – sex – and was giving me an opening on the topic. It was consistent with the watchful eye he kept on my development. Watchfulness was the point of the trips to the county dump – man-to-man time, bending the twig to properly grow the tree. He couldn't have been blind to the discomfort I must have revealed in unguarded moments, or blind to my disinterest in the things that he felt all boys should love. I simply had nothing I felt I could say, though it was clear something was expected of me.

My mother had a talent for sewing, patience, and a focus on detail that allowed her to make curtains, dresses, and even fully-lined sports jackets. I studied her closely as she pinned the delicate paper shapes of Butterick patterns onto lengths of fabric and cut along the blue tracery lines into tissue and cloth: right sleeve, left sleeve, yoke panel, facing, and cuffs. The footer on the Singer fed the pieces under its stitcher as she turned, refolded, and restitched them. She kept the iron warm on the ironing board because it was important to flatten hems and seams once they were made. In careful imitation of every new trick I could learn from her, I was soon making A-line skirts and shifts for all the dolls that my sisters, and Sue and Sarah Fudge across the road, would bring me. I had the patience for small stitches, the curiosity to learn the principles of assembly, and a heady love for all the lovely fabric textures and colors among the remnants of Mom's projects. When I started third grade, my father took my impressive sewing kit away from me. I knew, when he told me to put all the scissors, needles, thread, and cloth on the dining room table and walk away, that he was addressing a core failing, a reason I was a misfit. The sewing that had been so satisfying to me suddenly brought me shame.

That Christmas, in his enthusiasm to help me find my inner macho, my father gave two pairs of boxing gloves, one pair to me and the other to my younger brother Glenn. When I opened them, I remember thinking, "how odd!" I set them aside and moved on to more appealing presents. But on New Year's Day, he cleared our small kitchen of its table and chairs and, feigning an enthusiasm that seemed to spring from nowhere, he dressed Glenn and me in "boxing shorts" and assembled my mother and two sisters for the big fight. I still cringe at the memory of that odd tableau, that moment Glenn and I realized what was expected of us. As if we had rehearsed it, we both stared at our father with incredulity. Then in slow, quiet embarrassment, we slipped the gloves off and slunk toward our bedroom.

I offered disappointment in other areas as well. For two seasons, my father brought me with him to his archery club meets. I worked my way through a series of increasingly larger and stronger bows. I loved making my own arrows, gluing the fletching onto wooden shafts, shaping them on a lathe that seared the feathers with a hot electrical wire pre-shaped for optimal flight. It smoked and sent up the primordial stench of burnt flesh. I earned a few ribbons and an occasional medal at those Saturday morning meets, competing in open fields, far from the road, walking from a paper bulls-eye strapped to a hay-bale stack to the thirty-yard line, the fifty-yard line, and the hundred-yard line. As I improved, Dad became more intent on critiquing my stance, my grip, my release, and my very desire to win. His face loomed closer and closer, keen on the competition, on the disciplined hard work that I must sustain if I really wanted to be a winner. His intensity and my lack of it led him one day, in exasperation, to say, "You don't really want to do this, do you?" I was relieved to hear myself say no.

He had tried, and he had failed. It was his best effort, and I don't gainsay it. He bore the failure mutely and without rancor.

I adored our Principal, Sr. Lillian, and by the time I entered fifth grade, she was my teacher. Her face and her hands, all I ever saw of her flesh, were always pink and clean. Her smile, her wit, and I liked to think, her partiality toward me, made her my obsession. She was wrapped in great authority. She composed music, taught piano, and was an admired vocalist. She hinted a little at her accomplishments during her summer recesses, enough to give us to understand that people traveled from near and far to hear her sing.

But she, too, was capable of breaking down under the rubric of purity, the isolation of a small midwestern town, the grind of needy, messy children, and the chilly, disapproving manner of her housemates equally starved of affection. One spring morning, against the usual background of whispering, and shuffling, and sniffling, and desktop banging, she simply snapped.

"How," she asked us, "could I possibly go on with people like you?" She stormed out of the classroom and locked herself in the library.

At first, we took this as license to break into chaos. But after giving full vent to pandemonium, it slowly dawned on us that it would fall to ourselves to get a grip on the situation. We acquiesced when Steve, the school bully, wrested control and imposed order. We knew this was the only possible solution to the crisis, and we submitted. There descended on the fully assembled fifth, sixth, seventh, and eighth-grade students of St. Mary's Elementary School an air of calm and camaraderie. Like small adults in a cordial town hall meeting, brandishing the respectful manners of give and take, we discussed what should be done. Ultimately, we decided that Steve should go to Sr. Lillian and tell her we were sorry and that we would change our ways. He came back after a few minutes to tell us she wouldn't open the door to him. We sent him back to apologize through the key-hole. Again, she simply refused to deal with us.

The standoff lasted all day. Contrite and confused, we spent our time copying from our readers, self-imposing the standard punishment assigned to recalcitrant students. She never once appeared, and at the end of the school day, we quietly packed up our things and went home. I said nothing that night, nor did Lee Ann. This was a private matter. On the next morning, we were back at square one, with Sr. Lillian locked away and Steve disciplining us and making the occasional fruitless diplomatic sortie toward the library. It was an electric time. The air was charged with all kinds of possibilities, all kinds of dread.

In the end, to a man — to a boy and to a girl — what we came to see was how much we wanted things back the way they had always been. I have no idea what Sr. Lillian came to see. After two days of this, she returned to us at morning Mass, and we all resumed our normal routine. No one ever referred to the incident after that.

Memory is illusive, susceptible to mutation over time. I am certain of a few things: Redcap, the boxing gloves, the sewing kit, and Sr. Lilian's exile in the library. I can affirm their existence; the memories are clear. But we experience things at a mad, onrushing pace. We assign to them their significance later, in rumination.

Five

IN THE AUTUMN OF MY SIXTH-GRADE YEAR, MY FATHER BOUGHT property in the western part of Clinton County, a former maple sugar camp on 17 acres of land in the Wildcat Creek river basin. It was listed by the realtor under the name Springwood. The prior owner was a botanist who converted the dwelling into a multi-roomed cabin that shed rain and cold without offering further creature comforts. The cabin was set down the lane a good bit back, off the gravel road that ran past the entrance. With its dense tree cover, it was invisible to passing cars most of the year. From inside it, the passing cars were invisible, too. It sat in its own quiet world, nestled in an old-growth forest fronted by a large stand of evergreen trees.

From the moment he first saw the place, Dad referred to it as paradise. Mom said nothing to him when he did, but she muttered to us her reservations about its isolation and state of disrepair. I was in love with Springwood, too. In the end, Dad's enthusiasm bore more inertia than Mom's caution. We were all eventually seduced by it. The woods lay at the eastern edge of a major watershed. Rivers began their formations there, flowing south-west and taking on increasing force. Unlike the ditches of the featureless flatland east of town, these streams were permanent and, after a rain, insistent. Over the millennia, they had carved out hollows and glens in an unimpeded flow to the Wabash River, on to the Ohio River on Indiana's southern border, and ultimately into the Mississippi.

A few gravel roads sliced up and down the surrounding hills, bending and curving. They crossed tall bridges arched over roiling waters. Wildcat Creek ran along the northern edge of our acreage. It teemed with fish and water snakes. The surrounding woodlands sheltered deer, raccoon, and a variety of other mammalian species that had survived the onslaught of the DDT pesticide decimating midwestern wildlife since just after the war.

There were fields under plow, but they were small and irregularly shaped. Given the topography left by the Wildcat's erosion, not even the industrious stripping, burning, and clearing by several generations of homesteaders had been able to clear cropland all the way to the horizon. Viewed down upon from high ridge-land, the isolated fields laid out finite geometries hemmed in by thick woods. Some of the fields abutted grassland outcropped with stone. These were only good for grazing cattle or sheep.

The creek beds had sandy bottoms. They ran clean and clear. Redbuds glowed pink in spring. Jonquils ran a rampant yellow. Wild violets sprawled in large beds under the cover of tall shade trees. Half-hidden morel mushrooms poked their spongiform heads out from under may-apples. June cottonwood showered everything in tiny silken parachutes. The pine trees exuded a resinous Christmas scent all summer.

Large waterfowl by day – and owls by night – had sufficient prey to keep themselves and their offspring fed. The streams hid crayfish and turtles. The woods above the riverbank sheltered sassafras and paw-paw trees, a habitat that in its turn sheltered flying squirrels. Gnarled beech trees stretched mature, intricate silver branches out over steep hollows, their equally complex root systems nakedly holding fast to the slopes. And, topmost, the tall pillars of tulip poplar, the Indiana State tree, craned up from the creek basin, trunks impossibly straight and branchless, to form the ultimate canopy.

The cabin had dangerously outdated electric wiring and fixtures. Sub-floor structural weaknesses needed repair. All the plumbing had to be replaced. More bedrooms were needed. Mom and Dad pored over plans, drawn up then redrawn several times, calling for insulation, new joists, studs, and plasterboard to wall out proper living quarters. Dad hired Norman, a general contractor, to guide him through the work of making the house suitable for the family. The two of them would take on the project by themselves in the evenings after their day jobs. I was brought along to help. The cabin was 20 miles west of our house on a road leading out of the other side of Frankfort called The Farmers' Gravel. Throughout that dark, cold winter and spring, we renovated the place. We framed out an open living room and a large, separate kitchen. We punctured the roof to add two dormers as the girls' and the boys' bedrooms. We finished part of the basement with a washroom and shower. We dug a new patio into the hillside and faced it with a stone wall for outdoor living space. We kept at it each evening with hammer, sledge, crow-bar, and trowel until we simply couldn't go on for fatigue. We came home to the glass of warm milk Mom insisted would help us sleep so we could pick up our other lives the next morning. I went to the site two or three nights a week as work sped up. Silent and observant, I learned the basics of cement-block work, studded walls and plasterboard construction, plumbing, wiring, and tiling. Norman was a low-key, gentle man. He and Dad often worked silently side by side, their instructions to each other punctuated by grunts of physical exertion. Sometimes they would take up a news item of the day, and I would thrill to adult conversation that comfortably included me in its orbit.

We moved into Springwood on June 20, 1960, a date I still remember, so strong did I deem my good fortune. Its setting offered a perfect geography for adolescence's nascent and inchoate inner stirrings. The summer passed in an idyll. I was happy to join in play with Glenn and Maureen, still enrapt in childhood. We didn't know any of the neighbors, but we were adapted to country living and accustomed to making our own amusement. Indiana summers are warm and lush. We had Wildcat Creek to explore. We had our own small rills running between steep-sided hills. We had all that luxuriant pine.

As if reverting to type, we soon began construction of another fort across the steep rift behind the house. We pilfered discarded cabinet doors and two-by-fours left in the shed after the renovation. Our plans were ambitious enough that we laid out street patterns. The fort morphed into a town. We named it Pineville. We dragged up dozens of metal pipes, old galvanized plumbing that had been torn out and replaced. We laid these underground with elbow extensions rising up within each "house." When someone spoke into his end of the pipe, he could be heard from the open ends in the other huts. It was a make-believe place, suitably scaled to our small frames, that grew out of earnestness and desire for predictability and dominion.

We built rafts, and we launched them into the Wildcat. It took several attempts to design one that could stay afloat. Each model required someone to pilot it. Maureen was the lightest of the three of us, and for each maiden voyage, the navigation fell to her. We pulled her out of the snake-infested water several times before we succeeded in keeping a raft from sinking. We fished the Wildcat and caught mostly carp and catfish, tossing the carp back in as they were deemed inedible. Catfish, on the other hand, were highly coveted in Indiana, where a few towns earned state-wide fame for their catfish restaurants. Live catfish have subcutaneous dorsal rays which they can protrude at will to puncture your hand if you hold them the wrong way. They have a mud vein that has to be stripped away when cleaning them. We had to be careful, but we were a fish-for-Friday family, and catfish was a prized meal.

We gathered morels in season and stalked the occasional intruders who were also collecting them. We were coached to be reasonable, to tell each trespasser, "I'm sorry, but this is private property. Those are our mushrooms." It was awkward, not to mention potentially dangerous, but it had to be done. We understood that if someone hurt himself on our land, he could sue us. It seemed unfair – the concept of being liable for an "attractive nuisance" – but I cited it as the reason the intruder should "kindly leave." We picked black raspberries in late summer so my mother could preserve them as jam. They left our hands and faces scratched and bloodied as we fought their aggressive thorns, all for rather mediocre produce, to my thinking.

Throughout all of this, Lee Ann was often absent. The move to Springwood was difficult for her. She had established friendships with Sue and Sarah Fudge, and she now knew no one but her boring siblings. Lee Ann spent a lot of time in her room listening to the radio, teasing her hair into the bouffant style that was fashionable then, and polishing her tennis shoes to an immaculate whiteness. There were days when I couldn't connect with Glenn and Maureen either, when I found myself out of sorts. On those days, I sought the solitude in Springwood that I found in the rest park in the eastern part of the county. I was fumbling with puberty, wildly happy, then numb with boredom. I read more science fiction and began supplanting it with historical fiction and magazines: *Time*, *U.S. News & World Report*, and *The New Yorker*. I plowed through these by inferring the meaning of unfamiliar words and building up a mental picture of a larger world where there were many different ways of being.

I still had a considerable capacity for silence, for mute observation of nature: how leaves rustle in the canopy, how flotsam works its way downstream in the small creeks, how the plants in the ground-cover deepen their greening as summer moves on. There was a silken patch of grey-green fox-grass over the wire fence that delineated our woods from the neighbor's. It was under a stand of walnut trees with a broad view of the Wildcat, out of sight of almost anyone at any time. There I took my books and magazines and had my deepest reveries. There I fretted over imponderable things.

With no bus service to Frankfort, St. Mary's school was out of range as an option for us. In our new district, Washington Township, the public school was in Jefferson, a few miles south of Springwood. Jefferson sat between State Highway 28 and the Nickel Plate Road, the two arteries that sustained the entire county and were its *raison d'etre*. Jefferson had less than a dozen short streets in a standard grid. When Indiana was granted statehood in 1816, its citizenry expected Jefferson to be chartered as the county seat. It lost out to Frankfort in 1830 and had to content itself with an ancient cemetery, a large grain silo near the railroad tracks, a public school, and a vague air of defeat.

I was intimidated by the idea of going to public school. Adding to the nervousness were tensions over the 1960 presidential election. It was increasingly clear that John Kennedy, the Democratic candidate, had a real chance of being elected. Rumors began that a Catholic president would mean Vatican-driven foreign policy, a revival of the Roosevelt welfare state, and the end of religious freedom. These fears filtered down to us obliquely, mediated by what Mom and Dad did and didn't say in front of us. A few days before we began school, they coached us on the topic of the election. They were careful to avoid reference to the Catholic-Protestant culture war still emitting its creedal fog. Dad simply said he thought they should say something to us, mindful that people would make assumptions about us "as Catholics." It didn't then occur to me that they, too, knew few of the neighbors and they, too, knew the challenge of fitting-in. This coaching was part of their effort. "If anybody says anything, or anybody asks," he said, "we are not voting for John Kennedy. We are voting for Richard Nixon."

I was stunned to hear it. After the announcement, I sat at the dinner table, staring at the clutter of empty dessert plates in front of me, trying to understand such betrayal. There was a measured seriousness in Dad's tone and in Mom's silent nodding. I couldn't fathom why they would not vote for the Catholic, for one of us. I suppose Dad was simply holding true to his tribal upbringing. His father had railed against the Democrats – especially the Roosevelts – when he was a boy. He once quoted the refrain he grew up hearing, mocking Eleanor Roosevelt: "I'll kiss the niggers, and you kiss the Jews." He had taken for himself his wife's religion;

he had raised his children Catholic; he had seen to our proper religious education. But, he would not abandon the Republican Party. That was a bridge too far. Mom closed ranks with him. I don't know if she shared his opinion, or voted as he did, but it was made clear that evening that this was the family position. It was on record.

And so more bus commuting, now to another school. The hours spent riding a bus and sitting in classrooms made for a long day. Traveling with kids who were in those classrooms offered some continuity, as if the two worlds cross-pollinated each other. Friendships formed on the morning ride meant familiar faces at school. Our corner of the county was sparsely populated. Seventh-graders like myself, uninterested in elementary kids, had a small cohort of potential companions. We were direct with, but tolerant of, each other. The early hour and the sheer number of times we rode together meant we came to know each other well. I can't say many of them showed much interest in how I saw things, or what school had to offer, but I was happy enough to settle for their tolerance.

The school was a large 1920s brownstone, a two-story building with outsized granite quoins framing its edges and set back on a lawn 15 or 20 yards from the street running parallel to the highway and train tracks. It had several rooms on both floors flanking central hallways, each room with remarkably high, multi-paned windows overlooking the grain silo in the rear and the broad, porch-fronted bungalows across the street in front. Large stairwells opened to those hallways, and the classroom doors were topped by transoms high enough that they required extension cranks to open them. The ground floor, where grades one through five had their classrooms, also housed the principal's office. An annex perpendicular to the main building held the gymnasium where the sacred Hoosier rites of junior and varsity basketball stoked the hearts of every living soul in Washington Township.

Jefferson School was a repository of visible stains and scratches, entrenched smells, and ghostly generational memories framed in photographs. It was a sturdy monument to the value placed on a good, solid education, one that wouldn't lead to ideas that challenged the status quo. The kids who lived in the village itself formed their own clique. Those of us who were bussed in from the hinterlands were considered part of a lesser crowd. If a community of 90 to 100 people could claim a special *savoir-faire*, we, the kids on the bus, lacked it.

I had my own way of not fitting-in. I came from a parochial school where the academic performance of every student had been everyone's business. At St. Mary's, when our schoolwork fell short, the nuns used shame as a pedagogic technique. If we were slow with an answer, they would ask someone else to answer for us, demonstrating that we were shirking our duty of study, passing that onus onto another child. The coercion was intensified by the ethos of strict moral formation and the certain knowledge of right and wrong, of virtue and sin. It instilled a collective eagerness to acquit ourselves well in the classroom. For a brief period, Sr. Lillian used this shaming technique on my sister, who in class was shy and reticent to respond aloud. Sr. Lillian would ask me to answer the question Lee Ann hadn't. Eager to shine and thoughtless of the consequences, I piped up with the answers. After a few such incidents, Lee Ann gave tear-laden accounts at the dinner table of how I made her look bad in school. I was admonished to refuse to answer any questions put to me in such circumstances. There was a corrective parent-teacher conference over it as well. I remember the guilt I felt at making my sister cry. I also remember the hurt, injured look she wrapped around herself for weeks thereafter, as her entitlement for such injustice.

The skill we developed in garnering teacher approval at St. Mary's was called brown-nosing in Jefferson and did not serve me well. Seventh-grade Geography class was taught by Mrs. Hurt. I liked her classroom. It had a remarkably complete set of roll-down maps that charted the entire world. One day Mrs. Hurt began a new textbook chapter by pulling down the atlas of Australia and asking who could name the large bay on its north side. I immediately threw my hand up into the air several times, as if casting a fly rod and looking for the perfect stream bed. For further emphasis, I threw in several hissed urgings of "Sister! Sister!" The room went deathly silent, and I soon realized Mrs. Hurt and everyone else in class were staring at me, shocked and amused by such an off-the-wall response. The word "Sister," shaming because so Catholic, echoed off the walls.

The alternative, then, was to play it cool. I had already been exposed to the entire seventh <u>and</u> eighth-grade standardized curriculum at St. Mary's. My fellow students at Jefferson were, in the main, having trouble with the seventh-grade curriculum. Even worse, they didn't seem bothered by their slowness. My refuge was laconic silence and smuggled supplementary reading material hidden in textbooks. Most of the teachers, unsure of how to handle me, accepted my high test scores along with my disengagement as being of a piece. But my English teacher, Miss Spangenberg, mistook me for a cheat.

A few weeks into the first semester, she assigned an essay on some since-forgotten topic. In my response, I set up a "straw man," an initial argument I then refuted point by point, something I learned from the magazine editorials I was fond of reading. In her rejection of the essay, she focused on my use of the word "adept." She returned my paper with the word circled in red ink, the same bright red color she wore on her fingernails. The word *adept* sat like a stray dogie, lassoed on the page. There was no grade on the paper, simply a note that we would discuss this matter.

In fact, we didn't discuss the matter. Miss Spangenberg called my father in for a conference, showed him the offending paper, complete with the circled "adept." It's clear I hadn't written the paper, she told him. Had he? I wasn't part of the meeting, but in his later retelling, he would chuckle. Not at the notion that I had put forth a cogent argument or shown off my vocabulary, but that he would have deigned to write an essay for me.

There were other indignities, both mysterious and gratuitous. In Mr. Robertson's Music class, a once-a-week event that, for some reason, included only boys, while singing Christmas carols, I sang out a high tenor descant line on the last chorus of The First Noel. That was how we always sang it. Mr. Robertson stopped playing mid-bar. The other boys started giggling and snorting. It took me a moment to realize that Mr. Robertson was angry, and even longer to realize he was angry with me. When I realized it, I blurted out something akin to, "Why? What's wrong?" He never answered my question. I sat out the rest of the music period that grey December day, in the wide and empty hallway, swollen with self-pity. I had committed the sin of "ornamentation," clearly a Papist tendency.

I never felt like anything but an imposter at Jefferson, as if the mismatched expectations that I had for school, and that Jefferson had for me, proved there was something incomplete or mistaken about me. But that was to be my only year there. A new consolidated school, Clinton Prairie, was under construction a few miles to the south. It would accommodate all the students in grades seven through 12 from Jefferson, Mulberry, Colfax, and Antioch, the entire western half of Clinton County. I was to be dealt a new hand once again.

Six

PINEVILLE LAY ABANDONED THROUGHOUT THAT JEFFERSON school year. It bore signs of winter's siege and nature's intrusion. Root-sprouting plants and burrowing creatures had invaded all of the dwellings. The houses themselves were muddied, rank, and more cramped. The telephone system was flooded, irreparable with our limited technology. We began a reclamation. Glenn was elected mayor. I was the newspaper editor, owing to my small wooden hand-stamp press. It had three horizontal grooves into which I slid moveable-type letters, a box of those assorted rubber letters, and an ink pad. That first day back in town, we formulated our plan for renewal. I have a copy of the May 26, 1961 issue of The Pineville News, dated for posterity. The limited number of letters in my type box, and what might be thought of as our rush to deadline, made for brief articles. Each one is quoted here in sequence and in its entirety:

- A new lunch bar, bank, general store are to be built at Pineville soon.
- Wanted: One windowasher. Call Mommy.
- Glenn and Dan went to the first 4H meeting on May 25th.
- Mrs. Paul Juday visited her mother on May 24th.
- Mrs. Juday will add another member to the Juday family soon.

I stamped this news onto small paper squares, thereby willing town renewal into place. I willed that there be a newspaper, that we have a bank, that Maureen open a general store. The very language exposes that willfulness. "Are to be built" is a future passive infinitive claim on things that did not exist. More remarkably, the news account contains one of the most egregiously buried leads of my attempts at journalism. My mother was pregnant, yet it is the last thing I mention.

But that was to be overshadowed by further breaking news. Within days of publishing this first, and as it transpired only, issue of The Pineville News, my father told me, almost as an aside as I was putting away the lawnmower, that I was 13 years old now. A teenager. It was time I had a job. I would work for him.

My father's stockyard was in the industrial outskirts of Frankfort, next to a spur of the Nickel Plate Road. The vacant slaughterhouse attached to it once fed the local populace but was no longer viable in terms of scale. Big commercial meat-packing corporations on the East Coast were buying hogs in semi-trailer loads. They slaughtered and processed pork carcasses, established regional and national brands, and shipped product to growing markets across the country. A burgeoning trucking industry and improved refrigeration made this feasible. Dad's business model was to buy small lots of hogs from local farmers, sort and re-aggregate them, and sell them in large lots to out-of-state meatpackers. There were two men on staff to look after the customers, clean the yards, and keep the livestock in place. Neither liked cleaning the pens, the "shit work." I would be their break from it. I began my working life on the first Monday of June 1961.

Someone told me, soon after I started working in the yards, that the nose adjusts to ambient smells within twelve minutes. I suppose it's true, but I didn't particularly mind the earthiness and was soon inured to the stench. What I liked was being useful, being the lone boy among men, eager to show I knew what to do, to show I was part of a larger, grown-up enterprise. That these men would allow me to share their camaraderie was sufficient compensation.

I worked the off-load chutes, built to accommodate the farmers' small, low truck beds. I drove their hogs down an alleyway and onto scales that could pen up to fifty at a time. I drove each lot to their holding pens. I soaked the cement floors and power-hosed the acrid effluent into a sewer system that ended in a cesspit behind the yards. In the afternoon, large semis pulled up to the on-load chutes in the back. There the truckers and I ran the hogs up steep, shit-slick ramps into three-level trailer beds that held more than a hundred head. Hogs are naturally reluctant to go up and down inclines. To get them to do so requires yelling, whipping, and electric prodding from behind. If I had qualms about driving thousands of sentient animals every week to their certain destruction, my mantra was "people have to eat." I took refuge in my father's rants against vegetarian arguments. Certain basic proteins, he insisted, were found only in meat. But on quiet afternoons, perched on top of a stockade fence, watching those corralled animals interact with each other in such forced proximity – fighting like overwrought people in an angry crowd to determine who had squatter's rights, who would feed first – I saw their kinship with humankind. I saw the interrelatedness of all mammalian life forms on our shared evolutionary journey. At a cosmic level, all living things appear to be variations of the same, one thing willing life itself. I saw I was employed in a dispassionate system that brought intelligent creatures from farrow-grate to butcher's counter with a total focus on maximum efficiency. I watched highly social animals spend their last days in stockyard pens and on livestock trailers crammed nose to tail in frenzied terror. The frenzy was contagious. I was never totally numb to it.

Hog are self-protective and keenly aware of their surroundings. The herds passing through were undergoing a nightmare journey into dread. The idealized lifecycle of farm animals, illustrated in children's storybooks, is one of birthing, suckling, weaning, and fattening. The emphasis is on comfort, routine, and fondly remembered and illustrated settings. The hogs I watched from my roost, counting them in twos and sometimes threes, were part of a millennia-long tradition of animal husbandry. There is a nod to this in Genesis, where we are assured that "mankind shall have dominion."

The religious tradition handed down to me elevated sacrifice. Every morning of the school week, on many First Saturdays and on every Sunday, I witnessed the Sacrifice of the Mass, a mysterious re-enactment founded on pre-Christian rites comingling the slaughter of animals with obeisance and victim offerings to a higher power. But the on-load chute that enabled the afternoon herding of hundreds of hogs in a fevered, screeching rush into sometimes two and three semis a day was far removed from that ancient human rhythm. It was – and is increasingly so today – a mechanized harvesting of flesh on a vertically integrated corporate scale. I place no particular guilt, if any is to be meted out, on myself, or my father, or any of the farmers engaged in all of that. I simply relate what I have seen at close range, what is done in our rush to feed the global markets that can afford commercially produced pork. Perhaps it is pointless to struggle with moral justification for what is a biological imperative. Life voraciously feeds on itself. Perhaps civilization depends on our ambivalence.

For the several summers of my adolescence, and on school and Christmas holidays, I spent my weekdays rising early and passing long hours in rubber boots running up and down cement alleys. The open barns were hot in summer and cold in winter. There were mornings and afternoons when I was alone, lost in vivid, morphing reveries. Time passed less tortuously once I learned to stop thinking about its measure. I earned a dollar a day that first summer. There was a large barrel in the office filled with peanuts soaked in brine. It was there for the customers, but I kept a regular hand in it. I also had indoor chores to complete alongside the men in Dad's employ, the commercial truckers, and the farmers selling their livestock. In cold weather, I found frequent reasons throughout the day to seek the office's sheltering heat. I learned its tacit rules.

When a farmer came in to sell hogs, the initial talk was low, nearly murmured. It had to do with hundredweights and market quotations, what was heard on the radio or read in the farm report. It was quiet conversation, usually just with my father, man-to-man talk with eyes cast downward and gaps left open to mutually assess the reasonableness being shown on both sides. Sometimes the seller was Amish, in which case a wife might accompany him. With women present, the talk was particularly sedate. Bracketed by long silences, each topic was self-policed for propriety. Opinions were phrased with concern for "present company."

With no women present, the language was looser, opinions more forceful, and the subject matter more wide-ranging. My presence had no diminishing effect on any of it. I was below the radar. Once the transaction was complete and the deal settled, there followed a handshake, a collective exhale, then a ratcheting up of volume and change of subject. Voices grew louder. Politics were debated. General grievances were aired. Many men tossed in expletives to further punctuate their assertions. They chose their words for impact. I was stunned the first few times I heard the talk enter this dark territory.

Someone in the heat of an argument would claim, "You can't trust that mother-fucker." A brief silence would ensue. The word hung out there, both semi-permissible and semi-offensive for most within hearing. Ultimately the listeners would accede to the crudeness, and a few would be spurred on by it.

"The cock-sucker doesn't know what he's saying. He can kiss my ass."

A thirteen-year-old boy growing up in a town, among other boys, might have been accustomed to this language. I wasn't. It was as if someone slapped my ears. My word for it would have been naughty, but that didn't rise to the occasion. Naughty was "damn," or "shit," the kind of adult word a child filters out but secretly stores away for future use. The sexual intensity of the office language was something new. I struggled with a literal understanding of the terms. Why would someone fuck his mother? What would make him do that? Why would you call someone a cock-sucker? Did people do that? What else could it mean? Why would you want someone to kiss your ass? What was the purpose of that? Wouldn't you be embarrassed to have someone do it?

Where was my father in all of this? Certainly not an active participant. He was running a business. He was the boss, and

70

he set a tone that discouraged excessive indecency. He seldom uttered anything beyond what would today be considered mild cursing. The phrase he used frequently – I suspect it was his device to avoid stronger obscenities – was "bear's ass." He used it in syntactical niches that might otherwise have been slotted for "bull shit." "Oh, bear's ass," he'd say when someone was trying to assert what seemed patently outrageous. The phrase still puts a smile on my face. But he wasn't deaf to the foulness of the words thrown about. He listened to them impassively and then steered the conversation back to the topic at hand. I sensed his keeping an oblique eye on me to judge how this man-talk was registering with me. These things are in the air, he seemed to say, and there's no preventing them. Stand up tall and let them wash over you.

My father was happily sexual. He was unguardedly demonstrative with my mother at home. In the evening, he would slide up behind her at the stove and wrap his arms around her, nuzzling his cheek against hers. He'd whisper something suggestive enough to make her say, "Oh, Paul," and smile at its boldness, naturally affirming that physical affection was a good and welcome thing. In his office in the stockyards, he hung a Playboy calendar on the back of the door. With the door ajar, it was barely visible from the public area. The sudden appearance of an Amish wife required only a slight shift of the door to prevent her being offended by the image of a naked young woman audaciously arching herself to display her pert, pink, airbrushed breasts. The assumption was that any man would be grateful for a glimpse of Miss June or Miss July. The full issue of *Playboy* magazine was often sitting on Dad's desk. I wasn't overtly encouraged to ogle it, but it was there for me to look at, and I sensed my father's indulgence when I did.

Tolerance of sexual imagery was different from the aggressive language I was hearing. *Faggot* was the worst the men in the stockyards hurled – rare enough that it never lost its punch. I recognized faggot. The boys in Jefferson had a fanatical focus on faggots. At any random moment, any one of us could be accused of being one. It was the worst thing to be. A faggot was a queer. The whispered secret among those in the know was that queers wore green on Thursday. The rumor gave rise to cautious sartorial monitoring on everyone's part.

A queer was a failure at sports. Queerness was ignorance of the subtleties of sex. I had a subliminal assessment of my own level of queerness. Naivety was the entry level, and my effeminate giddiness, which I had to constantly guard against, indicated a deeper level. My love of designing and sewing clothes, my dread of boxing, and my aversion to rough-and-tumble was more evidence. I knew that much. It hovered in a distant corner of my mind. I could not disown this truth, but I could refuse to claim it. I could let it drift out of focus and avert my eyes.

But standing behind the sales counter in the stockyard office, I heard grown men excitedly call other grown men cock-suckers. I could not avoid the obvious fact that this had literal roots. It had sexual implications. These men knew something I didn't. They couldn't refrain themselves from repeating it. They found it somehow both fascinating and deeply maddening, severely vexing. Everyone clearly abhorred it but brought it up again and again in moments of pique. What they were saying was, indeed, there were genuine faggots, and they were repulsed by them. Faggots were to be called out for shaming.

That first summer of steady work meant that I no longer fit in with the rhythms and routines of the house. I was set apart from all of it. My days started before my siblings awoke and were spent away from Springwood, away from Pineville and the Wildcat, alienated from those who still belonged in those spheres. My father woke me wordlessly every morning, silently putting his hand on my shoulder so as not to disturb Glenn, and went back downstairs to fry our bacon and eggs. He expected me downstairs by the time breakfast was on my plate, and he moved at a faster pace than I was used to. He cooked with a high flame under the skillet, a manifestation of his impatience to get on with things. His bacon and eggs were quickly fried, brittle, and crispy as a result. He stood over the stovetop with a composed and quiet countenance. We spoke little on those mornings. The rest of the house was asleep, and his mind was on the day's business, the month's financials, and the market trends. I had little time for conversation anyway, tasked with eating breakfast and getting into the soiled boots and freshly-washed uniform kept next to the basement shower stall without delaying our departure. My thoughts were on the stockyard's feedbags and power-hoses.

Adrift in the hours spent at those tasks, I had a private place to ponder my mother's pregnancy. My parents told us on a Friday, after dinner, near the end of the school term, that a new baby was coming. Mom was at the start of her second trimester. This gave us the weekend to absorb it before going out to inform the world. It also gave us time to decide what we thought about it. The household consensus was that this was exciting news. We were a family that knew happiness, and the idea of another family member offered the possibility of more happiness. Maureen, at nine, was the youngest child. If she felt threatened losing her status as the baby, she never let on. She was eager to be a big girl and seemed genuinely happy with the news. Lee Ann felt owed an additional deference due to her reinforced status as eldest. She looked at the prospective baby as one more subordinate sibling. Glenn kept his silence.

My inclination was to go along with the consensus. I made appropriately eager sounds, but privately saw two major problems. The first was that my mother's pregnancy was clear proof of my parents' ongoing sexual activity. I never had another sex talk with my father after the peanuts-in-the-jeans chat, but my understanding of these things was relatively clear by then. The sore point was not that they were sexually active, but that everyone would know they were sexually active. Nearly 40 years old, what compelled them toward such things?

The second problem, beyond the public shame, was the risk that the baby would be deformed. My seventh-grade class pored over black-and-white science textbook images of children with Down's syndrome, conjoined twins, and hydrocephalic babies. There were any number of distressing possibilities in Mom's pregnancy. But everyone was smiling, congratulatory, and solicitous while we could very well be standing on the brink of real tragedy.

Within the orbit of our close family friends were two families who had severely challenged children. One girl, Karen, had a starkly deformed appearance, her thin and awkward limbs seemingly mis-joined to her body. We were told she was born backwards. She was my age and seldom went to school. She had few words to express what she was thinking, communicated poorly and infrequently, and took notice of very little around her. She and I got along well, and I was happy enough to tolerate her tugging on me, grunting things, and looking pleased to be acknowledged. But she needed constant monitoring and special care, even for simple things like getting up steps or eating food. Another family had Janet, an angelic-looking girl who had a sweet smile that hid severe, uncontrolled tantrums, fears, and destructive habits. Because we often visited both these families, I knew that life for everyone living with Karen and Janet was difficult. In their siblings,

I could often see a kind of stoic coping, extra energy spent getting an ordinary day back on track after an accident befell them or an emotional scene played out. I worried that the new baby might bring that kind of sapping, perpetual drama to our house.

One Saturday afternoon that summer, my mother arranged her new maternity wardrobe to display it on the living room sofa. I suppose she intended to engage with the girls about the new clothing, but my interest in fabric and design drew me to inspect each item. I pored over them. What struck me was the darkness of the colors she chose and the heavy weight of the material. It was a collection of two-piece outfits, skirts and matching tops. The skirts had hidden under-panels that would allow for the abdominal protuberance that was setting in. The tops were designed to hide the panels and diminish the protuberance. They were short-sleeved and trimmed with large bows or over-sized buttons. They had darts and pleats along the front to finesse what would become an expanding silhouette. The clothes were well-tailored, but there was something prim and matronly about them. They were designed to hide the pregnancy and struck me as heavy-handed and theatrical. I don't know why I didn't like them, but lied and told my mother I thought they were beautiful.

I came home to the long, lingering evenings of that summer exhausted, rank with livestock odors, and ravenous. I tried to slip back into the household rhythms as best I could and chatted with my mother while she prepared dinner. I draped my lengthening frame from my grasp on the overhead kitchen cabinets, just as I had done throughout the school year. There were new things to tell her, but somehow stockyard work was of less interest to her than the things my teacher said and what I thought of them. I was no longer the young boy decompressing from his school day, sorting over its minutiae for tidbits to offer his mother. I was the adolescent who spent his day in his Dad's world, occupied with things outside of what concerned her. She and I were going through changes simultaneously but separately. Our worlds were diverging, and it was hard to re-establish the rapport with her I so valued. At times she seemed to be listening and responded to my enthusiasms. Other times she let me know with her busied silence or distracted unresponsiveness that she needed space. She needed quiet, and sometimes I had to be prompted to recognize this with, "Please, Dan."

So much changed that summer. Each change felt charged in a novel way. The one automobile I knew better than all the others that came and went from my earliest memories was our 1950 Chevy sedan. My father drove a series of leased cars that were newer, sportier, and more stylish, but the Chevy was a member of the family. With an even larger family coming on, Dad decided it was time to replace it. He was upgrading to a family station wagon – even more perfidiously, a Ford. The night before the buyer came to claim the old sedan, I snuck out to the carport to look at it once more. I saw its black, curved metal trunk-lid arced downward like a tail between its legs in a protective crouch against my father's betrayal. Just above the trunk latch, it whispered a cursive "Chevrolet." I came very near to talking back to it, to bidding it goodbye. This was my childhood's companion, and at thirteen years of age, I was learning that time has hinges on which it sways and closes gates behind us.

That summer was the first time, though not the last, when I would walk into the quiet living room and find my mother sitting in a chair in a dark corner under the open staircase. She sat still, slippered heels joined, feet aligned and pointing slightly to one side. Her hands were palm-down on her knees. She was looking at her knuckles in silence. It was disturbing to see this woman, otherwise always busy at something, sitting so still. One of her abiding principles was that each of her children be treated with a careful show of evenhandedness. This required a curated detachment, a steady distancing. None of us would have expected, or even attempted, to get special privileges from her, but that summer, seeing her so withdrawn, I wanted her confidence. I wanted her to talk to me in a way that she would not have ever been disposed to speak to any of us. I wanted her to tell me what was wrong. I wanted to console her.

Of course, I see now I wanted her to console me. I had the habit of seeing the world as immutable. I reflexively melded anything new and unfamiliar into my personal narrative of stasis and reliability. There would be changes and turns of luck, as a matter of course, I reasoned. But now, increasingly, I could no longer cast those changes as mere oscillations within a fixed world.

The laws of the marketplace obtain for every good and service, even in the marketplace of familial love. And those laws only record what they never can control – the seasonal imbalances, one way or the other, between supply and demand.

St Josephs

Wildcat Creek

Birthday Cake

Ms. Grishams' Class

79

Seven

ON FRIDAY AFTERNOON, OCTOBER 20, 1961, I CAME HOME from school to an empty house. We had been on alert for weeks, and I ran straight to Mom and Dad's bedroom to check for the hospital suitcase. It was gone. So, it was happening now. She was having the baby.

For an anxious hour, we fidgeted, climbed up and down the stairs, bounced on the sofas, and tried to out-voice each other's predictions. With two boys and two girls in the family, the sole topic was about which sex would be in the majority when the baby came home. Glenn and I were supposed to be rooting for a boy, Lee Ann and Maureen, seldom united in any sentiment, said they wanted a girl. In truth, I just wanted a baby without the congenital deformations that had worried me for months. The banter was oddly intense. As Lee Ann bore down on the gender question, the competition ceased being fun. Somehow dread loomed over the issue.

Our telephone was mounted on the pine-paneled wall of the TV room just off the hallway. Its central location highlighted the public nature of phone calls in a house of six people during a less-mediated age. It was an early 20th-century model, a sturdy assemblage of wood, metal, and Bakelite. A crank on the right side would ring the operator with one long, continuous turning. A black bell over the speaking tube rang when the operator wanted to reach us. Our identifying ring was four short bursts. Other combinations, some shorter, some longer, meant the call was for someone else on the party line. The decency with which we were raised was all that kept us from lifting the ear cup from its cradle when someone else's ring sounded.

However she managed it, Lee Ann was nearest the phone when the four short rings sounded and seemed delighted with herself.

"Hi, Daddy!" *Pause.* "Really! That's wonderful." *Pause.* "Ok. Ok. Bye."

And then the smuggest look I had ever seen on my sister's face. She folded her arms across her chest and stood there, mute and immobile. At last, I burst out. "What is it? What is it?"

"I'm not telling," she smirked. She walked out of the room as though she had some purpose in mind other than deeply upsetting the rest of us. She kept up the silence for half an hour, roaming around the house, feigning tasks. The news was monumental, of course, and not hers to withhold. We had as much right to it as she did. Torn between the demands of justice and a desire to avoid a real fight, I finally confronted her. "This isn't right. And you know it."

She blurted, "It's a boy." Oddly, she didn't seem unhappy with that result. Instead, she looked strangely pleased. She yielded the information with a gloating *so, there!* look on her face that was at odds with all her earlier cheerleading for a girl. I felt a swift emotional wallop at the news. We had a family agreement that if it were a boy, the baby's name would be David Michael. I went upstairs and sat on the edge of my bed and said, "David Michael Juday" aloud. It sounded odd. I had never known a David Michael Juday. There had never been one, and now there was.

Mom, with this late-in-life delivery and four children at home, was kept in the hospital for a few more days. Dad returned home that evening and, by default, suddenly had us in his care. We carried on as always, washing the dishes, doing the laundry and ironing, and scrubbing the kitchen and bathrooms. The housework ran on without interruption. Perhaps in an effort to make some gesture toward his temporary role as chief-cook-and-bottle-washer, Dad opted, on the Sunday after David's birth, to fix a pineapple-upside-down cake, a family favorite. The recipe called for a preparation of brown sugar, butter, and pineapple rings in a black-iron skillet, into which he poured cake batter. He set the oven to his default setting of high, the same full-scale assault on cooking he made when frying breakfast, and baked the cake. The kitchen soon filled with black smoke pouring out of the oven vents. We laughed through our scurry to open windows and get the by-now-flaming skillet out to the patio. The smoke hung in the air like a portent. There had been an inherent rightness to things as they were up until then. Now, unreliable, makeshift arrangements would have to be cobbled together, and some wouldn't work.

On the day our baby came home to the bosom of his family, we cooed and awed continuously – both as a group and in turns, as individual siblings. David Michael paid little heed, staring off into space with opaque, milky eyes, pursing impossibly tiny lips ready for his next feeding. I was taken by how compelling a newborn is, how small and delicate. He had microscopic, perfectly formed fingernails on the ends of such tiny fingers. Mottled skin and remnants of the umbilical cord were proof that this fretting, writhing life had indeed emerged from inside the chambers of my mother.

It was arranged with Fr. Mueller, the parish priest, that Lee Ann and I would be godparents at the christening. I was just shy of 14 years old, canonically too young for the role. Dad, raised in the Protestant dispensation, saw church law as negotiable. He argued for an exception. I don't know what persuaded Fr. Mueller, but he acceded. The Sunday afternoon that we brought little David Michael to the baptismal font, Mom slipped me a ten-dollar bill saying it was my job as godfather to thank the priest with a remuneration. I did so with as much nonchalance as an altar boy could manage, palming off cold cash to the god-like presence of his parish priest. Grace and mercy and eternal life had been earned for us through Jesus' death and resurrection; it turned out that a ritual sprinkling to welcome a child into that grace and mercy required further emolument.

I had made my First Holy Communion at the altar rail of that same church with Rev. Leo J. Scheetz, Parish Priest, administering the sacrament. The nuns had warned us not to let the unleavened wafer stick to the roof of our mouths. They encouraged us to look for signs that Jesus was entering our souls. On the day, I strained mightily, squeezing my eyes shut against the distractions of the material world, waiting for some bodily sensation that the change was complete, that Jesus was now living inside me, and I had been made stronger and holier by His presence. A few years later, at the same altar rail, I was ceremoniously slapped by The

Most Reverend John George Bennett, Bishop of the Diocese of Lafayette-in-Indiana, who came to confirm us in our faith, ritually demanding that we declare ourselves soldiers for Christ. I was rehearsed to say I would, although I knew by then I wasn't really soldier material.

Now here I stood again, next to the baptismal font near the entrance to the church, across from the dark wooden confessional booth where I had whispered so many petty failings – fighting with my sister, forgetting my chores, touching myself. I was holding my baby brother for another sacramental milestone – my godson-to-be. I was committing myself to look after him and to concern myself with his eternal soul, should anything happen to Mom and Dad. It was a serious charge being thrust on a reluctant soul who knew his own weakness only too well. I trembled as I held him over the small font of water, willing myself to be his defense against Satan and all of Satan's sorties and sallies against this newborn infant. I knew I was unprepared for such clear-headed, true-hearted valor. I wasn't even equipped to do so in my own defense.

Lee Ann began a gradual, extended turn away from aloofness and toward periodic, full-bore tantrums. She always had a big-sister bossiness about her, but the Friday night David was born, with Mom and Dad out of the house, was the beginning of a determined campaign for control. The new baby may have been the catalyst. Maybe it was caused by those few days without Mom's presence, a kind of usurpation. Whatever the cause, her temper grew in intensity from then onward. She mastered eye-rolling out of Mom's line of sight and would suddenly wail out protestations or refuse to come down from her room for dinner. Her complaints were varied but, to my mind, strange and obscure: one of us startled her in the kitchen or embarrassed her on the bus; Mom asked her to do something in the wrong tone; Dad questioned her about her attitude. Any annoyance could lead to a scene.

While I was mystified, I marveled at her daring. She knew how to push Mom and Dad to Armageddon's edge without incurring major punishment. Even when reprimanded, she seemed pleased with her performance. Hers was an entrenched grievance, in stark contrast to my constant need for approval and comity. I knew I lacked the defiant boldness she showed. I also knew I wouldn't be allowed the kinds of scenes she pulled. I didn't know what was at the root of her distress, but her resentment offered no hope for any kind of prolonged peace in the house. It served, intended or not, to further fray the fabric that held us together. It made us withdraw from each other just that little bit, encouraged us to lean out and away from a now volatile center. Tension settled in, taut like a tripwire, liable to flare into tearful scenes, especially when Mom and Dad were away.

PART II

Faith

Listen to the jingle,
The rumble and the roar
As she glides along the woodland
Through the hills and by the shore.
Hear the mighty rush of the engine,
Hear the lonesome hobo squall.
You're traveling through the jungles on
The Wabash Cannonball.

—Traditional American Folksong

One

MY FATHER ANNOUNCED ON A FRIDAY NIGHT IN SEPTEMBER that we were going to build a lake in Springwood. What he described was more appropriately called a reservoir, created by a dam across the lower end of the creek behind the house, looming above where its waters reached the Wildcat. He had the backing of the Army Corps of Engineers. Our collaborator in the effort would be Walter, a hired hand. I don't know where or how Dad and Walter met each other. I thought it odd that he was so much younger than Dad, younger than any of Dad's other friends. When I first met him, Walter was eager to let me know how much he admired Springwood and how happy he was to be working on the project. He was older than I was, nevertheless, and he was full of instructions – on equipment maintenance, on coffee brewing, on the growth of hardwoods – so I saw him as a mentor.

Walter's regular job was working on railroad and utility crews, felling trees and clearing underbrush and overgrowth. He was tall, long-limbed, and notably laconic. He had a mastery of ropes, winches, pulleys, and chain saws. He could scramble up the tallest trees or stand at their base and plot where they would fall, like calling a pool shot. He was the most daring, wiry, agile man I ever knew.

Over the course of that autumn and, after a mid-winter hiatus, resuming in the early spring, we cleared the brush and trees from the would-be lakebed up to the projected water line. From early morning frost through the low-slanted light of late afternoon, Walter dropped debris from the canopy. I learned to stay alert to the ropes and branches overhead, and I enjoyed yelling "timber" when another tree fell. When Walter gave the all-clear, Dad waded into the tangle of leafy branches and cut them into smaller lengths with his own chain saw. Glenn and I dragged those onto the fire, our misery's only relief on cold autumn and winter days. In the terse and awkward way of men basking in hard labor, high risk, and virile display, not a word was uttered about which direction we would work in or what we might accomplish for the day. Grunting and the occasional false laughter at a branch welt across the cheek – or a side-stepped disaster – were the only exceptions to the silence. Men don't talk, and boys don't ask.

All the while, serious hardwood tumbled around us. The steep embankments of the ravine had been carved out from alluvial soil over millennia. The creek bed at their base was populated by crawdads, water-striders, and any number of fingerling fish in its flow. I loved every rock and tree-root of its course. I had often poked and prodded my way along it. But I was now engaged in a man's work, building a lake, and I shrugged off the numb of regret

I felt at all the destruction. The dam was completed by the Corps by June, but it burst open a few months after the lake filled. All that accumulated water was released at once, overpowering the Wildcat and temporarily flooding the adjacent fields. The Corps returned to reconstruct and fortify the dam once more, insistent that it belonged there now.

After the dam's restoration and the refilling of the lake, I came to see it, on the one hand, as something lovely and pleasing. It offered boating and swimming – or ice-skating in winter – and its surface reflected seasonal changes in the surrounding foliage under its open sky. Fresh, cool water flowed across its surface, over the dam spill-way, and into the Wildcat. At the same time, I saw it as the watery grave of a forest bed I once knew and loved, now irretrievably submerged. On warm summer evenings, after dinner, I sometimes went down to its shoreline. I would wade in and stand in the tepid lake water up to my chest, quickly running my hand, palm downward, back and forth across its surface, hydroplaning. It was mindless sensory play that in its way confirmed both the existence of the lake and the secrets of a world I knew lay beneath its surface.

In the autumn of 1958 while I was still enrolled at St. Mary's School, Pope Pius XII died. The framed photograph of him on the back wall of our classroom, in fading color and three-quarter profile, was all I knew of ecclesial authority. It was fathomable – although terrifying – that he should die and go to heaven. Any other destination post-mortem would have been unthinkable. When people I knew died – a list that included only Great-Grandma Juday and Great-Grandpa Diamond – no one asked who would replace them. That would have been a meaningless question. But now we needed to find another Pope, someone else to become the final word on right and wrong.

So momentous was that search that Sr. Lilian had some men haul a television console and rabbit ears into our classroom. A block of network TV time was being devoted to covering the papal transition. An announcer supplied Vatican trivia while the camera looked up the Via della Conciliazione and into St. Peter's Square at a seemingly endless series of interchangeable columns and windows and statues. Probably no more than an hour a day was allotted for the coverage. I suppose Sr. Lilian saw this as a chance to assure us of our rightful place in the public arena. And it would, of course, have relieved her of the need to prepare lessons for that day. To the boys and girls in grades five through eight at St. Mary's Catholic School, it meant that a part of our private lives was being aired in black-and-white for everyone else to gawk at. My personal concern, aside from the Pope's mortality – and by extension, mine – was the television announcer's unfamiliarity with the way we pronounced the Latin language. *Sanctus*, when he said it, sounded, incorrectly, like *sang-toose*. *Agnus Dei* became *agnes-day-eye*. Rather than feeling affirmed, I began to question the accuracy of everything I had seen and heard on television up to that point. If they could get so wrong what little I knew to be accurate, what else might they be wrong about?

After eleven ballots, which deliciously dragged out the national obsession with the papal enclave for a few days, we had a new Pope. He was Pope John XXIII, a short, roly-poly man with a big nose who donned fabulous, gem-encrusted capes and gloves and a pointy, golden miter. He won me over with these visible proofs of the eternal verities of the faith. Ultimately he wouldn't last long. After calling a world council of bishops to modernize a church still mired in the 16th century's Counter-Reformation, he died during the first year of the Ecumenical Council's four-year deliberations. I was in public school by the time the Council sat.

A televised synod in a public school curriculum would not have been approved by the local Board of Education.

I read about the Council in TIME magazine, amused by the possibility that Cardinal Martini might be chosen to replace John XXIII. Mom liked martinis, so we teased her about that. On Sundays, as part of his weekly sermon, our parish priest kept us abreast of the basic events, along with reports on the proceeds from last week's collection baskets and any announcements of banns of marriage. My parents were quite animated about the council, speculating with each other down the length of the Sunday dinner table over the morning's Vatican news. My father was enthused at the talk of freedom of conscience and ecumenism. He had gone so far out on a limb when he converted. Here was a suggestion that his exile could be ameliorated. Then we started hearing things like the de-canonization of certain saints, including St. Christopher, whose image was pinned to the sun-visor in the family car. There followed news of translating the lectionary and the Roman missal, the core texts in the mass, "into the vernacular." To a church slavishly adherent to one, sole iteration of its sacred rites, this was revolutionary. Some people feared things might not hold, that the universal church could break into smaller, language-specific churches. For my part, I thought vernacular was a splendid word. I imagined all the vernaculars of the world, great and humble, being read out to everyone who didn't speak Latin. That would, of course, have been everyone.

My mother's position was that we were throwing out the baby with the bathwater. Over the course of the next few years, I discerned that "baby" – presumably the essence of her faith – included Benediction, novenas, Forty-Hours devotions, and Latin incantations she never really understood. St. Christopher fell somewhere between baby and bathwater. These were phased out – or marginalized – over time. She lamented the loss of each.

She was not alone. She was baptized – as was I – in St. Joseph's, a splendid red-brick Prairie Victorian building on South A in Elwood. Its two steeples – one slightly shorter and differently embellished than the other – pierced the town's low skyline. Inside were three wedding-cake altars painted glistening white: the main altar in the center, Our Lady's on the left, and St. Joseph's on the right. Mounted high on the walls on both sides of the nave, interspersed between the ogees of the windows, were intricately detailed plaster stations of the cross in high relief and vivid colors, lovingly maintained, and dolefully revered by the descendants of the German and Irish immigrants who had paid for them out of their meager finances. In his zeal to bring everything into the modern era, the bishop ordered the removal of this "dated religiosity." The parish revolted, refusing to strip its sanctuary of its treasures. The diocese had no choice but to cave. Under the guise of a "diocesan shrine of special devotion," the church retains to this day its stained-glass, three altars, flesh-colored statuary, and filigreed ceilings.

I was an altar boy in parochial school and remained serving as one at Sunday mass after I left for public school. There was a natural order in the old Tridentine Mass that enshrined what I had been taught of the world. Mass was a great thing happening, to which I merely bore witness. I was subordinate and should be subservient. If my presence on the altar was a minor elevation putting me in proximity to that great thing, it was only at the beck and call of someone greater, someone worthier and wiser, fluent in the arcane language in which that great thing occurred. It was the priest who said *hoc est enim corpus meum* (*this is my body*) and brought on the transubstantiation. It was only necessary for me to be at the right place at the right time, holding the right vessel, ringing the right bell, so that it would all come off properly.

We trained by rote and accomplished an impressive amount of memorization. The caste system among altar boys was under the tutelage of the *fifth server*, usually a seventh- or eighth-grader who knew everything that was supposed to happen. He cued us with a cutting look or a barely audible clearing of his throat. In the lull before mass, as we dressed ourselves and laid out the priest's vestments, the routine aggressiveness of boys – the thrown elbows, the slurs, the deference earned through prior jousting – held sway. But from the moment the priest appeared at the sacristy door and throughout the entire mass, we were transfixed with an earnestness that was never breached, never mocked. Its rigor flowed from the no-nonsense attitude of the priest. He never spoke to us while vesting. Indeed he had a set of whispered prayers to recite as he donned his alb, his cincture, his stole, and chasuble. Our job was to maintain the solemnity, to form a quiet, respectful cushion around him as the celebrant.

His vestments were kept in wide, shallow, smoothly gliding drawers. Each drawer was broad enough and deep enough to hold a full set of smoothly pressed altar robes and ancillary articles—these sporting beaded or *lamé* motifs appliqued on *moire* silk. More than a dozen indexed drawers were stacked one above the other to accommodate the prescribed liturgical colors: green in ordinary time, purple in lent, red on Passion Sunday, and white for high holy days. The most impressive were the black funeral vestments, now gone out of fashion. We altar boys learned the color rules, the proper handling of wine and water cruets, the lighting of the ciborium's coals and incense, and how to get candle wicks, buried in hardened beeswax, to re-light. During communion, the server followed the priest up and down the communion rail, far enough back to avoid stepping on his cassock, but close enough to get the paten under the chin of a kneeling communicant before her pink tongue shot out to catch the host. These were complicated things and doing them properly required full attention. We executed them in our own cassock and surplice, maintaining a gaze of wonder, mute chorus to daily miracles.

When the first English translation of the mass was released, Fr. Mueller called me aside and asked me to read the lector's part from the altar. I showed a comfort there that I didn't feel in other venues, and he recognized it. But the vernacular was unnerving. I knew the Latin responses were rote supplication, but they sounded like groveling when I read them in my native tongue. They felt sycophantic. The Kyrie and the Gloria, invigorating in their Greek and Latin, deflated into "Lord, have mercy," and a series of "we praise, we worship, we adore." New words crept into the printed instructions – words like *congregation* and *assembly*. This was the Protestant language under which I squirmed at Juday family reunions, words leading to an emphasis on *fellowship*.

The tables had literally been turned. A new, low altar was set in front of the steps that lead up to the taller, proto-gothic altar still visually dominating the sanctuary and now meant to be ignored. The priest stood behind the new altar and stared out at the assembly across what felt like an aggressive lack of adornment. It contradicted our sense of decorum. Servers knelt behind the priest, so we faced the people, too. I was intimidated by kneeling and facing people who looked back at me. I learned not to focus on anyone and to assume a ceremonial gaze. These were people among whom I once sat in anonymous comfort, slipping into my pew without looking directly at any of them, mumbling into my missal while they muttered over their rosaries, each of us intense in his devotion, on his own. There was both tedium and reassurance in being huddled together like that. I knew which of them would queue early for communion and then surreptitiously slip outside, just as I knew I was to show my manners by waiting in place until the end of the recessional.

We adapted an English vocabulary transliterated from Latin. "The *lector* stands at the *lectern* and reads from the *lectionary*" – phrasing that underscores the tautological rigidity of the dead language from which it came. As lector, I read the epistle, the psalm, and the prayers of the faithful. Each required the people's response. I spoke into a microphone; my amplified voice meant to encourage that response. The parishioners were uncertain of the new order. We all stumbled through with improvised cues. I would raise the back of my hand when they were to respond. I would motion my palm downward when they should sit or kneel, palm upward when they should stand.

Contemporary hymns began seeping into the music mix, new hymns in English. Their focus meandered away from the old European paeans to Mary, Mother of God, or the Immaculate Heart of Jesus. Some patently Protestant tunes snuck in. This trend disconcerted the women of the parish. The men seemed to go along with what was on offer. They were less perturbed, I suppose, because they weren't singing anyway. The only hymn to get them in a robust chorus was "Come, Holy Ghost," one we had always sung in English. It was set in a low register, the notes easier for them to reach, and it always came at the end of Mass when most were happy to see an end to it.

Because we were no longer enrolled in Catholic school, we were expected to go into town on Tuesday evenings for CCD, religious instruction under the aegis of the Confraternity of Christian Doctrine. We were only a few students – no more than a dozen, of mixed ages. Most of the kids in the parish were townies and still attended St. Mary's school. Traditional catechetical rigor was beginning to leach out of the curriculum. Experimentation encouraged by the Vatican Council through its *aggiornamento* shaped the new approach. A young assistant priest, a short, intense, dark-eyed man named Fr. Salvatore, was saddled with the CCD classes. Tuesday evenings began with a few prayers, followed by his reading of an excerpt from the upcoming Sunday's gospel. He attempted to stoke group discussion with aimless follow-up questions: "What do you think?" "Have you ever had this experience?" We were not inclined to tell Fr. Salvatore what we thought about much of anything.

His posting to St. Mary's was long enough to include joining in on a strange Easter holiday trip. He and Fr. Mueller took me and a couple of other boys to St. Meinrad's Abbey, a then-already 100-year-old Benedictine seminary in southern Indiana. We were escorted through a tour of its impressive grounds and beautiful, castle-like building nestled in rolling hills, and laid out in Benedictine adherence to *ora et labora* – prayer and work. The monks there had farm duties, garden duties, prayer duties, and study times and – *this is something you'll get used to, pretty soon, and really come to appreciate – rules against idle chatter and rules to ensure obedience to all the other rules. Isn't it beautiful? Many of these boys and young men are studying to be priests. Some of them have been here since they were 13, just like you.*

I remember the long, silent ride home that night in the back of the Smith's station wagon. I felt sick. As we rode the highway back north, I drifted off into sleep and had strange dreams of small rooms and high walls and encircling moats. I was back to more quotidian concerns by the following Sunday. After Mass, Dad called me into his den, a room he seldom used. In his absence, it had become the kids' playroom. He and I sat on the sofa, side by side, and he asked me about my trip to St. Meinrad's. I tried to be as descriptive as I could, as if this were an oral book report. But the room started to spin when he interrupted me and asked, "Do you want to be a priest?"

I had not anticipated the notion. It seemed to fall of its own volition into the space on the sofa between Dad and me. The question was obviously planned, but its actual utterance caught both of us short in the moment. Only much later did it dawn on me, reflecting on Fr. Salvatore's and Fr. Mueller's eager endorsements of the abbey, that there was a plan afoot to ease me into a seminary. It didn't take much longer for me to see, somewhere in the rest of that conversation on the sofa, that the force behind the plan was my mother. She saw my awkwardness, my softness, my lack of the stuff that boys are made of. Her response, her cultural reflex, was to find an appropriate place for me – for my own good. The seminary was where boys like me belonged. Later, musing over my terror on that sofa, I saw how her own discomfort, too, made her want to send me to the wooded hills of southern Indiana, behind the abbey walls, far away from any need to explain me to anyone else.

"No, I don't," I answered my father quickly, definitively. Self-preservation sprang up from some deep, hidden well. My panicked state must have been clear to him.

"Then we'll hear no more about this."

Dad had spoken. Putting boys in seminaries would not have been his idea, but he had done his part. He had raised the question. He then made a judgment. He listened to me and threw me a lifeline, for which I am still grateful. And we heard no more about it.

Two

IN THE SUMMER OF 1961, AN INVITATION ARRIVED IN THE MAIL.
The upper left-hand corner of the envelope bore a miniature line drawing of a modern two-story building with attached one-story wing: Clinton Prairie Junior-Senior High School. Everyone in our part of the county had been finding reasons to drive past its construction site for months. The invitation was to one of a series of orientation sessions preceding its opening for the new academic year, sessions designed to prepare us for change in the offing. The merger threatened potential diminishment for those with high social status – basketball heroes at Jefferson, Jackson, Mulberry, and Colfax. Big fish in little ponds might soon find themselves small fish in this larger pond. But I was eager for change. I saw its promise. At the orientation, I found myself among students I

didn't know, thus beginning the mixing process. We gathered in the administrative office and were each handed a mimeographed sheet of paper that bled purple ink-stains onto our sweaty hands. It was a schematic of the school layout: music rooms, gymnasium, cafeteria, classrooms.

The guidance counselor was a wan man with a hairline receded to well back behind his pale crown. I was attracted to the notion, implicit in his title, that he would guide and counsel us. I was disposed to let him lead us through an introduction to this brave new world. The five-man school board, he was happy to announce, had decided on our mascot and school colors. We were to be named the Clinton Prairie Gophers.

I thought it might be a joke and waited for his follow-up. None came. I was deflated and alarmed. The county powerhouse schools were the Frankfort Hot Dogs and the Clinton Central Bulldogs. Compared to those, a gopher was liable to ridicule, not fear and admiration. How could we hold our heads high against Hot Dogs or Bulldogs? Had the school board gotten too literal with the prairie theme? Weren't there serviceable alternatives? What about Bisons?

"The bad news," he added, failing to fathom just how bad the news already was, "is that the school colors will be black and red." Another general sigh went up. "I know," he lamented. "It sounds like a nigger school."

When I was a small boy, an Elwood playmate told me the town used to have a sign at its border on Main Street that said, "Nigger, don't let the sun set on you here." He cited this as if it were a fun fact to know. My literal mind immediately wondered how sunset was calculated. What happened if they didn't leave on time? But I also understood from this that the town wanted to have *them* kept apart from *us*.

What little I knew of black people I had absorbed from *Amos' n' Andy*, one of the first shows broadcast on television. The cast was black, but the show was adapted from an earlier radio program voiced by white men feigning a southern black country dialect to amuse a presumably white audience with their characters' naiveté and risible pretensions. I loved the show for its quirky, carefully chosen vocabulary. Amos and Andy would have said "bodacious" vocabulary. Their timbre was low and unhurried. When they used a word like "bodacious," they savored it in their mouths. The women had names like Sapphire and Ruby Begonia. Their exaggerated facial expressions required conversations be kept to a slow and deliberate pace.

Who *they* were, exactly, was a bit vague. Indiana had not been a slave state, and there was no tradition of black farmsteads. For reasons made clear by the Elwood sign, there were no black people in Elwood, or Frankfort for that matter. There were no black kids in any of my classes at any of my schools, but there were black people in Indianapolis. Indeed, there were entire black neighborhoods settled earlier in the century as part of the great migration north toward work in the auto industry and away from Jim Crow. I often saw smartly-dressed black men and women promenading up and down the streets when we drove through the capital.

Black musicians were getting air time on the radio. My mother's car radio played Fats Domino's *Blueberry Hill*, and we sang along in the back seat. I listened to him without context and unaware of his race. My father and I sometimes went to the yards in Indianapolis on Saturday mornings to feed hogs held over for Monday shipment. On the ride down, Dad would tune his radio to listen to Dinah Washington, her unforgettable voice intensely caught up in lament over *This Bitter Earth*. I had no idea she was African American. She was a faceless voice performing out of a musical tradition I knew nothing about, one that spoke to me with its timbre and delivery, one that ran, unbeknownst to me, back to Billie Holliday and Ma Rainey, back to slave camps and to West Africa.

Dad brought home 33-1/3 LPs to play on our new Hi-Fi record player. The album covers showed Johnny Mathis and Harry Belafonte. I was drawn to their faces. Dad called Johnny Mathis one of the best singers he ever heard. I could certainly hear the beauty in his voice. My mother said she thought Harry Belafonte was handsome. I couldn't have agreed more. He was the most beautiful man I had ever seen.

I saw black men in the yards who worked as "yard-boys" on weekends. They lowered their voices when we passed and looked down at the ground or off into the distance. I misread this as a particular deference toward my father. He never acknowledged them. My mother spent her childhood years in Chicago where there were many hundreds of thousands of black people. She never spoke about that.

Hearing the term "nigger school," then, so casually thrown out in our shiny new Clinton Prairie administrative office, startled me. I knew the word was ugly. Negro and colored were the terms used on the nightly news, its steady coverage of civil rights protests nurturing the hopes of the demonstrators for a better life. The guidance counselor's sneer was urging me on a subliminal level to rally around "whiteness" and to dread what those marchers might usher in. His sneer was a dismissal of those outside our tribe. It said it was important I be someone who belonged inside. But I had my own private fears. Skin color was not the only criterion that people used to measure belonging. If full scrutiny were applied, I could be exposed for deviation myself.

My new school routine began with the same walk up the hill from the house to catch the bus. But when we got to Jefferson, the younger kids climbed off the bus and headed into what was now Jefferson Elementary school. I rode on a few miles further south down a flat secondary road to the new school. I would repeat this journey, by bus or car, autumn, winter, spring, and summer for the next six years, going to classes, band practice, basketball, and football games.

The building, fenestrated in plate glass and clad in aluminum, glowed incongruously and deceptively quiet in the early morning light, surrounded by cornfields. Inside, wide hallways were lined with tall, narrow lockers. My first assigned locker was just outside the chemistry room, far to the back of the building. I oriented my day in relation to that locker. It took me most of the first semester to sort out who the people were in my classes and what they might be like. Each of the consolidating schools had been of comparably small size so that any one of us would know only about a quarter of the students that made up our new cohort—so many new faces. I avoided eye contact, meanwhile carefully grooming a few new friends to help me learn about the others, face by face and name by name. With ninety students in my class, piecing together who was who and from whence they came required a good deal of whispered consultation.

The building roiled with us, its intensity thrumming from eight in the morning to four in the afternoon. A wall of noise washed over everything, sometimes punctuated by a locker door slamming shut when some girl gasped aloud what she had just heard from a friend. In the back hallway, boys occasionally burst from the bathroom in mad pursuit of one another. It was a happy chaos that gave no quarter to silence or personal space. All the while, we were reliably constrained within established norms of civility, more than 500 adolescents showing up every day to try on constantly evolving personae, each straining toward adulthood.

Mr. and Mrs. Egli started a music program from scratch. They launched an aggressive recruitment drive. Everyone had to take Music three days a week, where we sang *Camptown Races, She'll Be Coming Round the Mountain*, and *Green Grow the Lilacs*, American standards from a previous century, deemed by music book editors as having universal appeal. I didn't know any of the songs. We were trained in pitch, tone, and tempo. Within the first semester, those who showed any promise at all were pulled aside, one by one, and quizzed about their interest in playing in the band. I was offered my choice of instrument. It happened so fast. I thought saxophone players on television looked cool. A letter went home to my parents explaining the terms of purchase. Financing was arranged, and I soon had an alto sax hung from a strap around my neck.

I determined to improve my social standing, taking heart at the idea of a fresh start. There were things in play working on my behalf. Kennedy won the 1960 presidential election, and the country survived the shock. If his being Catholic worried our parents, to us, he was a modern, energetic man with young children and a beautiful, Dior-dressed wife. He was the embodiment of our new era, one reflected in the sleek straight-lined functionality of Clinton Prairie Junior-Senior High School itself. Kennedy was cool, *and* he was Catholic. There was a chance, then, that I could be cool, too. My first week in the cafeteria line, I was recognized by one of the women who worked the Jefferson cafeteria line the year before. With an absolute minimum of fuss, on Friday, she offered me fish sticks as an alternative to the meat on the daily menu, a sign that this might not go so bad after all.

The administration divided us incoming eighth-graders into four class levels: the most studious; the least so; a mixed lot; and the truculent – those who saw school as so much nonsense to be endured and so much authority to be challenged. I was cast among the studious, among kids who didn't think it un-cool to be interested in the larger world, who read assignments and came to class ready to talk about what they read. We policed our own study habits. There were things to be learned; learning them quickly earned status. Unprepared was un-cool.

Our teachers were a mix of tenured holdovers from the consolidating schools and new hires coming into a new system. Mrs. Hurt, in whose Geography class I had abased myself in Jefferson, was eased out of the classroom and assigned as librarian. She assumed a falsely solicitous bearing there, offering visitors ambiguous hospitality, anxious to help us find what we were looking for among the stacks, but fearful about what we might get up to in her new and otherwise peaceable realm.

My English teacher was the mother of one of the boys in my English class. I felt sorry for them both, compromised, as I saw it, by the maternal bond that didn't fit in with free-flowing discourse about great literature. Their blood-tether hovered over every discussion. It left the rest of us feeling constrained and awkward on their behalf, discouraged from saying what we thought about what we'd read. We were, of course, pushing against the residual umbilical forces in our own lives, which fed our sense of inappropriateness.

The new teachers seemed younger, more in sync with our own take on things. They came at the textbooks from unexpected vantage points. They had a more relaxed sense of humor. They flattered us with apparent interest in what we were thinking. Some of the women teachers were less than ten years older than we were. Private ratings of their hotness were feverishly transmitted among the boys.

I gravitated toward the Music Department. Being a member of the band felt assuring and inclusive. I learned to read musical notation and blend in with the band's dynamics. It pleased me that my one contributory note built chord structures that needed all the others' notes for full effect. Every day for an hour's practice, we sat as a cohesive unit, focused on creating something jointly, outside ourselves. Over time we came to recognize a growing proficiency that provided pleasure in and of itself. Sometimes, at the end of a well-performed piece, we would settle our instruments on our laps and grin at what we had just managed.

People extol sports for providing team-building experiences, too. Perhaps they do. But then, so does marching onto a battlefield. In Indiana, basketball was king. I had no interest in playing it. I saw myself as awkward – an image deeply embedded in my understanding of who I was. I didn't recognize my physical speed and agility, the eventual loss of which I can now only look back on and sigh over. I didn't like athletic competition, all that vying and going-up-against, all that running and sweating and hitting and colliding. It seemed risky and brutish, painful and unnecessary. I worked long, hard days at the stockyards and at endless chores around the house and yard, my days filled with physical exertion. I found no attraction in spending my scant free time dodging baseballs and head-tackles. Sport seemed to me a pointless preoccupation with numbers, scoreboards, and the begrudgery that comes of winning and losing.

I signaled my ineptitude, and the boys who did well at sports read those signals. I was seldom shamed publicly, but I was often among the last to be called to make up the team. That appraisal was shared by – and learned from – the Phys Ed teachers, former high-school jocks who loved coaching on the court or the field but who had minimal interest in formal instruction. They were so disengaged that they never explained the rules of basketball to us – double-dribbling, free-throw shots, or regulations against fouling. It did not occur to them that some of us didn't know the rules. The inference was that our ignorance was our own fault. Basketball ignorance is decidedly non-normative in Indiana. In my first Phys Ed class, I was told to play a 15-minute *skins-vs.-shirts* game. I showed my cluelessness about the relentlessness happening up and down the court by hanging back. And so the cycle reinforced itself.

I accommodated my own marginalization. I refused to try. I deliberately held back. I actually hurt myself a few times in gymnastics by not going all the way through with a leap or a tumble, stiffening up in mid-air, and falling awkwardly–pulling into a tight ball as if to remain unobserved. Fit and strong, I was nonetheless awkward in the presence of physically developed boys. The awkwardness thwarted my every attempt to overcome it.

The worst part of Phys Ed class was after the workout, in the locker room, standing totally unclothed among the other naked boys, some of whom were maturing, fleshing out, and muscling up. I was consumed by a deep, wordless attraction toward them. I tried to appear nonchalant as I furtively eyed them undress, soap themselves, and gleam under the shower-head. They padded on bare feet back to the benches surrounding me, dabbing wet skin with fresh white towels, slowly drawing on their clothes. Throughout the whole mesmerizing process, I struggled to do the same without giving evidence of enthrallment . It demanded continuous eye contact and a disengaged attitude. It required zen-like concentration. It often resulted in shortness of breath.

To do otherwise, I knew, would be to expose my deviance. I knew what it was to be an outcast. I was working to recover from just that state. I was not going to slip into it again.

Aloofness required endless effort. To muffle the seductive appeal of bare flesh I put a psychic wall between myself and the others. I dared not let fascination with those naked bodies surface to a conscious level. I could only hope the depravity would eventually go away. I was both at the mercy of desire and in horror of that desire, cognitively short-circuited. There was no way to express it, no language for it. I simply lived in fear of it. And in denial, when I could muster denial.

This anguish was worlds away from the chaste thoughts the nuns had urged on me, a violation of their every exhortation. Internalizing the conflict, my own voice ran through my head as if it came from elsewhere. As if I were split in two in a kind of civil war in which one brother turns on the other. One of me sneered to the other, *you are sick.* And sometimes, *you should die.* Death in innocence would be preferable to life mired in guilt.

Once those thoughts crept in, the disapproving world had done its work. I no longer needed the censure of others. My guilt evolved into shame, and I took up the task of self-loathing. No one else could have been more severe or more complete in my condemnation. An ever-fresh scab of self-hatred encrusted me. At times, when I was alone, furious with my essential self, wandering the secluded footpaths of Springwood, I spoke my disgust out loud. I wallowed in obsessive, repetitive despair. Sometimes I threw myself down onto the ground in retribution. That was where I belonged, I reasoned, like a sick animal. Even more cravenly, I feared I might hurt myself in the act of falling. I wanted to punish myself, but I was too cowardly to endure anything truly painful.

There was no one with whom I could talk. I could think of no one who wouldn't have condemned me. I look back on my terror now, not with shame but with compassion. How can I not want to console myself, still, over the agony I felt then? I remain to this day sad for that boy who came to hate his very nature. I was not alone, of course, but I did not know there were others. A half-century into the healing process, for that boy and me, for those other boys and girls, now men and women, the remnants of that sadness still linger.

Up to then, I had what felt like conversations with God. We spoke privately, obliquely, unconcerned with the particulars of how the dialogue worked. We carried on in our makeshift manner. But now, all conversation was inappropriate. I was undeserving. I dared not beg for understanding.

And yet, there was that other part of my now-split self. When not tormented with such thoughts, I went about negotiating my social life. I sought friendly groups who might welcome me and my lunch tray to their cafeteria table. We had no foreigners, no racial minorities, no rich kids, and no gangs at Clinton Prairie Junior-Senior High School. Everyone was presumed a member of the Protestant majority except the three Catholic and one Jewish families. If there were others who felt alone and isolated, the outward signs weren't there. We all partook of a stolid, midwestern, middle-class ethos. We lived in rural houses or in villages too small for traffic lights. Even against these odds, phantom cliques formed around subtle identifiers: attractiveness, bookishness, athleticism. Some maintained fealty to the kids from their home school, associating solely with them. Some boys saw themselves primarily as farmers and kept to their own company. Others self-associated out of resignation to their marginal social standing.

In a different world, one I could imagine only decades later, I might have identified boys with whom I would want to keep company, with whom I would want to talk between classes, in whose attention I would have reveled. There were a few to whom I was strongly drawn and whose interest would have elated me. I say this now in rue. It would never have occurred to me then. The heart is a hungry thing, but it cannot pine for what it cannot conceive.

Full integration into society required a girlfriend, and I had a lot of friends who were girls. I was comfortable among girls. Every culture lifts up its perception of womanly beauty, and I was aware of which girls were regarded as pretty. My indifference meant the process of finding a girlfriend was unfettered by the erotic. Some socially connected girls served as allies, setting me up with so-and-so in the dating game. I had a knack for enlisting their help. For them, I suppose, there was a satisfaction in knowing they were furthering the social churn. I approached the question of a girlfriend like many Old World fathers approach marriage for a son. Who would bring honor? Who would confer status? Boys naturally drawn to girls might ask the same thing, but they also have more urgent and intimate goals. My approach, cerebral and self-interested, was to look on girls as if they were wards in a royal court, debutantes on display, ripe for the choosing. Ironically, in many ways, both the girls and the social milieu in which we found ourselves colluded in that attitude.

Early in those paring-off efforts, my girlfriend-of-the-moment and I were too young to go out together. If she responded positively to the suggestion that we "see each other," I would walk with her along the school hallways, stammering out banter that I hoped was sufficient to engage her, acting as if something unspoken were passing between us. Nothing much passed between us, in reality, spoken or unspoken. I would dance with her at sock-hops and sometimes, though rarely, share a cafeteria table. There was very little else involved. It was posturing on my part. My vision of our coupledom was from a remote angle, appraising our mutual attractiveness, our social adeptness, my own personal fitting-in. Early on, there was Connie, and there was Debbie. And who else? Or are my memories fooling me? Did I aspire to Debbie and Connie, and was I spurned? How quickly did they tire of my vapid patter? How much time did they allow me to make my move before despairing? I don't remember the eventual split-ups or what prompted them, but each was bound to happen. Posturing wasn't sustainable over the long-term. Even if I were not seriously interested in the opposite sex, the girls were. I was playing charades. They were playing for real.

Three

THERE WAS SOME IRONY THAT, AT THE SAME TIME THAT LATIN disappeared from Sunday Mass, I started to study the language at Clinton Prairie. Latin was the last relic of an older, classical curriculum whose remnants survived from one of the schools that amalgamated into Clinton Prairie. The lone remaining Latin teacher was Miss McDaniel. She was a spinster, rumored to be almost 60 years old. She wore black, wide-heeled shoes that rose nearly to her ankles and flower-print dresses with white lace collars. She had steel-grey hair permed into finger waves like the ancient Roman women in our textbooks. She was shy and blushed easily. The shyness gave her an odd power over us. Latin was an elective course, and its reputation as a difficult subject frightened off any trouble-makers. The result was a calm classroom in which we wrestled with the ablative and accusative with sincerity. Miss McDaniel's diffidence put us at ease, let us time-travel back to her ancient world to wonder at how Caesar divided all Gaul into three parts. I suppose I felt drawn to a language I considered part of my patrimony. I took Latin for three years and got involved in state-wide Latin contests, drilling myself in irregular conjugations and declensions. This earned me some private tutoring time with Miss McDaniel, and I came to treasure her. I wanted to shield her from harm. I think the innocence she emanated affected everyone. We devised terrible, irreverent nicknames for most of our teachers, but I don't remember any for her. She retired at the end of my Junior year and was never replaced. The joke was that old Latin teachers never die; they just keep on declining.

We were told when Latin disappeared in the fall, along with Miss McDaniel, that the language curriculum was going to modernize. Spanish would be offered. French would normally have been considered a more proper academic subject, and I wager no French teacher could be found. So Spanish was pitched as a practical option. It was promoted by the guidance counselor as a language we would find useful. As if it might encourage us into the tomato fields to converse with the migrant labor. I'm certain no one did.

In middle America, any skill worth acquiring demands its competitive display. I traveled to other high schools for music contests, just as I had for Latin contests. Each year we competed in all day, county-wide judging for instrumental and vocal soloists and small ensembles. The rating was for individual performance, but we students compared Clinton Prairie's medal-and-ribbon count against that of Frankfort and Clinton Central. Preparation began by having Mr. Egli point out everything you were doing wrong on your chosen piece so as to strip away any self-satisfaction. I had no self-satisfaction and so began with a severe confidence deficit. My first entry was a saxophone solo. I later moved to saxophone quartet with companions in the band, where the saxophone section numbered about eight by my Junior year. We competed to see who would compete. We practiced endlessly, even over Christmas vacation. In my senior year, I opted to sing a tenor solo. It was an art song whose opening line still brings a spasmodic gulp to my throat: "The golden sun was shining…"

The morning of the contest, my stomach churning, half-nauseated with dread, I lost my sheet music minutes before it was time to leave home. I was near madness with worry. Grandma Boyle saw my state and told me to join her in a prayer to St. Anthony. I did, and within a few minutes, the sheet music was discovered under a sofa cushion. In the rush of gratitude for the miracle, I failed to question how it got under the cushion, who might have already known it was there. I came home with a first-place medal in voice and two for instrument. They felt hard-earned, if not for excellence in performance, then for surviving the anxiety the performances brought on. My mother, in an audible aside, commented that too many awards were given at these things. She didn't say it just once, but whenever the subject arose over the next few weeks as if making certain it got read into the record.

I think this may have been prompted, in part, by her disappointment bound up in the large electronic organ that sat in our living room. Mom and Dad were fond of the music played in the cocktail lounge of their country club. They said the organist was somehow related to someone of standing in the music world at the time – Chet Atkins or Les Paul – someone of a stature that impressed them. Jazz organ had peaked in popularity in the late 1950s, but Mom and Dad still loved it. Noting the time and attention I gave to music, they thought I might have what it took to learn some cocktail music for them at home. An electronic organ appeared unexpectedly, complete with a full octave of foot pedals. I feigned enthusiasm for it. Equally suddenly, I was brought into Frankfort for private lessons with the organist who had the famous bloodline. He told me right off to call him Jerry. The man had no pedagogic or interpersonal skills whatsoever, and I had no keyboard training. He soon despaired over my failure to get a left-hand rhythm, a right-hand tune invention, and a foot-pedal beat all going as smoothly as they seemed to go for him. Soon enough, the lessons stopped, and any reference to them stopped as well. There was whispered concern on Jerry's part about my lack of talent.

After this ran its course, the organ remained behind, left to dominate the living room. I was intrigued with the tonal variations I could create by adjusting its stops. I started collecting sacred music – Palestrina, simple Bach – whose scores featured tight harmonies and chords that shifted one constituent pitch at a time from major to minor and back to major. I never developed proper fingering and had no comprehension of harmonic theory. My performance was all arrhythmic hesitance and pedal-swelling chords. But I sat at the organ bench on Saturday evenings after chores were done and blared away nevertheless. I was aware how little I knew about the classical canon and brought home 33-1/3 LPs from the library to expose myself to some of it. I would load these into the hi-fi, sit directly in front of its cloth-covered speakers and let Wagner, Debussy, and Rimsky-Korsakov wash over me. All the while, my brothers and sisters watched *Bonanza* on the television upstairs in the den, volume raised to cover my din.

On Friday nights during basketball season, I sat in with the Pep Band. The saxophone was perfectly suited for the music we played. We played all the popular "fight songs." Our school's was a wordless version of *On Wisconsin*. Our repertoire included several other outdated carryovers like "Running Wild" and "Hold That Tiger," loud, punchy tunes that stirred the team and fans at breaks and half-time. Here was something I could do, something I was good at, and some way to contribute to the overall conviviality, so I gave myself over to the performance. I could rally the players and rally the kids in the bleachers without actually suiting up and going onto the court. The auditorium acknowledged with rhythmic clapping. We were joined together in a competitive spirit. I fit in.

The basketball games were almost always followed by a sock-hop, lightly chaperoned events intended to provide release after the excitement of the evening's athletic contest, come victory or defeat. When the parents and children dispersed, wending their way out of the gym, the lights dimmed. Someone in the audio-visual club piped in the music. I changed out of my band uniform into street clothes, and the basketball team changed into theirs. The cheerleaders kept on their circle-skirts and matching sweater outfits, lending a signature authority to the mix. We went out onto the polished wooden basketball court, shoeless, to protect the highly-waxed surface, and we mingled as one undifferentiated student body. Steady couples clung to each other and swayed slowly. Dance fads – the Mash Potato, the Watusi, the Twist – came into fashion, then disappeared. Simple, loosely defined movements, their physically-demanding pace provided a means of dissipating hormonal energy. We preened and gyrated and otherwise partook in the kind of primal display that millennia earlier would have been centered around a communal fire. We were sweaty, happy, and claiming the here and now as our own.

Four

WHEN WE STILL LIVED IN THE HOUSE ON HIGHWAY 28, I PICKED up occasional glimpses of the larger world from things left behind by rest-park visitors, mostly men who stopped there to stretch, eat, relieve themselves, then move on. On one occasion, I found a small black-and-white magazine. I picture it as dog-eared; that's the kind of thing often said about such magazines. I'm not sure it was dog-eared, in all honesty. What comes back to me about this little magazine was a black-and-white photograph, set in a blur of grey-colored text, of a woman with no blouse on. She might have worn a skirt, or slacks. I think I remember a belt somewhere below her exposed breasts. The image was cropped so that most of what was below her waist, clad or unclad, was not in the frame.

This was my first, furtive encounter with pornography, tame as it was. I had been pondering the conundrum of women's breasts for years. When I was six or seven, after hours of reflection, I told my mother I was unsure what to call them. I announced that I would, in the future, refer to them as milk bottles. She seemed unfazed by this declaration, and the afternoon continued with no further comment on the subject. It was clear women had breasts and men didn't. Sexual differences were a constant subtext to everything – every fairy tale, love song, product advertisement, and family magazine of the era. Men were tall, had square jaws and broad shoulders. Women had tiny waists, coiffed hair, a bit of cleavage, and flared-out skirts. Men worked in suits and came home ready to be fed. Women stood on one high-heeled foot while the other kicked back in delight. That these clichés didn't match my particular world made them no less persuasive.

Now here I was, seated at a picnic table in the rest park huddled over a small black-and-white photo reproduction of an adult woman, as unknown to me as was I to her, and I was staring – ogling – at the unavoidable reality of her breasts. Large breasts. I am certain of no more detail than that. I stared for some time. I then discarded the magazine in a trash barrel, got back on my bicycle, and rode home, soon distracted by other mysteries.

What came back to me later that night, as I drifted off to sleep, was not so much the flesh in the image, or any prepubescent stirrings it might have engendered, but the notion that I had looked on something that was forbidden. Worse, I had sat and stared at it. It had come to hand through no fault of my own, but guilt crept in when I didn't immediately, on realizing what it was, throw the evil thing away. There were several nights of such self-recrimination.

A Catholic childhood has a built-in mechanism for dealing with self-recrimination: the confessional. Confession was not on offer during the school week. Each day began with early Mass, followed by the cold breakfast, then classes framed by lunch-hour and recess, and ended with the scramble to get transportation home. This scheduling didn't allow for time in a confessional queue. Weekend arrangements had to be made for that. Confessions were heard from 4pm to 6pm on Saturdays, presumably to ensure cleansed souls for Sunday communion. The assumption at home was that we stood in regular need of it. The weekend shopping or a deferred errand would be scheduled to allow a Saturday evening trip to town and a visit to an eerily empty church whose back pews held a handful of sinners waiting to be shriven.

I sought out confession a few weeks after the bare-breasted lady began haunting my conscience. The confessional box had all the appeal of a doctor's syringe, but I bore both with unquestioned confidence in their efficacy. Sometimes there would be a visiting priest to hear confessions, but most often it was Fr. Scheetz. I knew his voice, of course. Father Scheetz would have known my voice as well, but I was focused more on the unworthiness I was about to name than on what the priest might already know. Inside the booth, I took assurance from the lattice-like screen that separated us, each in his own chamber. A further gesture toward anonymity was the linen cloth pinned against the lattice. I stared at it in my terror. I can see it still. I thought of it as a handkerchief because it was an era when women could not enter a church with their heads uncovered. At the same time, they were increasingly forgoing hats and headscarves for all but formal occasions or inclement weather. A handkerchief secured with a bobby pin technically complied with church protocol, and if push came to shove, even a Kleenex, similarly pinned, met the basic requirement.

The thinnest tissue separating a woman's hair from God's and the public's prying eyes would suffice, just as the thin linen cloth between my abject sinfulness and Fr. Scheetz's omniscience made the confessional bearable. The promise was that I could be heard and not seen. Ironically this was my grandmother's dictum for a child's table-manners turned on its head.

"Forgive me, Father, for I have sinned. My last confession was three weeks ago…" At some point, I worked up the nerve to tell Father Scheetz about the naked lady. He had the patience and, since he knew me, the perspective to ask how I came across it.

"I found it on a picnic table. At the park."

"And were you curious?"

"Yes, Father."

"A sin is something you know is wrong, something you know to be wrong, but you go ahead and do it anyway because you want to. Did you want to sin?"

"No, Father."

"Then you have not sinned."

This was a novel – and potentially quite useful – formula. It brought immediate relief. Nothing can be more exculpatory than to have your parish priest tell you that you haven't sinned. Of course, I hadn't. What was I thinking? And how might this be applied further down the road? What Fr. Scheetz offered in his line of reasoning, if looked at slightly askance and with one eye, was a Jesuitical argument on the nature of sin that afforded emotional distance from the *act itself*, as the catechism called it. It didn't exempt so much as give breathing room for the anxiety I often brought to moral questions. There were moral questions everywhere.

By Junior High, most of the boys in my class were entering into puberty at about the same time. It was our rutting season.

If you listened knowingly, there was always someone making a funny but veiled reference to a penis. It was all the more hilarious if it humiliated someone else, humiliation being the highest form of wit at that age. Sly comments, vague enough to be ignored but clear enough to be understood, were, in effect, invitations: *If you show me yours, I'll show you mine.* The penis was foremost among the things we considered, both in idle moments and in settings that permitted shared intimacy. None of this ever seeped into locker room discussions, of course, where our manhood was on such public, vulnerable display. Penis-talk was something we never heard the adult world publicly engage in, and we honored that silence. The silence was also honored at school and in church. I wasn't sure what the Protestant boys were being told.

Any advice I got – scant, whispered, and always as a knowing aside rather than a principled assertion – was that I ignore my sexual urges, that I think about anything but my sexual being. The Church's instruction on human desire was to honor and satisfy the drives for food, shelter, and clothing. All other drives were to be sublimated and turned to God, an unhelpful concept for a thirteen-year-old with a nearly constant erection. Opportunities for further discovery were rare, but they existed. They bore no malignance beyond sexual impulse, whatever that was, and curiosity as to how it might be sated. There must have been a few precocious boys among us who enjoyed such exploration with girls. For my part, I didn't suppose girls to be interested. The academic notion of sexual orientation was of no interest to groping hands. The hunt was for warm, tingling, and immediate gratification. That objective, no matter how carefully phrased, would have been solemnly denied; the rutting took place, nonetheless.

In a farm down the road toward Jefferson lived a boy I will call James. He was an only child, a year younger than I. He was quite a braggart and had a flippant manner he assumed with everyone, even his own mother. I stopped in to visit him on my bike one Saturday. We sat behind his barn, casually balanced on the top fence rail. He began deriding a series of absent schoolmates, smirking at how ignorant they were or how miserable their lives must be. It was shame talk, and it held a certain power over me. I knew well what it felt like to be an awkward outsider. James told me these things, I reasoned, because he didn't think I had such low social standing myself. Or, if he did, that I could rise above my station by seeing how risible the others were. It was a deft ju-jitsu that flipped self-contempt into contempt for my neighbors. During his rambling critique, James let his waving hands sweep toward me, tapping my leg for emphasis. Soon enough, they rested there, then slid upward, triggering an electric and paralyzing state. There was that wonderful tactile warmth again. He didn't talk about what he was doing. I followed his cue, hypnotized by the sensations that coursed through me as talk veered off into silence. We proceeded to unbuckle, unzip, and explore each other. It felt as if I were in a large plaster-of-Paris cast, unable to move my limbs beyond the fixed postures into which our activity conformed me.

It was unanticipated. I tried to accept it as something that happened. I thought about it with dread and shame over the next few days, but I looked forward to repeating the experience. It did happen once more, and with more abandon. I found myself back in his farm lot, focused on how to keep my cool, how to encourage conditions under which it might recur, and in spite of my other-worldly physical state, how to act as if nothing remarkable were happening.

Both encounters had a certain inevitability. We were curious, half-formed, with healthy hormones pumping through healthy veins. A shoulder shrug, a tsk-tsk, and a what-can-you-do sigh has always been sufficient when boys go "girl crazy." The encounters with James sprung from the same source – nature unfolding. I might have given off signals that I was approachable. Or that might be what today we call victim-think. I can't be sure, but I was undeniably curious. I was open to physical exploration. James saw his chance and was bold enough to make his move. I didn't flinch, so he persevered. I knew no more than a fern knows to uncoil or a bud knows in what way to open. The uncoiling, the opening, is genetically programmed and is always going to occur. It is simply a matter of time.

The experience was something oddly private, as if not really shared with James. I later asked myself if it was wrong, if I knew it was wrong, and if I wanted to go ahead and sin anyway. I avoided coming to any conclusion. I moved on as forthrightly as I could. I learned little from it except how to avert reckoning for things that unsettled me. I also learned enough about James that after the second encounter, I knew not to continue coming around. He had a nasty side to him. On the bus or during the school day, we avoided each other. Without coming to an understanding of what passed between us, I buried the experience. I put it in a box, put it away, and chose not to dwell on it. I nearly succeeded in expunging it.

I had my own circle of friends. I knew most of my classmates, and I knew how they responded to me. That loop of behavior and response showed me where I stood in relation to them. I saw myself as projecting wit, with a slightly daring edge, and I offered an acceptance of most everyone's foibles. I was good for a joke, and I tolerated being the reasonable butt of others' jokes. I was good for an easy smile in the hallway. It was a pleasant place in which to reside that allowed me to ignore the shadowy parts of myself. I had a benign and comfortable perch well above the undercurrent of dread and longing underneath. I worked at dissembling any doubts I felt. We all did. We sought detachment, freedom from any anxiety about what we harbored inside. We wanted to drift along on the current of normalcy.

Other guys were dating, going steady, and exchanging class rings. The girls wrapped their boyfriend's ring with yarn to keep it from slipping off their finger. The ideal wrap was angora wool, brushed out into little bird-nests around the ring setting. The boys wore their girlfriends' rings on a chain around their necks. This was becoming slightly passeé, but it was a fashion that still lingered, and I was intrigued by it. I was ring-less and studied the pairings-off. Hallway gossip monitored the latest couplings and un-couplings. I see now how much of the personal drama I missed. I saw the ring-bearing as public display; the more desirable the couple, the more glory found in the coupling. What I didn't appreciate was the powerful urge compelling these would-be lovers to pair off. It didn't occur to me that the boys were besotted with the girls who were developing womanly shapes – teenage Delilah's with near-total power over their Samsons. I was merely trotting along the edge of the herd, feigning when they feigned, grazing when they grazed, and fleeing when they fled, enchanted with simply being of their number.

But I was not of their ilk, and few of them were of mine. I knew of one, for sure. His name was Francis. Francis was dark-haired and short, with large lips and ears that jutted out from a wide-set face. He was quite overweight – a rare thing in that land of lanky teens – and he suffered from poor hygiene. I had known him since my year at Jefferson. He lived south of Jefferson but was related to kids in the village, which set him apart from those of us on the bus. The guys privately mocked Francis for his effeminate bearing. Francis the Fairy they called him. He never pretended to be anything other than who he was. He was witty and showed a puzzling detachment from the pressure the rest of us felt to fit in. He played deaf to the whispered slurs and ridicule. I avoided Francis like most everyone else did. I was reluctant to be associated with him. I held it against him that he was such a sissy. I see now he was insistent on staking out his ground, fighting to be himself. But I disapproved the degree to which he did. Why did he have to behave like that? Why didn't he try to fit in, be more like everyone else? His refusal to be someone other than himself made me nervous. He was a living admonition.

My sophomore year, I "went with" a girl named Judy. Judy was a private soul, more fearful than aloof, but talented enough to be a regular pianist for the Music Department, including the full choir that rehearsed in the gym on Tuesday and Thursday mornings. She was small and thin and wore dark-framed glasses and kept her black hair heavily sprayed into the era's bouffant-and-flip style. She was an only child of retired and protective parents. Judy was two years older than I. Pairings in which the girl was older than the boy were rare, but they occurred. Never the other way round. Yet, she and I never spoke about our age gap. Our conversations were awkward, serious talks between two high-strung adolescents wanting answers to questions we hadn't clearly formulated yet. My parents watched us out of the corner of their eyes, relieved I was dating, if unsure what I was doing with this girl. I can only imagine what her stern, Lutheran parents must have thought. They kept tight vigil over us whenever I was in their house.

In the spring, Judy asked me to the Junior-Senior prom. The weekend of the prom, Dad was gone on a fishing trip. Mom followed me out to the driveway as I left that evening and took a photograph of me standing next to the open car door, recording this milestone on my road to manhood. In the photo I have of that moment, I am preening a bit in a white tuxedo jacket, on my own, poised to claim the girl and take her to the ball. I see myself standing in a dream that I knew would so please everyone, especially Mom and Judy.

I was nervous going to the prom as a sophomore, mingling with an older cohort. As it turned out, the mingling was quite limited. Judy was socially disconnected, and I was out of my league, below most everyone's radar. We were announced by one of the teachers over the PA system, no more and no less special than every other couple similarly announced as they entered a gymnasium decorated for "An Evening in Paris." We danced. We posed for a photo in front of a roll-down canvas with an image of the Eiffel Tower. We sat at a round table and made polite conversation, mostly between ourselves. When I drove her home, I found myself standing in her screened-in front porch, wondering what was supposed to happen next. It seemed the best thing to do was to kiss her. Unsure how to proceed, I asked her for permission. She said, "Yes, you may." I can still hear her say it. I reached out my left hand and promptly crunched her stiff bouffant hair beneath it, leaving it flat on one side. Then I drew this nervous, fragile, intelligent girl toward me in a movie-inspired embrace that ended by smearing her heavy foundational makeup onto my rented dinner jacket.

And yet… we felt that we were maturing, that we were one step closer to our inscrutable destiny, to the person we were meant to become. We were gelling into shape. Clinton County was a static place, few families moved in or out, and as time passed, we became quite familiar with each other. We settled into the roles assigned to each of us by some general consensus. I aced exams. Others scored basketball victories or track ribbons. Boys who once were game for a dare or a jibe were turning taciturn, more interested in talk about cars or livestock. Girls grew more circumspect, speaking of private things among themselves, unimpressed with hallway gossip. We accepted these roles because they offered a release from attenuated self-introspection. Each role was an available seat in the life-game of musical chairs – a safe place to sit. Change was falling down on us like dust from a future attic. We sought, if not certainty, then some kind of courage in a first, rude appraisal of who we were.

Camaraderie was in generous supply. We mingled un-self-consciously. We all rooted for the Gophers on the football field in the autumn and on the basketball court in the winter. We flowed through the crowded hallways with precision, skillfully navigating the cross-traffic, focused on the few faces of immediate interest. On Tuesday and Thursday mornings, Music students from grades nine through twelve assembled in the gym bleachers for choir practice, nearly fifty voices warming up, learning to listen to each other, establishing the tonic, building the chords scored for the SATB harmonies, segueing through key and meter changes. Over time, with earnest application, we had learned to read sheet music, and we had learned to keep relative pitch. Mr. Egli would arrive after the bell, we would all settle onto the steeply ramped bleachers, and the warm-up would begin.

It was just such a morning, toward the end of my sophomore year, while people still milled around, while Judy sat at the piano, hands in lap, waiting for the bell, in a brief lull in all the chatter, that James blurted out, as loudly as he could. "Hey, if you're looking for a blow-job, ask Dan Juday."

A cold silence shot through the gymnasium, lasting somewhere between a few seconds and the rest of my high school days. It reverberates even now. I lost any train of thought, intently aware only of where I sat, simultaneously clueless as to where I was. Quiet people sat all around me. I don't know where they looked. I simply looked forward, and I saw nothing. My immediate thought was that this was a lie – well, an exaggeration, anyway – but that made no difference now. I knew instinctively it could never be unsaid.

Mr. Egli arrived, Judy played an intro, and we began our warm-up routine.

Five

SUMMER NOW MEANT WORK AT THE STOCKYARDS MONDAY through Friday, but evenings were free. And I had access to a car. At fifteen-and-a-half, I took a driver's education course; at sixteen, I got my driver's license. We were a three-car family during the years between my getting that license and my leaving home. The Ford station wagon was the family car, although we seldom went anywhere as a family anymore outside of church on Sunday or a rare trip to Elwood. In my Junior year, my father, confident about business and fond of new things, bought the first Ford Mustang to appear in our part of Clinton County. It was a trendy, unapologetically sporty car, a calibrated middle-class indulgence on wheels. He announced that it was Mom's car, and she used it all right. But sometimes – on some delightful, unexpected, and highly cherished occasions – she handed me the keys, smiling to let me know she understood how thrilling it was to drive and to be seen driving it.

A ten-year-old Oldsmobile sedan, well past prime but entirely serviceable, was my regular transport. Dad bought it soon after I got my license. It was "the kids' car," but I drove it most of the time. We called it Old Blue. It allowed me to keep my own hours at the stockyards, freed from Dad's schedule, and get to summer-evening band practice. I drove Lee Ann to the diner where she worked and ferried Glenn and Maureen to their events. It was a practical arrangement for parents with busy children whose extracurricular activities held little interest for them. I was deemed reliable and mature, and I was trusted to help keep the family on schedule.

A car brought the independence of mobility and unsupervised time. It offered adventure – what little that could fit into tightly-scheduled lives like ours. It also brought temptation and temptation's concomitant risks. I sneaked off to a drag race one night, south of school, to hang with the rough boys. At the designated stretch of tarmac, several cars were backed into fields, perpendicular to the road, their headlamps lighting the black-top. Two muscle cars sat on the road, revving and snorting, waiting for a flag to drop. When it did, tires screeched, and too much metal bearing too vulnerable flesh at speeds too reckless tore into the night. It was patently obvious those boys, boys I knew well, were flirting with their own demise. The noise the cars made carried across open fields, and we had to disperse as soon as the race was run before a deputy sheriff could be alerted from some lone farmhouse. I still associate acrid fear at the back of my throat and in the pit of my stomach with my first and last effort to fit in with that rough crowd. That fear clarified for me my natural niche – safe and well-behaved company. It also quenched any desire to witness another drag race.

A car also guaranteed the company of friends – if they could get away. In the summer, Patty, who lived across the Wildcat from us, often could get out. Her grandmother lived in town, providing a plausible destination if anyone asked where we were going. Patty was friends with Francis, and in the anonymity of summer recess, Francis was acceptable company. We often succumbed to the centripetal pull of the four streets framing the Frankfort courthouse, drawn there looking for action. Everyone else was looking, too, circumnavigating the square – usually counter-clockwise – for several laps: one block, turn left, one block, turn left, one block, turn left in a continuous loop. We drove slowly, scrutinizing the traffic in the oncoming lane and the cars in front and behind, straining to see everyone and hoping to be seen. Having possession of an automobile blurred any town-vs-country distinctions. We were all full members of the motoring community, equal participants in a promenade of reconnaissance and display. No one ever stopped to park at the courthouse on those evenings; no one ever cared that all the stores were locked and unlit. What mattered was the tempo of the traffic and the random assortment of people among which we found ourselves when the light turned red. What we cared about was which song was playing on the radio. What we valued was our running commentary inside the car about who we had spied and what could be inferred from seeing them. Summer nights were warm and lush under the town's streetlights, spot-lit by headlamps and languorous in their lack of structure.

Back to school meant back on the bus. Howard was the bus driver, the same man who had been driving us to Jefferson since the seventh grade. He was a stern, terse born-again Evangelical who eschewed worldly joy. Once, years earlier after Kennedy's election, toward the end of the bus route, after most of the kids got off, Howard pulled his bus over to the side ditch, pulled up the emergency brake, turned to us startled teens and pre-adolescents, and began to enumerate the wicked ways of the Catholic Church. He actually used the old Whore of Babylon metaphor. The few kids listening to him were quite amazed at his tirade, especially his use of the word "whore." All in all, I think at the time it earned me a bit of their sympathy.

I got even with Howard by withholding any deference toward him. Over the years, so much time spent together bred familiarity, which gradually introduced tolerance. We bantered with him. We complained there was nothing to break up the daily monotony of the trip. This prompted his one, begrudging concession – a transistor radio dangling from the lever that he used to swing the bus door open. The radio hung from a piece of twine wrapped through its handle. He soothed us – his savage charges – with pop music. It was a severe compromise of his religious convictions, and we gloated over it. As time went by, the music from the tinny speaker evolved from the adolescent angst of Leslie Gore's "It's My Party" and Mark Dinning's "Teen Angel," to Elvis and The Everly Brothers. It evolved further to the Beatles' "She Was Just Seventeen," and "I Want To Hold Your Hand," and the rest of the British invasion. I was riveted by the progression and spent part of my hard-earned stockyard wages one autumn – money meant to be saved for college – to make sure I had at least two mod, flowered shirts with rounded white collars, and a pair of striped bell-bottom trousers, anticipating the Carnaby Street revolution that, alas, never reached Clinton County.

It was, in part, through the evolution of popular music that the larger world came into view, demanding more of my notice. Bob Dylan mumbled his earnest, cryptic songs, and the lyrics were aired constantly, seemingly covered by everyone. It was protest music. Talk of the civil rights struggles in the South was everywhere too. I watched televised fire-hose assaults, police-dog attacks, and bus boycotts with one eye focused elsewhere. If anyone had asked, I'd have said it wasn't right that people should be knocked down with firehoses. I don't remember anyone talking about it. The riot scenes played out on the television as if the audio were turned down low. My parents watched TV in their room; we watched ours in the den. The images might have been beamed in from a parallel universe. I was distracted by Algebra and basketball sectionals. Nonetheless, for some reason I couldn't have identified then, a discontent began eating at me, provoked by Dylan's challenge: "How many times can a man turn his head and pretend that he just doesn't see?" Slowly, I began to see. The confrontation on the Edmund Pettus Bridge in Selma shocked me. And not just me, lots of people. In September, the Voting Rights Act passed into law.

It would be a serious error to underestimate the initial effect of this music, which has since been diluted, flattened into retro soundtracks for television commercials. It arrived earnest and fresh, and it unsettled the world with its uncomfortable moral prodding. Love lyrics, sha-na-na and itsy-bitsy, teeny-weeny bikinis were fading from the zeitgeist. War rumbled in Vietnam, a place where America dropped agent orange and napalm on bamboo villages. The music asked why the killing went on. Freedom riders were beaten and shot, and little girls were bombed in churches. Peter, Paul, and Mary sang freedom marches and asked us to hold to the belief that we would overcome. Mahalia Jackson poured her searing intensity into her spirituals in righteous anguish. It was not possible to believe that things were going well. *This land is my land, this land is your land.* Everyone sang for justice. Social injustice bred social guilt, a guilt shared collectively among us, beyond our own, separate, personal failings. Having been slow to see all that brought its own guilt, too, and a deep, impatient discontent with how things had always been.

From my days at Christ the King, I had been judged – and learned to judge myself – on "obedience," "truthfulness," "justice," and "charity." The way forward was not to abandon those values, but it required a new understanding of obedience. It once meant obeisance, listening to my mother and father. That obedience reflex was well ingrained. I valued being a good boy. I sought the harmony it ensured. But I had a new understanding of righteousness, a tentative understanding, as tentative as the confidence I felt in my right to espouse it. In Mrs. Estes' English class, we studied the tenets of critical thinking. We identified fallacies and logical errors that distort reasoned argument. I wised up to *post hoc ergo propter hoc*, the false notion that anything following an event was necessarily caused by that event. I saw how truncated and selective data misrepresented the measure and intensity of external influences. I felt my moral compass ought to be guided by what I reasoned rather than by what truths had been passed down to me. I pondered how this applied to war, race, and poverty.

Sadly, struggle continues to roil our civic life. In this cellphone age, I can watch internet clips of George Floyd, a black man accused of passing a counterfeit $20 bill, tackled to the ground as a white policeman slowly squeezes the life from him, kneeling on his neck as bystanders beg him to stop. And again I ask, "How many times?" The upheavals of the 1960s appeared to lose urgency for a while, but our unresolved disparities have ensured their return. People still go out into the streets demanding justice while others discredit those demands. Black Lives Matter is turned into All Lives Matter, a deliberate dismissal of a clear, urgent plea. There are days when I despair over what Dr. King called the moral arc of the universe. There are days, too, when I feel hope. Hope has so much more staying power than despair.

I brought my enthusiasms home to the dinner table, where my father prided himself on encouraging family debate. Some of what I put forth clearly rankled him. I'm sure he would have argued – but didn't –that he endured the Great Depression and World War II, that he rose to the moral challenges of his day. He went out, he would have said, to do what had to be done, and he came home to provide a better life for his family – for us – for me. He would have felt that earned him the perquisites of a peaceful life, the right to be left alone. I would have felt compelled to say – and did – that my new way of thinking would not be discouraged, even if he tried to discourage it. He would have heard in my arguments ingratitude for what I had – a stability and comfort he never had. I would have asked why a better life had to be so meanly apportioned, so fiercely defended, why so many had no chance to share in it. He surely recognized the intensity of adolescence and the dynamics of generational conflict beneath all I was asserting. They were of a piece with my struggle for independence.

To be young is to be unaware of that generational dynamic yet be driven by it. Of one thing I was certain: concern for others was mandatory. Nothing – no one – was permitted to ignore that. My insistence meant there was bound to be a further uncoupling between my father and me. It was always in the cards.

My social schedule reverted to the *status quo ante* – friendships drawn from among the kids in my classes. Ron was in most of them. He was from one of only three Catholic families in the school district, a fact that assured my mother about our friendship. Ron had a brother Lee Ann's age and another Glenn's age, which allowed us to think of his family as a kind of mirror-image of ours.

His father was a shadowy presence, usually off rooting around one of the decrepit outbuildings on their farm. His mother was cheerful, engaged, and extremely tolerant of our comings and goings. I visited Ron most weekends and delighted in his chaotic home life where everyone talked at once, no one much listened to each other, and the dishes were always piled in the sink. That casual and arbitrary ambiance appealed to me as an alternative to the well-regimented nature of life at home. At the same time, I knew my attraction to be a dalliance; I would have imposed order on things were I living there.

He practiced his guitar constantly. Spending time with him meant watching him with a six-string – and later, twelve-string – strapped around his neck, working his way through an expanding repertoire. He'd sing his standards, adjust the capo, and then launch into his newest piece. I accepted this as part of our friendship, even if sometimes I grew tired of hearing "Polly Vaughn" strummed at intemperate volume, over and over, week after week. At the same time, I admired his perseverance. I once told him I wished I could play like him.

"It's not any good to want to <u>play</u> guitar," he said, quite serious and notably intent on this point. "You have to want to <u>learn</u> guitar." Ron learned Dylan; Peter, Paul, and Mary; and scores of the old folk standards finding so much favor again.

Abigal – Abby – was from Jackson School in Antioch. She had a lovely round face, full lips, good cheekbones, and a piercing gaze emanating from clear blue eyes. We shared several classes when our schools consolidated, and sat near each other when seats were assigned alphabetically. She was smart, musically talented, and brought a rigor and precision to her singing – focused on pitch and tone long before those things registered with me. She had long, blond hair, and it was her hair that first caught my eye. She was one of the least frivolous girls in the class. She wasn't prim or dull; she was alert and ready to smile at something if it was witty, if it was worthy of one of her smiles. In my infatuation with her, I went to awkward lengths to earn a few of those smiles.

Eric was in most of my classes. He had dark hair, a broad forehead, strong jawline, and dark eyes that peered through thick, heavy-rimmed glasses. They somehow magnified the intelligence evident in his conversations, as though he saw things better than the rest of us. Eric was a bit shorter and a bit more muscled than I, a natural for the football team. He had athletic poise and a calmness about him that contained his gestures. He didn't speak impulsively like I did. He seemed absorbed in whatever was being discussed and, when not engaged in discussion, absorbed in his own thoughts. He applied himself to schoolwork, and he read as avidly as I did. I liked that about him. I was labeled an egghead for my enthusiasms and was sometimes resented for setting the grade curve too high for exams. I suspect the resentment also included my innate effeminacy. It was certainly aimed at my lack of physical prowess. Eric never talked about any of that. He let me know he, too, had enthusiasm for what we were studying, for knowledge beyond what was required for a test. In Spanish class, we were encouraged to assume a Spanish name to use in the dialogue sessions. One of us – I can't remember whether he or I – took the name Isidro. That I don't remember which of us bore that name is a measure of what the passing of years and the vagaries of the human heart can obscure. I had fallen under his spell.

I describe these friends in terms of their intelligence. I do not mean that others, to whom happenstance did not draw me close, were not intelligent. Intelligence is what sets us apart – if only in degree – from other complex living things. I focus on those friends' intelligence because, in the end, it is what I most loved about them. They were young. Youth has its native beauty, a truth that eluded me until well after my own faded. But I have always been drawn to that knowing spark that illuminates each of us. And I am always moved that it should be there, manifesting itself, the one part of ourselves we eagerly give each other.

Somewhere near the end of that Clinton Prairie football season, Eric was severely injured on the field. Rumors filtered through by phone, slowly, as it happened on a Friday. By Monday, we learned he had suffered cervical and nerve damage, that it was serious, and that he would be hospitalized, then bed-ridden for a long time. Full recovery was not certain. When, what seemed countless weeks later, he was released from the hospital with a hopeful prognosis, he was required to lie immobile in a mummy-like cast for an extended recovery. Someone devised an enterprising solution; Eric would have a microphone and speaker by his bedside at home. On the school end, in each of his classrooms, we would connect a portable speaker with a built-in microphone that allowed two-way-communication with him through the wires of the school's public address system, a precursor of an on-line connection. The speaker was as large as a toaster, a heavy metal box with a cloth filter over a small, static-prone tweeter. That "squawk-box" was all we would see and know of Eric for the next many weeks. It would need to be moved from classroom to classroom.

Because I was in almost every one of his classes, I would be responsible for the box-that-was-Eric. I would plug him into the speaker jack in each classroom and do the sound-checks to make sure he could hear us, and we could hear him. The teachers would throw a few questions his way in class discussions, so he felt engaged. After class, I would unplug Eric, then plug him into the next classroom – everywhere but Phys. Ed. and Band. I was an extension of this fallen hero, struggling to recover and return to life. He was my charge. His vulnerability and my attraction to him were of a piece. I developed a fixation, one not of his doing, nor, even from my perspective now, of mine. It was more like fate. Kismet. It was a private, personal fixation, a secret, one-way affair. If it had a tactile component, it was the heft of the squawk-box that held the thrill of repeated hellos from classroom to classroom while he waited for my voice so he could orient himself. I feigned detachment when we spoke; there was no eye contact.

Eventually, Eric made a full recovery. He came back to school paler and thinner and – was I imagining it? – socially more fragile, more cautious. He would need someone to lean on, and I would be there for him in the reintegration phase as well. As it turned out, Eric needed very little emotional support from me. Nor did he share my attachment. He had many friends he hadn't seen in a while. There were others with whom he had a shared history and interests. He needed no mediator.

I would find myself staring at the back of his neck, at that precious scar, that outward sign that he could have died or become a paraplegic. It made me both grateful for his recovery and resentful of his growing independence. A dark monologue sought voice in my head. I knew what it wanted to say. I didn't want to hear it. I knew where sanity lay, and I knew, with an exertion of will, I could rise to it. But I continued dreaming, suspended in a middle state between the unattainable affection I craved and the clear, unambiguous path to a decent, proper life.

As I worried about how to proceed, I clung to the metaphor of the picket fence, the border defining and containing a conventional life. A white picket fence encircled *Ozzie and Harriet, Leave it to Beaver,* and *Father Knows Best,* television sitcoms where black and white normalcy reigned. Inside that fence were a happy marriage, two children, and a life on Primrose Lane, where "life's a holiday."

Inside the picket fence, all was as it should be. Convention. Clarity. Anonymity. Approval.

The school year turned through its calendar. Marching band resumed. Mr. Egli approached me about being drum major. The few we'd had so far were girls who could twirl batons. My qualifications, scant in the twirling category, were my height, the length of my arms, and the abandon with which I dared fling them about. I was willing to march backward, blow a shrill whistle, and toss or spin the large crowned mace, something Mr. Egli wouldn't have asked of the other boys. He might have recognized something else in me, too. Everyone else moved in a straightforward, two-over-two cadence – left foot, right foot – stepping out in standard time; I seemed to hear an additional, phantom beat within that same measure. I would sometimes trip out a kind of three-quarter shuffle, partly in sync with the others, partly out, as if I were waltzing a two-step.

By March, we were all rehearsing for the Big Show, our annual variety program mounted for the general community's amusement. It ran for three nights. We sold tickets to pay the rental fees for the stage lights and the amplification system. Kids with talent, theretofore undisclosed, presented themselves at tryouts: interpretive dancers, singers, and flaming baton twirlers. It was surprising how many felt the need to put their talent on display. I sat in the stage band that backed up several of the performers. By then, Eric was fully recovered. With Ron on guitar, he, Abby, and I sang a set of folk and protest songs. We called ourselves The Group, and we felt we brought seriousness and moral relevance to the evening's bill.

A group of us in Mrs. Estes' English class mounted a parody of the "Ides of March" scene in Julius Caesar. It was standard buffoonery, the kind of post-vaudevillian clowning popular for decades across middle America, in which a Shakespearean classic is reduced to something farcical. I took the cross-dressing role of Caesar's wife, setting aside the compunctions I had about public perception. It was adolescent humor. I did not think of it as performing drag, something which has always felt to me self-alienating. The role was scripted. It called for camp, and I took the plunge. Once Brutus made his final dagger thrust into Caesar, I made it my task to ensure he was dead by pulling out the fatal knife. As I did so, I eyed its bloodied blade and pronounced him "a quart low." It passed as hilarious when I strutted across the stage in high heels. I practiced walking in those heels in the back of the English class for a couple of weeks while everyone else looked away as if it weren't happening.

My father showed up at the last dress rehearsal, unannounced. I was startled and confused that he should be at one of my school activities. He didn't come to our concerts and athletic events. Looking back, I presume that in my ceaseless commentary at the dinner table – or in response to someone else's warning – he learned I was performing while cross-dressing and wanted to assure himself I would not abase the family. After rehearsal, he came up onto the stage while I was still in dress and heels. He was subdued, which I attributed to his awkwardness over the venue in which we found ourselves. "Don't be vulgar," was what he said, then turned and walked away immediately after imparting his advice. He left as he came, separately, in his own car. I stood wondering what it was he found vulgar – the cartoonish flourishing of a stage prop knife as a dipstick on a stage corpse? Or his son dressed as Caesar's wife, playing it for laughs? He never commented further. Nor did he or Mom come to any of the performances.

Six

THE END OF MY JUNIOR YEAR WAS THE END OF LEE ANN'S SENIOR year. After her graduation ceremony in Clinton Prairie's gymnasium, a caravan followed us home, family and friends who had RSVP'd "I will attend" on the formal card Lee Ann included with her engraved invitation. In the long, open kitchen that ran across the front of the house, they gathered over a punchbowl and finger-food. Wine and liquor were discreetly available out of the direct view of our disapproving grandparents. The long dinner table stood chairless, draped and decorated for a party, and the house filled with aunts, uncles. These were outnumbered by church friends and bridge partners from over the years, some of whom, like my godparents, had been closer to me in childhood than blood relatives. It was an exciting evening, as remarkable for being the first graduation among my generation as it was for the assembled company.

People had their photographs taken with Lee Ann in her cap and gown standing next to them: Grandma Boyle, Grandma and Grandpa Juday, and the Linsmeyers. I don't remember seeing any prints of these later. Lee Ann took off her cap and robe to reveal the outfit she had chosen for this special occasion, a fitted-waist, gauzy, off-white dress in a small, pale green wildflower print. I remember the dress, remember watching her move about in it as she listened to the avuncular advice from people who had seen her grow up as a shy and half-hidden girl, the first born among their friends.

The tone of the party shifted slightly with the departure of relatives who drank one glass of punch and started dropping references to the long, 35-minute drive back to Tipton County. They were effusively thanked for making the arduous journey. As the kitchen thinned out, I felt increasingly awkward as the adult conversation grew louder. My friends were in their own homes, presumably standing next to their own siblings' punchbowls and navigating their own godparents. I found myself cornered by Mr. Bailey, a family friend from St. Mary's with whom I had heretofore never had a real conversation on any topic. He seemed earnest and deliberate, if a little slouched over. He asked me what I was going to do with my life, and I mumbled something about the coming senior year. Mr. Bailey moved his cocktail glass tighter against his chest, leaned closer toward me, and said, "No, I mean once you're on your own."

It was Dad, standing at the other end of the room, who had prompted Mr. Bailey's question. Dad was telling everyone about his firm and fast rule, one we had heard incessantly over the years: "Eighteen and out." It meant that, once we reached the fully mature age of 18 and presumably graduated high school as Lee Ann was doing, we were expected to move on, to go elsewhere with our lives. Lee Ann, raised under this dictum and in faithful response to it, had already made plans. She was enrolled in a training course in licensed practical nursing at Ball Memorial Hospital in Muncie. I chafed under Mr. Bailey's interrogation. As he probed further, I remember him at pains to point out that, in fact, I had no specific plan. Indeed, I didn't.

My parents enjoyed entertaining, and this later crowd included many people who enjoyed being entertained. Drinks and laughter flowed. Eventually, I slipped away from the hilarity to go upstairs and watch television. When everyone left, I went down to help wash the dishes, put away the food, and move the kitchen furniture back into place. I then climbed back up to my room, went to bed, and drifted off to sleep. I woke – I'm not sure how much later – to Lee Ann's anguished pleading downstairs, interspersed with Mom and Dad's patient but steady coaching.

"I don't want to leave. I want to stay here." She was sobbing and made no attempt to keep her voice down for those of us who were sleeping-another house rule. This earned me the right to sneak out to the top of the stairwell for a better hearing.

"Lee Ann, you've got everything arranged. Everything's in place. Just calm down."

"I don't want to calm down. I don't want to go. I want to stay here."

The news that she didn't want to leave home surprised me. She seemed proud to be following Grandma Boyle into a nursing career. I knew she had the temperament and work ethic for it. Everyone could see that. The surprise was that she didn't want to leave us, the very people she bitterly complained about for the last several years for intentionally thwarting and upsetting her.

She was inconsolable. Mom and Dad were unflappable. It was a standoff that had to be played out. This was the final round. Lee Ann was throwing down her last card. It was disheartening in a few ways to hear her do so. Did it mean she was admitting that much of her dissatisfaction had been a pose and that she was in reality content with the stasis of the last few years? Was she testing how much power she had to maintain that stasis?

A few days after Lee Ann's graduation party, Mom and Dad drove her to the nursing school in Muncie. The following weekend, on a Sunday evening, Dad drove me down to Indianapolis and checked me into the YMCA on North Alabama Street. I was to start working in the stockyards at the south-side terminal. Each subsequent weekday morning, Monday through Friday for the next six weeks, I would stand on the sidewalk on North Delaware waiting for Jack, Dad's business partner, to momentarily pause traffic while I hopped in and we drove to the yards. I worked under Jack's direction all day, putting on a clean, rented uniform in the locker room before entering the yards. I wasn't much help. I wasn't actually meant to clean pens. The "yard-boys" did that. I drove hogs from pen to pen, aimlessly walked the vast alleyways and suspended walkways of the yards, learned to chew and spit tobacco, and sat through numbing hours listening to one end of daily phone sales. If the idea was to expose me to the business end of things – the long-distance bartering over truckloads of hogs–there was little attempt at instruction. I left my soiled uniform every evening in a laundry bin in the locker room outside the showers. The regular company crew – four adult men and myself – showered together at the end of each day, silently milling naked among ourselves. We changed back into street clothes, and Jack brought me back to the YMCA in the evening, where he left me to fend for myself until the next morning.

I dreaded returning to the YMCA in the evening. It was heartless and dreary. The worn, randomly assembled lounge furniture matched the institution's comfortless, industrial air of make-do. A single television console sat against the far wall, wordlessly stared at by men I didn't know and didn't want to know. They were appreciably older than I. None of them seemed to know each other, either. There was a racial mix, some black, some white, the odd Hispanic. I remember feeling exposed in the lounge, and nervous taking the stairwell or the elevator to my small, single-bed room. I was absolutely terrified of the communal toilets and showers at the end of the hall. Someone was always lurking there. If I hated standing naked among my co-workers at the stockyards, standing naked among strangers in the YMCA shower was unthinkable. Simply relieving myself was frightening enough. A few times in the bathroom stalls and once from the hallway just outside my door, furtive invitations were made to engage in sex. They were wordless and coded, and it took me a while to recognize them for what they were. I remained paralyzed and mute, eyes cast downward from late afternoon and all through the night, still mute over my coffee and donut in the morning. I coped by napping for an hour in the afternoon after work, then slipping out to wander around downtown, away from the building. I learned to make peace with the unrelieved Indiana heat in the center of the city, where the most treasured feature was the lock on the door that kept people from getting in.

Over time I learned my way around. The city center was small enough then that it could be reconnoitered by a teenager willing to trace its sidewalks out to the limits of the commercial zones. Its architectural aspirations, remnants of an earlier urban vibrancy, were fading. Once fashionable avenues bore unrelievedly rapid, heavy through-traffic. After dark, long stretches of buildings sat closed and unlit. White flight was snuffing out the nightlife. As the earlier population moved out, wig stores and locksmiths were creeping in, set up in response to a new, mostly black clientele. There were a few small businesses offering what now would be obsolete goods and services, but these were closed by the time I started my evening wanderings. I watched the passing city buses open and close their doors onto the stench of grated alleyways. I learned to read waiters' faces across diner counters, gravitating toward those who appeared at ease with their clientele.

I discovered the Indiana Theater on Market street and attended the city premiere of *The Sound of Music*, a gala event that left me briefly in an uplifted, musical mood. For the next few days, as I drove hogs, I sang what I could remember of the film's musical numbers. After a few choruses of "The Hills are Alive," complaints rose from my fellow yard-workers. Word came that they were annoyed not so much by my singing as by my exuberance. I was the boss' eldest. The others, not much older than I, were struggling to get a start in the meat-packing industry. They took their role as working adults seriously and were put off by the sound of my show tunes. They resented what they saw as my privileged position. Their resentment was one more thing to be endured.

William H. Block's was downtown Indianapolis' flagship department store. Its proximity to the train station – and since-abandoned interurban rail system – had helped it build up a large middle-class clientele. Mom had once taken me as a first-grader to its Terrace Tea Room. A miniature paper parasol came with my banana split, confirming that Block's was the height of fine living. By the mid-1960s, it had lost much of its sheen along with its clientele. A faded elegance still clung on inside in spite of that, and the cafeteria stayed open until 8 pm. I spent many evenings browsing its book department, then lingering over short-order meals with my new reading material. I discovered Edward Albee's plays. I liked the absurdities he staged. They seemed as random and specific as the absurdities I was encountering. A fever came over me when I read James Baldwin's *Giovanni's Room*. I spent many nights that summer lost in Paris where David and Giovanni made love, while David struggled with his self-loathing and yearning for a conventional life. I wept in silence at the tragedy of Giovanni's death and the unrelenting subtext that such love is inherently doomed.

On Fridays, Dad came down to collect me. On the trip home, I filled him in on my observations. I never mentioned my fears in the YMCA or the week's tedium or loneliness. I reasoned that he needn't know what I was going through, although, clearly, I was going through what he intended I go through—eighteen and out. At home, I produced a running commentary for Mom and anyone else who would listen to my city tales. I tried to amuse them with impressions of people I'd met and with stories of all the awkward misunderstandings. It felt important I assure everyone all was well, that I was enjoying the adventure. I was good at that sort of thing; I was adept at misdirection.

On Saturday nights that summer, I could still get the keys to Old Blue. Patty wasn't around as much, but Francis was always ready to go somewhere. I'm not sure where – or if – he was working. My lack of curiosity was of a piece with my ongoing unease with his effeminacy. We simply didn't talk about what we'd done during the week. We didn't talk about many things, but he was still funny. I had to give him that. And he was insightful about people and willing to say what he knew. Francis knew the local gossip, and he shared it generously, chipping away at my naiveté. There was a lot more sex going on than I would have guessed, according to him. As we circled the courthouse square again, conversations were freer, critiques of others harsher than in previous summers.

One night Francis produced a small bottle of sloe gin. We used it to wash down some fried chicken. The next morning I woke to find I had gotten sick on my pillow during the night, too passed out to even take notice. I blamed it on the fried chicken and hand washed the bed linens so no one else would know.

The newspapers that summer began to take on a repetitive concern with headlines and photos of the escalating war in Vietnam. More Marines seemed to be dying each week. Robert MacNamara said the only way to win the war was to bomb and annihilate North Vietnam and its people. I pored over the military engagements they described, calling to mind my dread at scenes from *The Red Badge of Courage* and from war movies watched late at night. How could this be happening to the Vietnamese people? How could this be happening to American soldiers? In nine months' time, it would be my duty to register with Selective Service, to sign up for the draft. This could be happening to me. I would be eligible for a student deferment if I went on to college. I would certainly do that. I felt some shame at my lack of bravery, my unwillingness to enlist. Going off to war was a rite of passage to manhood. Dad had done it, and it would be expected of me. But no, I would protect myself with a student deferment, even if it was cowardice.

The Senior Class of '66 came back to school that fall with a swagger. We'd been waiting for this year as if it were a final flowering. As drum major, I marched the band around the parking lot, drilling them in the late summer heat, blocking out and rehearsing half-time shows for the football field. I pored over the yearbook, over its content and layout, and assigned people to draw up club rosters and organize photo-shoot schedules. We only had two days' access to a photographer. The one class I dreaded – other than Phys. Ed. – was Civics, a required course for every senior. Passing it was mandatory for graduation by Indiana State law. Mr. Ryan was the teacher, a holdover from pre-consolidation days, a spent and tired man. His pedagogical objectives were a methodical slog through a dry text and prolonged silences. These had a soporific effect. No one ever made more than minimal effort. I tried to enliven things. I feigned ignorance in a play for laughs. I was sarcastic, impudent, and occasionally rude. I was thrown out of class twice. The first time, I found the whole thing hilarious. It took a special intervention from the administration after the second infraction to get me reinstated so that I could graduate. What arrogance the poor man had to contend with from me – smart, cocky, and sick and tired of being well-behaved.

With both of us on an academic track, Eric and I once again shared a lot of classroom time. My obsession with him grew stronger with proximity. I spent a lot of time watching him, searching for clues about his feelings for me. I thought I detected an attraction – was it more fraternal or romantic? I was, in fact, intensely pining over him. One Saturday afternoon, when he came to visit, we walked down to the pier at the far end of the lake. I told him calmly that I thought I was in love with him. I heard my confession arrive to my ears as if I weren't the one speaking it. He listened with equanimity, then stood silent for a while in quiet reflection. Silence was not what I was hoping for. But he didn't mock me or gasp in horror, which is what I most feared. He looked at me in his steady manner, and said that it was probably just a phase I was going through.

What is he really trying to say? Maybe this is shyness? Maybe he feels the same way I do? He hasn't rebuked me. He loves me, he loves me not...

For the next several weeks, I clung to any sign that allowed this ambiguity to stay alive. I neither renounced my feelings for him nor reiterated them. We maintained our friendship as before and continued to talk about ideas, about books we were reading. He liked Joseph Heller's *Catch 22*. I found its ironic tone off-putting. I recommended Mary Renault's *The Last of the Wine*, whose two protagonists were men, lovers free to be just that in ancient Greece. He read the book and displayed no revulsion. I was certain a "normal" person would have been revolted. I had no awareness of simple tolerance; it never occurred to me there might be such a thing. *He loves me, he loves me not...*

I was a random chit in a board game. Each square around the periphery, like a trip around a *Monopoly* board, brought another loaded issue: eighteen and out; white picket fence; Eric; Vietnam. Pass go, collect $200. I rolled the dice, counted out the steps, and dealt with whatever I found. The game seemed to have no general purpose beyond keeping forward movement going. And avoiding fines. I roamed Springwood at night. Late autumn settled in, and the grey skies, the rust-colored foliage, and the dry, brittle grass suited my mood. I started to develop physical tics that eventually required coping mechanisms. Turmoil kicked at my ribs and churned in my bowels. These are not metaphors, but actual physical manifestations threatening what I had cobbled together and called myself. I pushed back with my gut when I heard the churn, and with my chest when I felt the throb. It happened every day, feeding on hormonal angst and a sense of being, inherently, a mistaken thing.

Coping mechanisms can't hold things back forever. One night it all snapped. I phoned Eric and told him I had to see him. I have no idea what I thought to say, what I thought would happen, what I needed to hear. I simply had to act. In fact, after the phone call, I realized I couldn't wait for him in the house. I walked down to the lake, stared at it for a while, then walked back to the house. No Eric yet. I went down into the ravine along the side of the house, looking for distraction. It was dark. Under the pale bit of light left in the sky, at the bottom of the ravine, the plant life was silent and unresponsive. I came back up to the house. No Eric. *He said he would come. He will. I know it. I should go up the driveway to meet him at the road. Better to be away from the house.* I waited along the Farmer's Gravel. The clouds moved relentlessly eastward, the thin grey moonlight appearing between their clotted shadows.

No Eric. I couldn't wait any longer. It was time to start walking. I turned west, toward the train tracks, toward Chicago. I would walk to Chicago. I remember establishing a military pace. A changing series of plans ran through my head. There was no possibility of going back now. At the next road, a side road I had never paid attention to, I turned south. I wouldn't try for Chicago right away; I would walk to Eric's. He'd be there, and we could talk. We could go through whatever had to happen. There was no plan now, except to keep walking, to leave everything behind, to go forward.

I remained in this manic state for at least two hours. It was a six-mile walk to Eric's. When I got there, I was more mentally exhausted than physically tired. I had no idea what time it was, only that it was late, that I had walked away from everything, that I was at Eric's now, and things would simply occur as they were meant to occur. I lay down on the side porch and rolled up into a ball. I was crying silently. There was no need to say anything.

Or maybe I did make a small noise. Or maybe a loud noise. Things weren't under my control. Whatever I did was without my awareness, without my intention. After a time, whether long or short, the porch light came on. I heard the kitchen door open and standing there, staring at me through the screen, was Eric's mother. She knew I had gone missing. Eric had come to my house sometime after I set out for Chicago, and told Dad that I asked him to come over. But I was nowhere to be found. There must have been some frantic yelling, frantic searching. Someone surely honked the car horn in the driveway, signaling me to come back to the house. Maybe after that, there was some slow driving along the county roads, someone at the wheel, someone on lookout.

Why do I wonder about these details? Maybe if I knew them, I could determine at what exact point I left my right mind, how long I wandered away from everything I knew in my determination to ditch it all and start again with a life built around a more palatable narrative. Maybe I would at least have a measure of how loved I was, that someone should care that I was lost, that I was gone.

Eric's Mom phoned Dad. She brought me into the kitchen and sat me under its overhead light until he came. If Eric was in the house, I don't remember him there. Was he still looking for me across the harvested fields? Was he worried? Did he hope I was all right?

Dad's car pulled up abruptly, as if from another time, as if from someone else's story. We drove home in silence. When we got to the house, he grabbed my arm as I stepped out of the car. He pulled me into the house, down the hall, and into his bedroom, where Mom sat on the bed, crying. When she saw me, she started a louder sobbing. She didn't utter a word and, when twice we made actual eye contact, she snapped her head away, shoulders still heaving.

"See what you did to your mother?" Dad spoke through gritted teeth. I was numb. I had the sensation of having something large frozen solid inside me.

The next day, a school day, Dad woke me early and told me I was going to the stockyards with him. Mid-morning, as I went through the motions of cleaning hog pens, refusing to consider what was going on both inside me and around me, I looked up from my work to see him standing directly in front of me.

"I don't know if I should take you to a shrink or just beat the shit out of you."

I had fallen into my own collapse, and nothing that occurred to me seemed worth saying, either in defense or as atonement. Everything was simply happening to me, as if I were silently witnessing my own criminal arraignment. Dad informed me I was not going back to school that week. Moreover, I should not expect to get paid for the week's work I would do in the yards.

It was a silent week at home, too. I knew I was on brittle ground, that I would have to find just the right posture if things were to hold together. The first few days went by as if the entire family were in mourning. Glenn, Maureen – even little David – knew things weren't right, without knowing what was wrong. Mom's only comment on the subject, days later, was an aside to me as we passed each other in an otherwise empty kitchen. She said she didn't think it right for Dad not to pay me for the week.

Nothing more was said about the event. Not by Dad. Not by Mom. Not by Eric. And not by Abby. When I returned to class, nothing was said to me at school. Everyone knew what I had done, and some rightly surmised why. But it was not spoken of. We all opted not to confront what had happened. I was left on my own to ponder the universal disapproval and the universal silence and to make of it what I would. It was a silence that spoke loudly. It was a silence that rendered me further mute.

Seven

I WENT BACK TO CLASS AND CAUGHT UP ON SCHOOLWORK THE following week. If Dad had acted on the first of his threats – to send me to a shrink – I might have constructively confronted my situation. But psychotherapy carried with it the likelihood I would say something to make Dad confront my condition, too. He was not prepared for that. Nor was he prepared to "beat the shit" out of me – his other threat. He was, at heart, a hopeful man. He had spoken out of frustration; he bore no animus. His burden was disappointment, and more embarrassment than he would ever admit to.

Eric and I were still friends, and we would carry on as before, but with a measured detachment. Our interactions conformed to the norms of our time and place. True to course, Eric seemed content with this. So, there was my answer. *Keep your cool. Keep your distance.* I determined to find a way to carry on. A semblance of dignity would be my shield.

By the Christmas holidays things settled down. Abby and I continued as if nothing had happened, as if, after a restoration, things were back to where they were. That seemed best. I valued the social standing being her beau provided. There were opportunities to ask her out, and I did. She said yes, and we continued dating. Things would be delicate for a while. What was needed was caution, patience, and watchfulness.

Graduation loomed. I needed a plan for the future, one that included college enrollment and a draft deferment. My English teacher told me the Journalism School at Northwestern in Chicago had a fine reputation. My grades were good. I was a national merit scholarship finalist and class salutatorian. That should count for something when pursuing scholarships. I met with the guidance counselor, the same man who years earlier sighed over nigger schools. He discouraged the idea of journalism school and reminded me that Dad had a thriving business in the livestock industry. I would be a fool, he said, not to claim a place for myself in it. That didn't appeal to me. It was clear I didn't belong in Frankfort, where I would always be "Paul's boy." And there was the draft. And there was that embarrassment about Eric. There were so many reasons why I had to move on.

By then, Dad was working out of a rented office in a converted storefront in northwest Frankfort, away from the stockyard toil and stench. It sat at an angle at the intersection of US 421 North and the Farmer's Gravel. Mom worked there as a part-time bookkeeper, along with a woman named Pete, who provided administrative support for the managers of what were now four separate and thriving subsidiary stockyards. When I told Dad

I needed to talk about my future, he said we should talk in his office. We arranged a date and time. Mom was sitting at her desk outside his door when I arrived. She made a show of packing up her things when I came in, and left for home without reference to my reason for being there.

I told him I was thinking about what I should do after my senior year. He sat attentively and remained quiet. By keeping his silence, he maintained the upper hand. After a few moments of "who goes first?" I told him what the counselor advised about my working in the livestock company. And what did I think about that? Like our talk about the priesthood, I felt there had been conversations among my elders to which I had not been privy.

I said I would like to go to Northwestern to study Journalism. Dad nodded calmly. He seemed unfazed by – maybe even in agreement with – my decision to go to college. My father expressed no interest in the subject area I wanted to pursue, or why. He simply asked how I was going to pay for what would be very steep tuition fees. I had no illusions about getting him to help. Eighteen and out. I said I would like to land a scholarship. If I submitted my academic record and declared my lack of financial resources and financial support, some funding source might become available, but he would need to fill out some forms. He shifted a bit in his chair. He said that, on principle, he was unwilling to fill out any forms concerning his financial position. His finances were his business, no one else's. He counter-offered to co-sign a loan at the Farmer's Bank. I would have to apply for it myself and convince the bank I had a workable plan for repayment. He had no further ideas about options to make Northwestern possible.

The bank told me out-of-state tuition was beyond their comfort zone. That meant going to an in-State University. I could afford any one of Indiana's third-level public schools, whose tuition back then would be considered minimal today. I investigated the requirements. With a student loan, I could make it happen. I had saved money for years. It didn't amount to a lot, but it would get me started. I would work every summer and find part-time work each semester for spending money. I had been working since I was 13. My peers already had plans in place. Abby was going to Ball State University in Muncie. Her brother was in the Music Department there, and she would follow him. The easiest solution was to follow Abby; at least, I wouldn't be alone there. I felt a sense of obligation toward her. I applied with the idea of earning an English major and a Music minor. I could consider journalism for graduate study. It was a plan. I needed a plan. And a deferment.

The remainder of the school year passed like a quick slide down a short chute. Events happened in their usual order but at a faster pace. I watched them go by, unable to grab them and slow them down. We marched for one last Indianapolis 500 race festival, parading through the city one day and then on the two-and-a-half-mile oval just before the poll cars got the green flag the next. In the street, parade viewers on the sidelines pressed in to watch us. A little girl thrust her balloon toward my hand as I signaled for a flanked turn at a street corner. I have always been nervous around balloons, alien in texture, and worryingly volatile. When hers squeaked against the back of my hand, I jumped sideways, abandoning the discipline we were so intent on displaying. There was tittering among the crowd.

Soon it was down to the last week of school. Then, the last day. On the final morning, we spent a chaotic couple of hours signing each other's yearbooks, cleaning out lockers, and patching up old quarrels, gushing out our heartfelt sentiments.

We mingled in nervous disbelief that all this was coming to an end. We promised eternal commitment to friendships that had no chance of being sustained.

On Baccalaureate Sunday, I remember standing on the risers with the rest of the choir singing "Walk On" while nearly blinded by tears. A charismatic preacher led the prayer. He had an evangelical style, and he exhorted us to bow heads, then hold hands. He began to utter "Jesus, Jesus," eyes closed as he rocked on the balls of his feet. I grew uncomfortable, as if I had stumbled into a forbidden rite. It was a novel awkwardness. That it stands out so clearly shows how well the issues of religious tolerance had been managed over the years.

I had written my salutatorian speech weeks ahead of time and practiced it again and again. The thought of actually standing at a lectern and delivering it aloud in a gymnasium full of classmates and family had me sick with worry. Unlike reading from the lectionary at Mass, these were my words, referencing my existence. On the evening itself, we entered to the sound of the band – minus us seniors – playing *Pomp and Circumstance*. We marched in cap and gown along heavy canvass tarps protecting the basketball floor against our dress shoes. The tarp ran down an aisle set between hundreds of folding chairs. Eric led off, alone, as valedictorian. I was just behind him, alone as well, proud to be his friend, wanting him to shine and be admired by all, still thrilled by proximity to him.

My typescript speech, pressed in the album my mother gave me, was predictably dutiful: "As each of us receives his diploma, he begins his own commencement, his next beginning. What we have done collectively is now behind us. It is what we do as individuals that must now be our concern." I don't remember Eric's speech that night. He delivered his, I delivered mine, we paraded across the dais and were handed a diploma. We moved our tassel from one side of the mortarboard cap to the other, and our families applauded. We went home to our celebrations, which would soon be forgotten among the distractions of the summer.

Eric went to Purdue University in the fall. I visited him once or twice over the following year and met his new girlfriend there. The last time I saw him was at his wedding, in the United Church of Christ, in Jefferson, a year or so thereafter. I never talked to him about how he felt about my professed love for him. I worried for years that I never apologized for what I put him through. Still, I don't think I was wrong to tell him. He handled it well – stoically and with aplomb. He had been confronted with no more than what many young people have to contend with in adolescence.

Too many years have passed to change any of that now.

Eight

ON THE LATE SUMMER MORNING I WAS TO LEAVE FOR BALL
State, my brother David insisted on walking with me up the lane
to the mailbox on the Farmer's Gravel, demanding I hold his
small, soft, not-quite-five-year-old hand. His short legs scurried
to match my gait. He was somber. He knew I was leaving, but he
didn't know why and didn't know how to address it. His watchful
silence caught me unprepared, and I felt powerless to console him.

I had enrolled in the university marching band and was mustered
up, two weeks before the start of the term, to drill for football
season. It was a hot, cloudless August day. Relentless sunlight
glinted off everything. The metal dashboard was too hot to touch,
and, even with the windows down and at seventy miles an hour,
the car was a rolling oven. Mom drove. Everywhere, indoors and

out, the muggy air hung limp and motionless. I'd been warned to hope I didn't get assigned to Waggoner Hall. Everyone called it The Zoo. It was a madhouse, I was told, where they dumped all the freshmen. It sat at the campus's edge. That was, indeed, where I was slotted. A sheet of paper taped to a door confirmed which was my dorm room. It said Steve was to share the room with me, but Steve hadn't arrived yet.

Mom helped me carry in a stack of folded clothes and the three boxes containing all my worldly goods. I saw her car pull away through the ground-floor window. Across a short side-lawn stood white wooden houses, laundry pinned to clotheslines, and one-car garages built on cinder block footings. It looked for all the world like any side street in Frankfort. I was not feeling a campus vibe. I turned to the closet and desk drawers I was claiming under "first-come-first-served" rights, distracted by what should go where. Within a few minutes, I jumped in startled reaction to a silent profile standing motionless inside the door jamb. It was my mother, returned. She stood quietly, both hands raised to her face. She was crying, an image that confused me more than unnerved me.

"Mom. What's wrong?"

"I wanted a proper goodbye," she blurted.

I rushed to her and instinctually put my arms around her. I kissed her cheek and pressed her hip against mine. I had given no thought to the idea she would miss me, and I saw now that it hurt her to have me go. I suppose I should have intuited this. Here was a measure of my self-absorption: my mother, distraught at losing her son, doubling back, weeping overtly, telling me so, wanting one more moment before parting. I walked her out to the car, my arm still around her shoulder. I was moved by what she, no doubt, saw as a display of her weakness. The moment stays with me still, so tender and so completely unexpected.

At some point Steve arrived with his things. He was a voice major, which appeared to be the most important news he had to announce. He was a baritone. He spoke from well within his chest, which amplified his air of authority. He was from southern Indiana, along the Ohio River, but pointed out that he bore no trace of a regional drawl. He seemed sure of all that he said. On the other hand, he was quick to smile and resigned to the idea that we had both been assigned to The Zoo. This put me at ease in the end.

Steve was mustered to campus early, too, but was exempt from the marching band. A baritone brings nothing of value to a parade. The next day I went alone to the practice field behind the Music building. Assistant directors and student assistants grouped us by sections: large brass, small brass, reeds, and woodwinds. As a former drum major, I found it deflating to now find myself marching in a row of saxophones again. The percussion section stood off at a remove, facing into a circle, drumming out an evolving set of cadences at varied march tempos. It was hard to hear over their din but pleasant enough to be enveloped by it. They set up patterns, modified them, alternated them, and then repeated them. Standing around waiting for things to come together, we all had a repetitive dip in the knees that kept time with the drummers, as if we were at an outdoor concert.

Marching is physically demanding. It depends on learning fast, repeating often, and keeping a steady eye on everyone around you – on your left, on your right, and in front. We rehearsed four hours a day, four days a week. By the end of the first two weeks, still nowhere near ready for the opening game, we were at least able to move at a snappier pace than I ever knew in high school. Breaks were introduced by the band director on a bullhorn bellowing from the top of an elevated chair where he sat like a lifeguard at the beach.

"If you got 'em, smoke 'em."

And so began a twenty-eight-year cigarette habit. Within two days, I had my first pack (Winstons, like Dad) and my first Zippo with its fresh cache of lighter fluid. Thus prepared for the next smoking break, I lit up on the director's cue, snapped the metal Zippo shut, and put it in the front pocket of my shorts. Lighter fluid seeped into the thin fabric of the pocket liner and clung, damp and sweaty, against my inner thigh. That night a painful skin rash broke out, hard against my scrotum, one that had to be endured for several marching days in the summer heat before it cleared up. Unenlightened by this omen, I kept on smoking. I liked the manly flair of pausing mid-sentence to pull out a cigarette and light up. It had a theatrical quality. I was evolving from Daniel Boone to the Marlboro Man. For the next twenty-eight years I kept smoking, driven by an addiction to steady levels of nicotine in my circulatory system. At the end, exhausted by chronic pulmonary congestion, I steeled myself against the full-body quakes and shudders that accompanied withdrawal and managed to quit. So much wasted money; such endless fouling of breath, clothes, rooms, and car interiors; such permanent damage to the lungs.

Life in The Zoo required accommodations. Steve was studious and not given to pranks, late-night card games, or lighting his own farts, something a guy across the hall had mastered, which others found unendingly hilarious. Meals were served within a narrow timeframe, but most of campus life was built around that timeframe. The food was decent, in spite of our tropes like "shit-on-a-shingle" and "mystery meat." The food intake requirements of healthy young men aren't difficult to calculate: at least a half-pound of protein, two scoops of starch ladled with gravy at every meal, and anything cloyingly sweet to cleanse the palate. Mealtime was structured by awkwardly standing in line with guys I didn't know. It was best endured by seeking out a friend to have someone to talk to while I grabbed a tray, got my cutlery, inched a few steps at a time in front of the steaming options, made my choices, thanked the ladies in hairnets, and found an unoccupied seat. Loud voices raised in forced hilarity bounced off the high ceiling of the dining hall, and every conversation required hearty narrating and strained listening. Unlike high school, there was no expectation of universal camaraderie. I knew some people, ignored others, and absolutely avoided a worrisome few. I got this sorted out in a few weeks, after which I maintained a routine that helped contain the chaos.

Waggoner Hall was a male dorm. Some were young men, some still boys. There were city boys who shared a smirky camaraderie with each other. There were farm boys with whom I had a natural affinity. Mostly, there were suburban boys, largely from the metropolitan areas around Indianapolis or from the south-side of Chicago, what we called The Region. Their talk was peppered with impatience at those of us from "the sticks." Most of us were white. There were a few black guys, most of them the first of their community to go on to college, hopeful pioneers determined to change the family legacy. They sat together at the mealtime tables and in the student hang-outs. There were mutterings among the whites about how this was self-segregation. I found it no more so than the privileged white boys who sought each other's company in the same way. I gravitated toward my own group – awkward freshmen whose rooms were near mine, guys I knew from the same hallway.

Bruce and Abrams had the room next to Steve and me. Abrams felt he had lost social standing by living this far away from New York, out in the midwest hinterlands. He could be quite funny and used that wit to ingratiate himself. Bruce came from the north-side of Indianapolis, from an affluent, socially desirable zip code. He was a competitive swimmer, tall and broad-shouldered with long-muscled arms and thighs, which he referred to as his delts and his quads. Bruce had fair skin, almost pearlescent. When he wasn't hanging out with other affluent jocks, he sat around one of our rooms looking for someone to talk to. Nothing too serious. He was up for easy banter and quickly put off by any probing conversation. He liked to walk around in his underwear. When he stood to stretch, with his legs slightly apart, he called to mind Leonardo da Vinci's *Vitruvian Man*, a rendering of an ideal body illuminating the unifying principles of beauty.

He showed an odd interest in me. With an indulgent grin, he sometimes inquired about what I was studying, coming up behind me as I sat at my desk and leaning over me. At times he lightly pressed his body against my back. Once, I felt his erection against me. It was not an unpleasant intimacy. I sat still, unsure what to say or what I wanted to say. I said nothing. I simply acquiesced. Others saw this behavior too. I have to suppose they spoke about it among themselves. But not with me. So there surely was talk in the hall the evening Bruce announced he wanted to spend the night in my room, suggesting Steve could sleep in his room. I must have been consulted about the arrangement and would have made no objection. Before lights out, some of the guys dropped in to see how things were playing out.

As we undressed, there was little talk. When I turned the lights off, I sat on the edge of the bed where Bruce now lay. I said I would lie down beside him if he wanted. He urged me back into my bed with a gentle, parental patience, as if I didn't fully understand what was happening. Which I didn't. I still wonder what he intended, what he was thinking. Maybe he was strolling the shore of a newly discovered seascape into which he was instinctively called. Maybe he wanted just to listen to its strangely lapping water. Maybe he wanted to slip in but found himself unable to for some reason. I wonder, too, about my own thinking. Certainly, I was compelled by his beauty. Certainly, I would have been sexually available to him if he had wanted. On the other hand, I don't remember being disappointed. Our proximity excited me, but it didn't frighten me.

Shelby and Jeff were two serious, socially awkward math students at the far end of the hall. They seemed well matched. I enjoyed talking with them. They were like people I knew, people who cautiously put forth ideas, tolerated disagreement, and avoided put-downs. Shelby was gaunt and had blond, curly hair. His conversations touched on many topics, always railed in by a natural politeness. I would go to his room some evenings where we listened to his stereo. He had an interesting collection of singles and LPs. Among them was Sam Cooke's *Ain't That Good News?* I knew Cooke's cross-over radio hits: *You Send Me, Wonderful World,* and *Chain Gang.* But sitting quietly with Shelby one evening, looking at the handsome young black singer on the album cover, I listened for the first time as a music student. I was amazed by the beauty and polish of his voice. Shelby knew all about Sam Cooke, his struggles and early death, and talked about him with reverence. It was the first night I really considered what *A Change is Gonna Come* was trying to say. I could hear it speak of struggle and hope, and of lament over the way things were. It was the voice of someone who wanted me to notice something was amiss.

One afternoon, Shelby introduced me to a black student who lived on the second floor of the dorm. He was sitting at Shelby's desk listening to the stereo. I don't remember his name; it was long ago and we never became friends. He seemed a lot like Shelby, a bit formal, a bit awkward, but ready with an open smile. Shelby introduced him more formally than the standard dormitory "how's it going?" It was a novel experience, talking to a black person in a personal setting. Shelby told his guest I liked Sam Cooke, clearly in an effort to introduce common ground. I knew little about Cooke, only what I had fleetingly felt on listening to his album. I became chatty and talked about my music studies. I talked about marching band. We had recently marched in a half-time show for the Chicago Bears. I wandered further afield, compulsively talking, bringing up the parade at the Indy 500 weekend. Shelby's friend listened politely while I described the excitement of it all, and of the moment I jumped out of formation when "the little pick-a-ninny brushed her balloon against the back of my hand."

Shelby and his guest froze. Shelby was the first to gain his tongue.

"Aw. Come on, Dan."

I looked at him as if to ask what prompted that remark. Meanwhile, the word *pick-a-ninny* ricocheted around the room, alien and offensive. It came to me in a rush that I had, without reflection, used a term with roots in my childhood – a rare word, as rare as black children in that childhood – and I had used it instinctively, for its specificity, for what I understood to be its taxonomical aptness: as if mares bear foals, swans bear cygnets, white women bear children, and black women bear pick-a-ninnies. I had dropped the word into our talk with the heedlessness of someone ignorant of its offensiveness, addressing someone vulnerable to such offense. My breath grew short, and my face flushed. I fumbled an apology, which was accepted under the lame pretense that I hadn't meant to be hurtful. But I had been hurtful by saying such a thing. I was stammering like Adam after eating of the tree of knowledge of good and evil, suddenly aware that I was naked.

My class schedule felt random and irregular. The order and location of each class varied throughout the week, and I missed the comfort of a standard daily routine. Venues were scattered among several buildings, each with its different architecture and distinct aura, as if I were going to several different schools at once. Biology lectures were given in a large, dim auditorium. Keeping up with the text we were racing through with all its slippery scientific nuance required copious note-taking from slides projected against a distant screen. I wrote as much as I could, as fast as I could, and hoped it would make sense later, away from the dark theater. Coursework for English studies was roughly mapped out by a series of Norton anthologies. In those days, the canon started with Beowulf and Chaucer and was charted through World Literature, English Literature, and North American Literature over the full course of undergraduate study. It was a canon that took little notice of the many diverse voices that have since been admitted – women, African-Americans, non-Europeans. Even so, it was daunting enough in that earlier, exclusionary form. There were several non-Norton supplementary texts rounding out each syllabus so that I was always fumbling with new or used paperbacks that did or didn't get read. I wondered that so much could ever be read. I supposed a full education to be commensurate with completing each and every syllabus, an achievement I cannot claim.

Saxophone training was a combination of one-on-one tutoring and lone practice sessions in small, airless, sound-proofed rooms, repeating the same runs and fingering exercises over and over again. This induced self-appraisal, like Forty-Hours devotions at St. Mary's when the Blessed Sacrament was on display: is my devotion sufficient to the moment? Is my response acceptable? Is it defensible under honest self-scrutiny? Music theory supplemented technique training. The notation part was obvious in a kind of mathematical way, but there were several hours of audio lab with headphones, listening to interactive, pre-recorded tapes. Two random notes played sequentially; the task was to correctly identify the pitch interval. This, too, took place alone, in a cramped booth. My instructor's name was Cecil. He was patient with me, but he had the air of someone beaten down by disappointments, and I felt as if I were one of them. The one chance to unwind and let go was in Training Orchestra. We chose an instrument at random, about which we knew nothing, and once a week gathered over an orchestral score to slog our way through it with the rest of the company equally at sea on their unfamiliar instruments. I played the tympani. I pounded them, often in error, eagerly, loudly, and happily most every Friday afternoon.

I gave myself over in varying degrees of earnestness to my weekly studies, separate pursuits in separate spheres, trusting that performing well would mold me into a complete college graduate. But questions haunt an 18-year-old. What is the meaning of life? Where do I fit into it? It may be such questioning that led me to the Newman Center, the Catholic campus ministry. On the other hand, it may have been nostalgia or reluctance to abandon a communal practice that had nurtured me. Whatever led me – I suspect it was the expectations of others more than loftier things – I went to Mass and social events there. The Center hummed with talk of liturgical renewal, as if we had discovered something that had eluded the theologians of the previous two millennia, as if we stood at a threshold, ready to formulate a new spirituality. I remember an enthused young nun – I don't recall her name – who was always happy to see me, happy to see any of us. She wanted to replace the devotional piety of our childhoods with something that spoke directly to what we saw as our newly acquired maturity and enlightened modernity. She held special events. There was the installation of artwork by Sr. Corita Kent, an artist/nun who traveled the country with a series of cardboard boxes daubed with simple graphics in primary colors. These were stacked into wall-like shapes in the center of large rooms and bore aspirational phrases like Love! Peace! Joy! and poetry from disparate sources. In overall effect, it felt fresh, even if it elided any precise delineation of a new vision. For a few weeks, we practiced Public Confession, a fad that quickly disappeared once it became clear how much it violated one's sense of personal space. But for those few brief sessions, there was the giddy experience of standing as one sinner among many publicly avowed sinners, each of us extending forgiveness to each other, albeit for rather attenuated admissions of transgression.

Mass was staged and scored in new ways, too. Acoustic guitars provided a strumming backdrop to homilies that bore less theology than they once had. New lyrics appropriated the melodic and harmonic structures of the American songbook, seeking a closer integration with the lives we led outside the cocoon of church. Every Sunday, after the priest raised up the bread and the wine, after he genuflected in adoration while we remained standing to demonstrate our personal autonomy, a young man sang out the Eucharistic Devotion in a beautiful baritone.

"God is love," he sang. "And he who abides in love abides in God, and God in him." And that felt like answer enough for the moment.

Nine

ABBY WAS TRAINING IN VOICE AND HARP AND STUDYING MUSIC theory as well. She walked the halls of the Music Department more often than I did. When we ran into each other there, which wasn't often, it felt awkward, as if one of us were intruding on the other's space. I shied away from following or commenting on her progress, in part because I knew her to be a better musician than I was.

To meet away from the music building required that we coordinate schedules. Dates were planned for the weekend, often to see productions staged on campus. She lived in a dormitory near Emens Auditorium. The Music and English departments, my two tangential worlds, were each housed in different annexes flanking that auditorium. Curfew for co-eds was 10 PM weekdays, midnight on weekends. References to females on campus were fluid, no less than for males. They lived in *women's* dorms, but they were expected, as *girls*, to be inside the dorms before ten. The custom was to return with their dates to a chaperoned lounge and sit with them until the clock struck the hour. A wordless ritual played out. Johnny Mathis crooned in the background while long-term or newly-met couples watched other couples cuddle and kiss – what we called making out. Abby's ground-floor lounge had exterior glass walls on three sides. Intimate physical contact was thus meant to be constrained by its being on full, public view. There were plenty bold enough to engage in heavy petting, derisively calling the lounge "The Fish Bowl." Their overt intimacy, in fact, helped to ease other couples' transition into sexual activity more than curtail it.

Another dorm tradition had it that the boys would erupt into spontaneous panty raids, driven by Fish Bowl ardor, at dates and times mysteriously telegraphed across campus. The role of the males was to stand below the females' dorm windows and demand they throw down bits of underclothing. This took place over a swelling sea-chanty of PANTIES! PANTIES! I stood in one such raid, half-amused by the enthusiasm stirring the crowd. But I slipped away after several minutes, fearful I might see Abby carry on with the charade and abase both herself and me by throwing personal clothing into the mob.

My freshman year unspooled in disconnected strings. At one moment, I was crossing a footpath on the Commons, distracted by dorm worries and struggling to remember what I read for the class to which I headed. In another moment, waiting at the crosswalk light, I stood wondering what the Psych prof was trying to get me to see. One thing ended solely because another thing started. Randomness was the only thing that seemed to sustain itself. I drifted through unconnected worlds: the stuffy, overheated

Economics classroom where I drowsed off after lunch; the Phys. Ed. class where I tread chilly, chlorinated water; lonely Saturday afternoons with nothing to do – that caged feeling that is the essence of dormitory life. Years later, when I first heard the word *compartmentalize* in reference to dissociative states, I immediately thought of my freshman year.

I also felt that the time and effort I was investing in music studies were leading nowhere. I no longer believed in my musicality. I sensed that the music I played didn't come from the right place. It resided in my head as studied technique, and in memory stored in my fingers through countless hours of practice. Music speaks in lyric, full-bodied truths. I was in rigid denial of my truth, and thus fearful of what might emanate from me, how it might expose me. Fear rendered me incapable of producing anything of depth.

Furthermore, music studies were not preparing me for an economic system that rewarded a skill for its utility. What value could be attached to a second-rate saxophonist? I had no potential as a music teacher; I couldn't play piano, and that was a *sine qua non.* I met with a guidance counselor and laid out my predicament. I acknowledged I had arbitrarily chosen the saxophone, and I was ready to abandon it. He considered my case and listed a few options. Among them was switching my minor to Spanish, given my two years' high school study. I was initially put off by the idea, recognizing it meant I would have to re-imagine myself. But I had to find some way forward, out of the present *cul de sac.* Always forward. I felt at home among words. Another language, full of new words, might be the right direction. The guidance counselor suggested that if someone asked why I changed minors, I could say that a second language was professionally useful in a shrinking world. As it turned out, no one ever asked me why I changed my minor. Within a month, I sold the saxophone and used the cash to buy contact lenses. I was tired of the bookish look that spectacles gave me. No one ever asked me why I did that, either.

One consequence of switching my minor was to put further distance between Abby and me. As music students we at least shared a few activities, a bit of departmental gossip, and occasional proximity. When I started intensive Spanish studies I left that world and entered another. The Fine Arts building was its new locus, and I had to get serious if I were to catch up to first-year, third-quarter fluency. There was an audio lab component here, too, more time spent with headphones, listening, repeating. I recorded my efforts at pure vowel sounds, trilled "rr's," and proper interrogative inflection. I had a good ear, I liked the sound of the language, and was happy enough to sit in an asbestos-clad booth repeating along with some faceless stranger, "*Le ruego que Vd. me perdone. ¿Sería tan amable de repetirlo?*" A most useful phrase for beginners: "I beg your pardon. Would you be kind enough to repeat that?"

A further distancing that spring was Abby's decision to compete for the Miss Ball State title, a preliminary round in the Miss America pageant. I don't remember when I first learned she had decided to do it, but it was well after she had signed up. She had been rehearsing for some time, practicing her musical number and, presumably, learning to walk in high heels and a one-piece swimsuit while maintaining a modicum of self-respect. By that point, we had been dating for three years, and I felt I should have been consulted. I didn't see how this project of hers fit into things. She had different thoughts about what I was owed.

The night of the final Miss Ball State competition, as she filed in across the proscenium of Emens Auditorium wearing a pale blue, off-the-shoulder gown, it hit me that I barely knew her. As the master-of-ceremonies placed the First Runner-Up sash over her head, her eyes glistening with emotion, I glimpsed what I now see clearly. I had kept our relationship in a box, one I frequently set aside, happy to watch Abby evolve in her personal sphere. All the while, I moved about as if I were alone in the world. I kept Bruce or other unbid distractions from her. I was coping through avoidance. Had I been confronted about this, I might have recognized these things couldn't fit together. But I wasn't confronted.

I was paying my own bills with my own borrowed money. I was acquitting myself on exams reasonably well. Summer break was coming, and I had a beauty queen for a girlfriend. Norman, the general contractor who had renovated Springwood with my father and me, offered me a job for the summer as his assistant. The wages were better than at the stockyards. I was a good worker; Norman would get his money's worth. If, on the downside, I was back in my old bunkbed in Springwood, in the small, cramped world of my earlier life, I had at least one manifestation of a new status: I was going to work with guys who didn't call me Pauls' boy.

I was only home for the summer, and therefore I stood on a new footing. We had gathered home for Christmas, grinning our way through once-significant traditions that were losing primacy, but the centrality of family was slowly fading. Over the last few years, Dad had been spending more and more time in the Upper Peninsula of Michigan. On one of those trips, he came across a log cabin in a deep pine forest that he claimed as his new paradise. We made an inaugural family visit there the summer I graduated high school. Now, Mom and Dad planned to spend the bulk of the summer at that cabin with Glenn, Maureen, and David. My function was to maintain Springwood in their absence, to keep an eye on things.

It was 1967, the Summer of Love. Every Top forty radio station was playing Scott McKenzie's insistent question, "Are you going to San Francisco?" It had a near-hymnal *cache*. I wasn't going, no, and I felt a bit irrelevant as a result. In June, the Beatles released *Sgt. Pepper's Lonely Hearts Club Band*, a collection of what were basically English music hall tunes twisted and morphed with a hallucinogenic sensitivity. It was undeniably bold and innovative. Aretha Franklin was demanding R-E-S-P-E-C-T. Youth-marketed media – ubiquitous radio and television programming and magazine articles – encouraged us to claim all this and more as ours. We were under thirty, still young enough to understand.

In the national news, there were race riots in Tampa, Buffalo, and Washington, D.C. I disapproved of rioting and failed to see its connection with Sam Cooke's *Change Gonna Come*. American troops were deployed in increasing numbers outside Saigon, part of a clear slide toward full-scale war. People argued that stopping the endless killing would be cowardly. The pressure was on for patriotic young men to take up their role in a self-perpetuating folly, to push further and further into chaos.

At the same time, it was a happy enough summer. I was doing construction work, manly work, freed from the Sisyphean stockyard cycle where hogs came, hogs shat, and hogs left, day after day after day. I was building things, making things. Norman showed me what to do. Each project had a before- and an after-state. A pool house needed new cement-work? Bring in a jack-hammer, tear out the old, pour the new. *Voila.* Plumbing needed upgrading? Cut the old galvanized pipes, sweat in the new copper pipes, test the fittings. *Voila.* The Monday after I bought – and endlessly played – *Sgt. Pepper*, staring at John and Paul and George and Ringo in their satiny circus finery against a crowded background of sly cultural references, I showed up at a worksite where our task was to rebuild The Milky Way, an ice-cream parlor and drive-in, after a large Pontiac sedan had crashed into its front wall late on a Saturday night. The car was still *in situ*, its front end plowed so deeply into the freezer behind the now-shattered walk-up counter that chocolate and strawberry syrup still dripped onto its front grille and hood. The scene seemed to echo and add to the general sense that everything was a novel adventure, with its own potential for hilarity.

Abby told me on the phone that she decided to compete for Miss Indianapolis. Again, she had already embarked on the effort and wouldn't be able to see me much, she said, at least for the first part of the summer. I asked if I could come down to see her in Indianapolis, where she was staying. Abby would have to ask her hostess; a convenient Saturday afternoon was negotiated. She advised me that our time would be short. She had so much to prepare for. I drove down North Meridian Street to the address I was given and pulled into a circular carriage drive in front of a two-story brick house with faux-gothic windows set in a formal garden. I was greeted at the door by a young woman who said she would let Abby know she had a visitor. Everything suggested I was out of place. When she arrived, Abby was on edge, distracted. I asked whose house it was. She said it belonged to a society woman, a friend whose name she didn't offer, someone kind enough to help her prepare for the upcoming pageant. I was more annoyed than concerned by the brevity of the meeting, annoyed at Abby's distance that afternoon, annoyed at this beauty pageant business. I would be glad to see the end of it.

Alone in Springwood, my weeknights were spent wrapped in the close, dark quiet that had nurtured me for years. I had the woods to roam, the lake for skinny-dipping, books to read – for pleasure rather than exams – and that old stand-by, the television. I sat in its blue glow, half attentive to the programming and half absorbed in the moths banging against the black windows. I had Old Blue, of course, the now seriously-aged Oldsmobile that offered my earliest independence. On weekends I phoned around for company. I didn't seek out girls' company with Abby out of town. Guys I knew spent their time with girlfriends. Francis was always ready to spend a few hours driving around, going to a movie, or dropping in on mutual friends. We sometimes went into town on a weeknight for hot dogs and root beer or, at the other end of Walnut Street, a McDonald's cheeseburger, fries, and a shake. I spent time with him, away from those who wouldn't have spent time with him. I didn't mind. Neither of us had to impress the other. Neither of us had to defend himself.

Sometime after the Fourth of July, I learned that Abby was crowned Miss Indianapolis. Her black-and-white photograph appeared in the *Frankfort Morning Times*, her hair now cut short and her lips more prominent with a lipstick several shades darker. I don't remember if she wrote or phoned to tell me the news. I was excited for her but she said, of course, this meant she would now be devoting the rest of the summer to her run for Miss Indiana.

I waited for a few weeks, then contacted her again for more information about the pageant. It was to be held in the newly opened Marquette Hall in Michigan City, up north on the Lake Michigan shoreline. I consulted maps and made a few long-distance phone calls to find a motel room I could afford for the night. On the morning of the event, I set out with a pressed suit, a fresh white shirt, and a tie hanging on the hook over the rear window. I barely took in the scenery, distracted by the import of the event I was to witness. I checked into my room in a low-ceilinged highway motel by early afternoon. I had hours to kill before the event, and there was little distraction in the bare room. No television, no refrigerator. There was one novel feature: a vibrating bed, activated by inserting a quarter into a metal box on the nightstand. The small print on the decal slapped against the side of the box said, "15 minutes for

25 cents." I hung up my suit on the curtain rod in the bathroom and ran hot water in the shower so that the steam would smooth out any wrinkles. Out of fear of getting lost and being late that evening, I made a practice run to the Hall, decided where I would park, then came back to the motel to rest.

I arrived at Marquette Hall for the second time that day formally dressed. I was surrounded by a crowd with whom I imagined I would mingle, striking up conversations that allowed me to mention Abby's name and my connection to her. *Yes, I'm here with Miss Indianapolis.* But I was alone, and everyone else seemed to have brought their own company. I took my seat without speaking to anyone. The emcee stepped out onto the front of the stage. He had polish, gravitas, and an excellent audio system. As he kicked off the event, it was clear from his insinuations, then his outright assertions, that the Hoosier State was poised to send off to Atlantic City its very own Miss America, 1967!

The competition was keen. I cheered on the twirler who never dropped her baton and the pianist who draped her floor-length skirt across the piano bench and sat erect as she flawlessly executed Beethoven's *Moonlight Sonata*. Then Abby appeared, already announced as among the top ten contestants. She stood under a single spotlight dressed as a waif, suitcase in hand, and sang "I Come from a Town called Mira," from the Broadway musical *Carnival*. Her clear, steady, warm voice carried across the PA system with startling purity. I sat in awe at her maturity, her poise, the rightness of her presence on that stage in that auditorium commanding everyone's attention. She seemed born for this. She was nineteen years old, and that evening she was crowned first runner-up to Miss Indiana.

After the final curtain, I edged up to the stage when the audience had mostly exited and the house lights had come up. Contestants were still in their places in "court" around the winner, congratulating each other, crying, laughing, and savoring their moment of glory. I stood patiently, waiting for Abby to notice me. I eventually climbed up the side steps onto the stage itself when I saw others do the same. I watched her hugging another contestant and posing for photographs. Eventually, Abby saw me. She looked askance for a moment, then simply stood still, her smile neither broadening nor softening. I walked across to her, beaming my satisfaction. I placed one hand at her back, a tad possessively, and kissed her on the cheek, which seemed to be in keeping with the evening's tenor.

"That was wonderful. Let's go get something to eat." I was eager to catch up with her after all the summer's separations. Things would get back to normal now. She blinked slowly, once, and said she was committed to an after-glow party that night. She would be busy the next day, too. I should call her later in the coming week.

I went back to my motel with all the pieces of myself that I had brought to the pageant gathered up against me, trying to keep them from dropping away. After-glow party – I had embarrassed myself. I had embarrassed her by being presumptuous. I was hurt, but I shouldn't dwell on that. This event was more important than merely how I felt about it. I considered how I might have better handled things, and I slipped into bed. Pleased to have the distraction of a vibrating mattress, I put in a quarter to have something to think about other than the faux pas I committed by ascending a stage full of beauty contestants, milling about among them as if I belonged there. I drifted off to sleep.

I woke up two hours later. The bed was still vibrating. Ultimately I had to get out, crawl underneath it, trace the wiring, pull the nightstand away from the wall, and unplug the machine from the socket to make it stop.

Ten

I PHONED ABBY THE NEXT WEEK, AS INSTRUCTED. BY THEN, ruminating on the weekend events, I had come to see where we stood. When she told me she wanted "some time away," "time for herself," I was prepared to hear it. She explained this as carefully as she could. She even did me the honor of a "Dear John" note as a follow-up. I knew the split was final. Her note was a full assault on what I wanted to believe to the contrary, and it helped me see that what I wanted to believe wasn't true. Nonetheless, something had been lost. If it wasn't something we shared, it was – more basely – something I thought I had secured. And because this new status would be known to my peers, it had a public dimension as well. How was I to respond to people who would hear the shocking news that Dan and Abby broke up? But in the loneliness of that isolated summer in Springwood, I rarely spoke to anyone other than Norman. I didn't need a response. I could continue to silently brood over what happened, what would no longer happen, what might happen now.

I wrote my parents in Michigan to tell them the news. Mom wrote back consolingly, urging me to hold on, assuring me we'd have a good talk about it when she came back. I was consoled to think she grasped the gravity of the situation. Her tone said she took the news seriously. But when the family moved back from Michigan, amid the distractions of settling back into the house and preparing my return to college, the topic never came up. There was general acknowledgment I was no longer dating Abby, but I spoke to no one about how that felt. I could have found an appropriate moment, alone with Mom, to make some reference to it, to give her an opening for the promised heart-to-heart. I didn't. She had similar opportunities, and she let them pass.

I moved back onto campus, into the same dorm room with Steve again as my roommate. I was eager to forget the summer's blow to my ego. The less I spoke of it, the less the abasement. With more than 10,000 students moving about campus, each engaged in his or her special interests, I knew I ran a moderately low risk of crossing paths with Abby. And, if I should, we had the comfortable cushion of knowing we last spoke amicably. I would forge ahead and pursue fresh possibilities. I decided to volunteer as a student host at the International House, thinking I would meet people with whom I could practice speaking Spanish.

The I-House was off-campus, a roomy, two-story mission-style house on a once-prosperous residential street. The adjacent, architecturally similar homes provided other student venues. Automobiles lined both curbs of the street for several blocks around. The front lawns, no doubt once well-tended, were paved over from sidewalk to front steps. In the rear, everything was buried under gravel, blurring any distinction from the alleyways, and a confusing number of restrictive parking instructions poked their signage over scores of more tightly parked cars. The lofty pursuit of enlightenment colleges promote is imagined as taking place on the Commons' broad and stately sweep, under its sheltering hardwood trees. But much of it takes place in annexes like the I-House, out of sight of the campus beauty spots.

The I-House was an oasis for foreign students, a place where they could make connections, get counseling, and ask questions. Its director, Mr. Orr, was not much older than the graduate students who were among his clientele. He was a slight man who sat in an upstairs office at a desk facing the window with his back to the door. He tolerated the few visitors who came up to see him, only because they gave him an audience for his rants against the university administration, its "mindless" directives, and all the documentation he was under pressure to produce to justify using the house as a foreign student center. I ingratiated myself with him by appearing Friday afternoons at his office door, a bit early for my evening shift and a bit before he left early for the weekend to avoid unwanted interaction with students. He would bemoan all the paperwork strewn across his desk, waving one or two sheets of typescript briefly over his head. He vowed that if he had his way, he would stamp the lot of them with "CHICKEN FAT," using the rubber stamp he had commissioned that said just that. I doubt that timid man ever dared to use his stamp.

The interior of the house had an open layout. Traffic flowed from the reception area into a front lounge, then a large dining space at the back, just off a kitchen well-stocked with cooking utensils. Overstuffed pieces of worn furniture broke up the flow, and folding tables and chairs were stored against the back wall.

I-House tradition was to hold Friday night dinners themed by the specialty foods of a highlighted country. A roster of volunteers cooked what they knew how to produce from their home cuisine. Everyone paid a nominal fee to offset the cost of the food being served. As host, I kept an eye on the kitchen to enforce safety rules. I greeted guests and sought out students who seemed to need assurance. English was spoken at various levels of fluency, and other languages lent assurance that here was an accepting community. Everyone was seeking company. The few stiff moments after arrival evolved soon enough into good-natured teasing over strange food and the struggles of adjustment. There was friendly banter and a general air of cohesion. For those eschewing the dining tables, dinner plates were balanced on knees or coffee tables or chair arms. At the end of each evening, my other function was to wash up, restack plates and utensils, and return things to their proper place. The responsibility for doing so, for securing things, made me feel at home among strangers who had simple expectations of me, less complicated than those who knew me better.

One of the Friday night regulars was Jacquelyn, who lived in a graduate dorm on the far side of campus. She was tall and self-assured, comfortable within her athletic body but deliberate and sparing in her movements. She remained largely still, rarely shifting among a few poses when she sat. Her face was broad-cheeked, flat-boned, and freckled, capped by a short gamine haircut rarely seen in Indiana in the '60s. In talking to her, I learned she grew up in a small farming village outside Rheims, in northern France. I spent more time talking to her as the weeks passed. We both had the country habits of politeness and slight indirectness. I was drawn to her both by those traits and by her exoticness. She spoke fluent English with a light, pursed accent that served to underscore how well she spoke, as if her fluency were the flowering of her education. She often had questions occur to her during the week and felt comfortable, she said, posing them to me because I was American. She was in this novel situation for only an academic year. Her curiosity was not easily slaked.

She wanted to see more of the town beyond the campus, and I suggested we meet on a Saturday and walk into Muncie Center. Neither of us had spare money, but walking cost nothing. When we came to the White River that runs between campus and town, I felt kind of a custodial chagrin that the downtown core just over the bridge looked so run down, so mismatched, and so outdated. There was little going on downtown in the way of commerce or public amenities. The economic energy once emanating from the city center had shifted out to its margins – to the University and the myriad auto plants and affiliated factories that now lined highways feeding its periphery.

"Muncie is an old town," I offered, half in apology.

"What do you mean by old?" I caught her irony as she grinned her question. She had studied at three different universities in France and Germany, and she knew the medieval and ancient history of each place. She was familiar with the historical role of the Cathedral in Rheims and the legends of the Gauls in their battles against Caesar. She didn't need to say any of that. All she had to say was, "What do you mean by old?" I was thrilled to have such a friend, someone older, wiser, more worldly than I.

Soon after that tour of Muncie, we began going to movies once in a while or for beer and pizza with others from the I-House. The Winter Olympics drew us to the color TV in the I-House lounge. She rooted for the European athletes, and I rooted for the Americans. Among the beer-and-pizza-crowd was Vera, an exchange student from Australia who identified with her native Georgia, still a soviet republic from which her family had been forced to emigrate under circumstances she would never discuss. Vera had her own apartment. On pizza nights many of us gathered there, listening to music, drinking wine, happy, laughing, and pleased with each other's company. We teased Vera about her name in the Cyrillic alphabet and christened her "Bipa." There was Sievert, a stocky, blond Swede whose great jawline lent itself often to a broad smile. He beamed out both complaints and awkwardly delivered jokes with equal intensity. Sweden was changing traffic flow to right-hand drive, he told us one night, and smiled as he described drivers forgetting to switch lanes and being maimed or killed in the resultant crashes. Jurgen came from West Germany. Dark-haired, handsome, blue-eyed, and suave in a kind of outdated, 1940's manner, fluent in what he called the useful languages. He joined us when he wasn't pursuing one of a series of women, most of them townies, it was rumored. We never met many of them. Jurgen had been in Muncie for some time already. Jacquelyn often brought her American roommate, Sharon, and Linda, a beautiful blonde Franco-Moroccan who seemed sad and lost. Mani was from Nepal, proud of his ancestry, deferentially insinuating himself into conversations after monitoring them quietly for a while. Faiz was an Afghani who made it clear that he was loving every minute of his student exchange experience. He must have had at least five different girls that year who moved in, then out of his place, sequentially. Those gatherings were my first taste of bohemia, a bit of French creeping into our conversation. Jacquelyn told everyone she preferred being called Jackie. She would especially prefer if I did so. As if we were an item. I was flattered by the notion, and with the social standing I gained within the group.

In the lead-up to Christmas, Mom invited me home for the weekend. She wanted someone to fuss with her over the holiday decorations, a task in which I had always been her ally. I asked if I could bring a friend, knowing Jackie would love to get off-campus and have a taste of American home life. While my motivation may have been a concern for my new friend, what else could Jackie's appearance have meant to my parents but that I was bringing home a girl for them to meet? That we had reached a certain level of seriousness? They were charmed, of course, when they met her. Jackie openly displayed her genuine interest in everything around her. She seemed happy to meet everyone and had frequent chats with my mother about domestic things. I could see, from things both Mom and Dad asked, that she was, for them, in part, a token of a fondly remembered wartime alliance, a kind of real-life Edith Piaf. Her crowning glory for Mom was that she was Catholic, if more in the French manner than Mom would have inferred. My parents nearly shoved me aside that weekend to ply their charm offensive on her. I was unabashedly proud that I should be capable of attracting such a fascinating woman. Our pairing looked charming. I so wanted everyone to be happy. I do not pretend to be ignorant of what was happening. But if I had set it in motion myself, I did not do so out of malice. Some other time, for all that worry. How charming it was to have a French girlfriend.

With the Christmas season behind us, I returned to my classes. Outside my major and minor studies, I was required to take a minimum of six Phys. Ed. classes, too. A few "easy A's" were offered; ballroom dancing, golf, and tennis were there for the future would-be country club members who comprised a sizeable part of the student body. There were more demanding alternatives: full-court basketball, soccer, and fencing. I pieced together a mix of these to meet my requirements and passed most courses with a heavy reliance on the written exams. Even the swimming class challenged me. I was a strong swimmer, but no one passed the class without diving off the ten-foot platform. After several red-faced balks, I managed to clear this hurdle by successfully pleading with the instructor to let me jump feet first. I discovered I had no natural grace for tennis; I loped and flayed about on the court like a Disney cartoon character.

Humanities class was structured on a syllabus provided by the professor, Dr. Taylor. More paperbacks and mimeographed paper to carry around. He lectured on mythology, religion, and the history of philosophy, from creation myths to classical Greece to modern thought. He did what he could to kindle discussion in the class. We were encouraged to respond to what we were reading and hearing by making a personal connection with the material. I wasn't the only one weaned on didactic, rote learning and multiple-choice options, who found this approach disorienting. It always seemed to me, when pressed to further clarify whatever idea I volunteered, as if I had missed the point. I enjoyed being part of the free-wheeling discussion and contributed what I could. I often felt galvanized by what I came across in the readings but didn't see where all this was going. I didn't feel in sync with the ideas being introduced. They felt like constructs floating out just beyond my ken. Sometime early in the second quarter, after one of our classes, I asked for an office meeting in the hope that I might discover what it was that eluded me.

I arrived early, nervous, and regretting I had asked to meet one-on-one. Dr. Taylor nodded when he saw me in his doorway and greeted me informally. He apologized for his distraction with something going on in an adjacent room. He showed me a chair with its back shoved against the wall, nearly abutting a desk that was pressed against the same wall. He excused himself for a few minutes. As I waited for him to return, wondering what I was going to say, I saw a paperback lying face-up near the desk edge closest to me. It was "I Have No Mouth and I

Must Scream," by Harlan Ellison. Nothing I ever saw or heard came as close to expressing my mental state as that book title in that moment. It had the effect of further impeding my ability to voice my confusion.

One Sunday evening at the end of March, sitting in Jackie's dorm lounge, talking and half-watching television, President Lyndon Johnson abruptly appeared in what seemed an impromptu press conference. He spoke of the war in Vietnam, of how it appeared to be a *cul de sac* from which there was no exit. War was the talk everywhere, the conversation of everyone, but there was something new in his tone, something odd in this apparently improvised appearance. Johnson spoke with unusual melancholy, as if no longer able to feign confidence. A hush settled over the lounge. His face somber, his hair slicked neatly back, his voice slow and tempered, he said that he must now devote all of his energy and attention to wrestling with this dilemma. He would not be distracted by anything else. He would not seek, nor would he accept, the nomination of his party for another term.

A cheer went up in the room. This was totally unforeseen. In retrospect I suppose it was connected to Bobby Kennedy's entry into the primary race two weeks earlier. As part of his campaign Kennedy was scheduled to speak on campus that Thursday. With Johnson suddenly out of the running, Kennedy had a clear shot at the nomination and, surely, the presidency. I had already made plans to hear Kennedy's speech, aware I was going to witness history.

Kennedy arrived late that Thursday afternoon. A crowd of more than 10,000 students and faculty was waiting for him in the men's gym. I was in an upper-tier section of bleachers, and as he passed below me, I looked down on his marvelously lustrous silver-brunet hair. I had to suppress the urge to reach out and tousle it, to touch the magic he brought into the room. He bore – because we projected onto him – the impossible promise of undoing the five-year trauma of his brother's assassination, the collapse of Camelot, and the loss of a keenly remembered optimism. He promised to end the quagmire, the slaughter and defeat in Southeast Asia. I cheered when he told us the war would be settled. He dared to tell us with our student deferments that he opposed student deferments and that there should be an impartial lottery system. I cheered nonetheless. That afternoon he took center stage; we stood at the periphery and set aside all reservations as he embodied our private hopes for deliverance from what seemed ceaseless social unrest. I had never known such exaltation.

At the end of the speech, taking questions from the crowd, one of the few black students in the auditorium wanted to know, "Your speech implies that you are placing a great deal of faith in white America. Is that faith justified?" Bobby answered, "Yes." He then added, "Faith in Black America is justified, too." It was unexpectedly electric. I walked back to my dorm room still floating on the afternoon's moment of grace. An hour later, I heard the bulletin on the radio that Dr. Martin Luther King, Jr. had been shot and killed in Memphis at precisely the same time that I was in the men's gym listening to Bobby Kennedy.

Riots broke out across the country. Kennedy went on to Indianapolis that evening, where he had been scheduled to address a primarily black-crowd rally at 17th and Broadway, the YMCA neighborhood of my summer three years earlier. There were fears of a riot once the crowd learned what had happened. But Bobby, who everyone knew had lost his own brother to an assassin, calmed the crowd when he announced the news. He quoted Aeschylus on "pain and despair and the awful grace of God." The crowd dispersed quietly.

Within two months, Bobby would be killed too, left lying in a pool of his own blood on the floor of the Ambassador Hotel in Los Angeles the night he won the California primary. The night he seemed nearly certain to become the next president.

Eleven

JACKIE WAS A FULBRIGHT SCHOLAR AND HAD SIGNED A commitment that, after her year abroad, she would return to France and not attempt re-entry to the US for at least two years. I had become enamored by the notion of us as a couple. I had a chivalric, if uncritical, commitment to the idea. I began to fret about what would happen when she went back to France. It was not something that preoccupied me at first, but as the end of the spring quarter drew near, as we made summer plans, as the perennial disruption that was summer break loomed large again, I worried about it.

I knew if I was going to learn Spanish, I needed immersion in it. I heard that again and again at the I-House. They said it was the only way to fully enter into another language. I was particularly encouraged in this by Jurgen, the older-and-wiser, polyglot West German who floated among us and doled out advice. He suggested I research exchange programs in Spain. France was not that far from Spain, he reasoned, and Jackie and I would have ample opportunity to spend time together throughout the academic year.

The Spanish department recommended an exchange program with the Universidad de Valencia. It was under the direct auspices of the University of San Francisco, but Ball State would endorse my enrollment and accept any successful credits earned. What sealed the deal for me was the price. The entire academic year, including airfare, tuition, room, and board, would cost $1,800, less than I would spend for a Junior year at Ball State. Here was a felicitous solution, resulting from an almost idle inquiry about study in Europe. I decided to seize it, with not much more thought than "why not?"

I cannot attest to Jackie's response when I told her what I decided. I assumed she would be thrilled, would be deeply moved at my gallantry, moved that I would pursue her across the ocean. She might just as easily have been dismayed. She might have seen the time we spent together in Muncie as a foreign adventure, one from which she could return to resume her life in France. It is entirely possible that Jackie could have felt she was being pursued against her will. On the other hand, she had every opportunity to say so. I was excessively attuned to the approval of others, and I saw no hint of reluctance from her. It's telling that I don't remember if we talked about the decision. Perhaps we did. Either way, I was making a unilateral move that very much affected her. We do such things, all of us, at certain slippery moments in our lives.

I told my parents over the Easter holiday. Once they were assured my student loan would cover everything, they seemed happy for me. Their lack of resistance made the moment even headier. I was announcing what would happen, and everyone was nodding in agreement. I told Dr. Taylor about my plan after class one afternoon. He asked me why I had decided to go. A fair question – one for which I had only partial answers. I was content with "why not?" It seemed rash, he seemed to imply. He asked if I wanted to talk more about it. He said he could meet me on campus, or we could go for a beer someplace nearby.

An adult conversation with a professor, face-to-face, away from campus, was a rarified event. I talked to him that evening about Jackie and about myself while I chain-smoked in the booth of a suburban diner. He must have seen something un-thought-out in my plan. He talked about himself, particularly about what influenced him as he went about evaluating moves he'd made in his life. His tone was casual, as if genuine concern were in the normal run of things. He asked me questions as if I were an adult. I felt bound to give the fullest answers I could. There was a steadiness to his tone and a seriousness to his inquiry. Explaining my reasoning – or my impulses – as an adult felt like acquiring a new skill, like smoking or drinking. It brought an onus commensurate with the heft of what I was contemplating. I knew, or was lucky enough to trust, that I had an interlocutor who took my words seriously, and that in speaking to him I was bound to do so as well.

After a few further office conversations, Dr. Taylor asked if I were free to help him with his two daughters one Saturday morning. I said I was. We rode to his suburban home, which I expected to be something manicured and maybe a bit posh, something somehow professorial. What greeted me was a sparsely furnished, split-level house sitting on an unkempt lot, with two small girls inside running amok and a wife in disarray and in a seriously foul mood. I was put off by the mess and by her frostiness. There was an edge to everything – to the domestic chaos, to the girls' agitation, and to his wife's disregard for my purpose in being there. Laurie, the younger of the girls, had been bitten by a wild raccoon. She was undergoing a series of rabies shots as a precaution and was frantic with fear over getting the next one. One at a time, they were administered over a series of 13 visits, directly into her abdomen. She dreaded the trips to the doctor, and my child-minding duties included keeping her as calm as possible while Dr. Taylor drove us there in his car. It was clear the man had his hands full and that his home life was taxing his reserves. He nevertheless continued listening to me as I rattled on about my life while I refrained from asking about his.

Jackie announced her summer plans, also somewhat unilaterally. She was going to buy a second-hand car and drive it across the country to California with Linda, the French Moroccan, and her younger sister, Chantal, who would come from France for the trip. She asked me if I wanted to come along. I wanted to, very much, but I knew I had to work that summer to afford the coming year in Spain. I explained this to her, and she said she understood, but I don't think she did. What I fundamentally needed, and didn't have, and knew I would never get, was Dad's approval for such a road trip. I knew better than to ask. It was, in part, a financial question. I paid for incidentals – clothes, movies, beer, and cigarettes – from money earned in the summer. I needed to replenish those savings even as I applied for an extension to my student loan. I knew Dad would never agree to my spending a summer without a job, without the meritorious buckling down to serious work that keeps one busy, out of trouble, and responsible. Many of my classmates used their summers – even spring breaks – to travel and see some of the world. That was out of the question for me. Easter break was spent cleaning hog pens, and summer break presumably would be, too. I was trapped in a middle state, dependent on parental approval, and unable to rely on parental indulgence. That is probably a fair description of most people's college years.

Dr. Taylor proposed I spend the summer in Muncie. I could stay at his house, and he would help me find work on campus. I could save more money. I could also cut the ties that were supposed to have been cut with "18 and out." It was clear I was not yet free of those ties, and what he proposed was a chance to effect that severing. I don't know how serious the offer was, but it seemed reasonable. He was performing his role *in loco parentis;* Mom and Dad were pursuing theirs. It was up to me to negotiate independence.

On a Sunday afternoon, I phoned Dad to tell him I wouldn't be coming home for the summer, that I found a place to live, and was certain I could get employment on campus. His response was he would meet me on campus Monday evening after work. He phoned me when he got to the dormitory lounge. When I came down, he suggested we go someplace where we could talk. I took him to the student cafeteria where I often idled away the hours between classes during the week.

What Dad laid out that night in the cafeteria, while I listened respectfully, was meant to sound more sales pitch than *dictat.* I was needed at home. He wanted me there this summer. It would quite likely be the last summer for us as a family; I was going overseas, and who knew what would follow? His company needed a summer replacement in the stockyards. It was important to the business. The final pitch: It would mean so much to your mother. I wasn't prepared to hear any of this and was beginning to see myself detached from Springwood, from a fixed place in the family order. I felt I was on the brink of my own life. Dad's impassioned argument undermined that. A raft of objections screamed loudly in my head, telling me to resist, to stand my ground.

I came home for the summer, of course. Conceding to do so, returning to family under those terms felt like abandoning myself. I remembered my grandmother in the wedding photo, the one where she looked as if she wanted to disappear, to make an exit, but couldn't. Things started out well enough. Jackie had to wait until her sister flew in from France before she could start her trip. My parents invited her to stay with us until Chantal arrived. The two of them then stayed on for another week. Chantal was a dark-eyed, quiet girl of 16. She avoided conversation, often even direct eye contact. We tried to pull her into group activities, but she preferred to spend her time with David, who was six years old. The two of them walked around together all day. Jackie disapproved. She wanted her sister to mingle with the adults and work on her English. Chantal was not interested. For the rest of us, a holiday atmosphere hung in the air as we sought out events that would keep our high spirits going. Mom and Dad invited Jackie and me as their guests to a dinner dance. Mom took Jackie to a dress shop in preparation, and they both came back with "little black cocktail" dresses. It didn't seem the kind of thing Jackie would do. The four of us looked country club-perfect on the night, the ladies in their new outfits, Dad and I in suit and tie. We sat at a table near the dance floor. Martinis were served. They were pure alcohol. Within a few sips, I felt myself floating up over the table, struggling to engage with the conversation. I was shocked by how intoxicated I was. I looked at Mom and Dad, neither of whom seemed fazed. When the combo started playing, I feared toppling onto Jackie on the dance floor in my woozy state.

Jackie and Chantal left in mid-June. We witnessed their depar-ture as a family tableau, waving goodbye while her second-hand car slowly made its way up the gravel drive and out into America's heartland, bound for sunny California. When they were out of sight, I felt the awkward silence. I felt the summer's weight on my shoulders; last summer's routine was this year's plan, too. Mom, Dad, Maureen, and David would go to Michigan. Glenn had a job with forest rangers this year, and he would be out on his own. Lee Ann was already living on her own. I would take care of the house and fill in at the company's various stockyards as vacation schedules dictated. Old Blue was gone, towed out of a country ditch near Muncie, where it had died late in the school term. I would be left with the Mustang, under the strict admonition to use it sparingly.

The manager of the Frankfort yards, Bobby, came by to pick me up in the mornings and bring me home in the evenings. Bobby was an earnest soul, grateful for his managerial position but stuck, as others had been in previous summers, with the boss's son. He had known me since high school and reacted to my earning a college education with a layered, resentful deference, initiating his strongly held positions with, "I'm sure you think otherwise, but…" He then laid out provocative conspiracy theories about the world. I took the bait a few times, until I realized he was looking to show me how thoroughly he disagreed with what he presumed were my opinions. I fell quiet soon enough on those rides into and out of work. This was especially true that morning in June when, as we rode into town, the radio announced that Bobby Kennedy had been shot and killed.

"No!" I gasped.

"Yup. They finally got him."

By then, Dad had already gone up to Michigan ahead of everyone to ready the cabin. I was sharing the house with Mom and the others for a couple of weeks. A dispirited funk hung in the air most evenings. With Dad away, the familiar rhythm was gone. Mom was distracted and easily annoyed. She deflected my efforts to start a conversation. Once, ignorant of the irony of her question, she asked me why I even bothered to come home that summer at all. I was well trained for the proper response to such a provocation; I made no reply. But her sullen moods and her accusatory tone irked me. I was offended. Normally, I would have tried to put her comments in a larger context to understand her point of view. That summer, my silence nursed the offense I felt. It stayed with me all summer, even after everyone left for Michigan.

I was "loaned out" to the stockyards in Crawfordsville, nearly two hours' drive from Springwood. I booked into a motel near the Crawfordsville yards from Monday through Thursday night. I drove down early on Monday mornings and back home on Friday evenings. The motel sat across a State Highway from a strip-mall where the cafeteria stayed open until 7 pm. A drug store stayed open late as well. The few other shops were always closed by the time I got back to the hotel after work, cleaned up, and crossed the highway for an evening meal.

Cheap motel rooms came without TVs. I drove around Crawfordsville the first couple of nights, but it seemed pointless. Nothing of interest was open in the evenings. I slipped deeper into my sullen state. Reading helped keep back the boredom, although I don't remember what I read. James Michener's *Iberia* had been recently published, but I found it dense and off-putting in my first go at it. I read it without geographical and historical context. The scenes were jumbled in my imagination, playing out as if they were set in Mexico or the southwestern US, landscapes and architecture familiar to me from movies and cartoons. I wanted someone to talk to, someone who knew where I was going, who could tell me what I would find there. I wanted someone's attention. I imagined Junior Montalvo, the dark-skinned boy at St. Mary's. He knew Spanish. I pictured him, now my age, at the edge of manhood. He was brown, smiling, and friendly. He would take me in as his friend. In my dark motel room, physical longing overtook me. I conjured Junior lying in my miserable bed, bringing comfort and companionship. He smiled with his dark eyes and offered himself to me.

I brought the funk home with me from Crawfordsville on the weekends. As in earlier summers since graduation, Francis was still around, and we still sought out each other for company, still drove the back roads of Clinton County, making half-hearted efforts to catch up on each other's lives. I always drove and Francis always rode shotgun. He had no access to a car. In my discontent that summer, in spite of what was never spoken between us, I allowed my talk to veer toward men and boys, toward their physical appeal. At first, little comments about someone's curly hair or muscular arms halted Francis's chat for a moment before he resumed. There was an involuntary element to what I was saying, as if I were merely riding along with things, too. Convinced we were approaching open talk about what had been stifled all those years, Francis was steady and measured when he said he always knew that I was queer. That was the word he used. Queer. It stung me. And it oddly consoled me. That was the name for what I knew to be my state. It was the correct term: a sexual disinterest in women, a sexual attraction to men—nothing to do with virtue. Francis simply affirmed that it was okay. He wasn't going to ridicule me. He knew what I was, and he was still my friend.

Late one evening, parked near his house, sitting on the warm hood of the Mustang under late-night stars fixed and mute over rustling cornstalks, we shared a half-pint of cherry vodka. We laughed over who in our class was "cute," who was probably queer, too, and who was hopelessly clueless about sex in general, and I accepted Francis as my friend. My real friend. It came as a revelation. I can still feel the way the muscles across my upper back started to relax, how suddenly I was longer and looser in the torso and the arms, how I had more lung capacity. I could trust Francis like a true friend; I could be myself around him. I was grateful to him. One day I would become my own friend as well.

Nothing changed in how Francis and I spent our time. We went to the movies. We drove to Chicago one weekend late that summer. I was stopped for speeding through some hamlet near the Illinois border. The state trooper led us immediately to a small-town courtroom where the magistrate, sniffing out our queerness, sneered throughout his interrogation with a scornful emphasis on my name.

"*Danny*, do you know how fast you were driving?" He grinned at the trooper standing behind me. "*Danny*, do you know what the speed limit is on that stretch of road?"

I was fined $150 on the spot. It was a well-rehearsed, speed-trap shake-down. It cost us most of the cash we planned to burn through in two days in Chicago. We pressed on to Chicago nevertheless and drove around for a few hours, daring a slow tour through a famously gay area in Lincoln Park, windows down, ogling. Then we drove home late that night, penniless. We laughed over that adventure a few times after that, but it was the end of the last summer either of us would spend in Clinton County.

Many years later, across the long stretch of silence that had accumulated between us, Francis phoned me when I was living in Washington.

"Francis, how wonderful to hear from you! How did you ever find me? Please tell me you'll come for a weekend visit. We'll have a blast!"

But Francis couldn't come; he wasn't able to travel. He was just thinking about me and wanted me to know that and how much he appreciated my friendship throughout high school, how proud he had been to call me a friend. He followed up with a letter written in his florid hand, large navy-blue loops across traditional, off-white stationery that reiterated how much our friendship had meant. Francis died shortly thereafter, an early victim of an AIDS epidemic that was to pull down so many lives around me.

Twelve

As early autumn set in, my family came back down from Michigan. Jackie and Chantal returned for a brief while, back from California, beaming over experiences that I "couldn't imagine." She sold the car back to the people she'd bought it from. I have no idea how or when she made all the arrangements: getting title to a car, getting an American driver's license, packing and shipping home a year's accumulation of clothes and books. She never talked about any of it. She simply made it happen, off-stage as it were, with silent aplomb. Mom was immediately cheered by her presence. The sadness she carried with her all summer lifted when Jackie was around. I was grateful for the return of the summer's earlier joy. I was exhausted from the turmoil of the lonely summer, the threat of my sexuality to future happiness, the discontent in the family home. What was needed was a decisive gesture to turn things around. I announced one evening to Mom as we set the table for dinner, "I'm thinking of asking Jackie to marry me." Mom beamed. My gamble was that somehow this was all going to work out just fine. I said nothing to Jackie.

The Democratic Convention in Chicago aired on television every night while Jackie and Chantal were with us for that last time in Springwood. Since Bobby Kennedy's assassination, there was no one I supported as a candidate, but I watched as Hubert Humphrey worked his way to the top of the slate. I was too young to vote, and, anyway, I would be overseas by election day. We watched the angry demonstrations in the park near Lakeshore Drive and the shoving and fighting inside the convention center. We watched as security personnel roughed up newsmen and convention delegates near the podium, the Chicago Police and the National Guard unleashed teargas on large crowds gathered outside the arena. It was riveting television, and I found it hard to disengage. Jackie found it tiresome, a distant event with little effect on her. I saw my parents' horror as Mayor Richard Daley, the police, the TV networks, and a broad collection of protestors – Abbie Hoffman and Jerry Rubin among them – ranted and tore at each other. The orderly convention process was in disarray. I could see the police losing their grip in the face of so much protest, poorly trained to control it. It felt like one more spate of chaos just as I was leaving, as if I were closing a book before reading the last chapter.

Dad must have felt all of this keenly: panic as the country spun out of control; sadness at Jackie's departure, to whom he'd drawn close; regret as I, his oldest boy, once his first and fevered hope, prepared to go overseas. The night after Jackie and Chantal pulled out of our drive for the last time, self-reliant and slightly out of synch with our anxiety, Dad wandered into the bedroom where Mom and I sat on the edge of the bed watching the chaos in Chicago. He was weeping copiously.

"You may not realize this," Mom turned to me to say, "But I've never seen him cry like this in all the years I've known him."

PART III

Self

"You must choose, Redcap.
If you want the open road, the road you shall have,
and we'll share the wandering life,
the cold, the poverty, the danger."

Rhoda Power,

Redcap Runs Away

One

IN A DEPARTURE LOUNGE AT O'HARE AIRPORT ON THE LAST
Saturday of September 1968, I watched my parents and godparents,
Anne and Louie, laughing and chattering among themselves. I
sat in silence as if on the other side of a one-way mirror, the kind
used to read focus group reactions. They were basking in the same
relaxed intimacy they had enjoyed with each other throughout
my childhood. They were on their way to the cabin in the Upper
Peninsula for a holiday and had taken Interstate 90 up through
Chicago to O'Hare en-route to see me off. I was to board a New
York flight, my first plane trip ever. I was leaving the country. I was
going to Spain. Alone. In the midst of my distracted companions,
who wondered aloud about what time they might get to the cabin
and where they would eat that night, I heard only bits of their talk.
They sounded far away, and my nervousness further muted them.

When the flight was announced for boarding, we all stood up at the same moment, steeled for the tender awkwardness of goodbye. Surreptitiously, my dear, dear godmother pressed two small cans of pre-mixed Manhattan cocktails on me, the fancy kind with pull tabs on the top. "These are for tonight," she whispered, slipping them out of her purse and palming the contraband off to me, her underage godson, as if in reassurance that this was what worked for her in such moments.

In the next moment, I was belted into an airplane seat, looking down on the tidy geometry of Ohio farmland, marveling at the sight of clouds beneath me, the summer-long anticipation now yielding its promise. I simply took it all in – the pressure on the eardrums, the nervous cigarettes, the mantra running over and over again in my head as I sat in an unreal place, looking down on a receding world: I am going to Spain, I am going to Spain.

I was booked that night at the Idlewild Inn, a low-end motel on the periphery of the recently re-christened John F. Kennedy International Airport. An Iberian Airline charter flight would take me to Madrid on Sunday. I spent my evening in the motel room distractedly working through a newsstand copy of *The New Yorker* while sipping room-temperature cocktails. The ice machine was broken. The next morning, in an era before what we are now encouraged to think of as security, I roamed aimlessly across the flat, weed-choked grounds just outside the fenced-off runways, clueless as to what to do with myself. By late Sunday afternoon, ready to burst from prolonged silence, I went to the featureless Iberia departure area two hours early. One other person was there among all the rows of empty seats, a pleasant-looking, short, olive-skinned young man with dark eyebrows and a goatee. He was reading from a breviary. I sat down next to him and in the intimacy afforded by the empty space around us, I asked if he, too, was going to Valencia. He was. He smiled and said he was glad to have someone to talk to. His smile was easy and appealing.

I would learn later that Ricardo, "*my friends call me Ricky,*" was a Benedictine novice. His superiors at St. Leo's Abbey in Florida were sending him to Spain to study, see a bit more of the world, and discern if he was really ready to take final monastic vows. He said he was Cuban-American and hoped to improve his Spanish, to "*speak it properly,*" unlike, he inferred, his parents, who were born in Cuba. Others, obviously students too, filtered in while we spoke, some prolonging their goodbyes with family members. Ricky and I kept talking and somehow managed to stay together during the open boarding process. I pointed out two adjacent seats that we might occupy, and we spent the all-night flight side by side, turning around occasionally to meet fellow travelers and introduce ourselves. We must have appeared to be old friends already. Early the next morning outside the Madrid airport, we transferred to ground transportation waiting for us, an old bus with a single rear axle, lousy suspension, and a rigid frame. Every exit and re-entry onto the highway to Valencia – during mid-morning breakfast, mid-day meal, or stops to facilitate physical needs on the long journey - jostled us, often creating a warm press of my knees and shoulders against Ricky's. I monitored for any reaction that would betray his discomfort with the proximity. He seemed content with it. As I drank in the novelty of low-slung mountain villages, two-toned with terracotta roofs and lime-washed walls set among undulating silver-green olive fields, every scene reflected Ricky in the periphery of the bus window.

Somewhere in the last hour, the bus left the highway and wound through high-walled and nondescript suburban settlements, then on to broad, palm-lined streets running between rows of mid-rise apartment buildings. We crossed a statue-lined bridge that spanned a dry river-bed converted to parkland and soccer pitches and reached the Torres de Serrano's medieval gateway to enter the ancient city of Valencia. I had an unobstructed view from my seat of second-story balconies with French doors behind dusty iron, the doors drawn closed against the dusk. I sat engrossed in the novel details, so different from what I had imagined. When we reached the gravel plaza in front of the university building, it was already dark.

I don't mean to say that I remember the exact French doors closed against the night or the specific broad streets on which we approached the city. But I remember the singularity of the moment, how unconnected it was to anything I had known before. I was jetlagged, hungry, and exhausted in a place where familiarity with my surroundings, which once served me well, was now gone. When I stepped down from the bus and onto the loose gravel under ornate street lamps, it was as a pilgrim tossed onto an alien shore.

Correspondence earlier in the summer laid out the plans put in place for my arrival. I was to have room and board that year with Da. Maria Cortona and was given her address. I wrongly inferred that "Da." was short for *doctora* and imagined her as well educated and worldly, there being few women doctors then. Maybe a single, professional woman? She might have a large house, perhaps one with a garden. A swimming pool might be too much to hope for, but it would be welcome. But there on the plaza Da. Laura, the guide who had been with us since Madrid shepherding us on and off the bus all day, introduced me to Da. Maria Teresa Esteve y Cambra. "Da.," as it turned out, was the simple honorific for *doña*, an adult woman. There had been a change of plans. Da. Teresa would board me for the year. My first thought was that I had given everyone the wrong address and was now completely cut off. Da. Teresa, short, pale, brown-haired, and animated, was all grins and matter-of-factness, rattling away in a barrage of words I was unable to connect into meaning. There was *piso*, there was *Mamá*, there was *conmigo*, and there was *taxi*. And with those, she ushered me and another student into a cab, and we set off into the night.

The other student was Tim, my new roommate. He was from Ohio and small-framed with curly hair, a thin mustache, and piercing green eyes. We were ushered through an apartment building's large outer entryway. The building appeared to date from the early 1930s. We were cursorily introduced to the *portera* who sat in a booth just off the hallway. She was tiny, dour, black-clad, and I soon learned she controlled access to the building. She wielded her limited power with aloof and chilling slowness. Da. Teresa, *"you will call me Mamá,"* pressed a button on a small panel. A glass-encaged elevator car, not much larger than a phone booth, came lurching down preceded by heavy cables dangling from its underparts. It moved noisily within the narrow space defined by a winding staircase rising into the darkness above. Our flat was on the seventh floor. The ride up with three people required dispensing with personal space, turning our faces away from each other as we pressed together. Da. Teresa continued filling us in on the details of life on Ruzafa Street, the neighborhood that was to be our new home. I strained to look at Tim to see if he was taking any of this in. He was not. It was apparent we both found the situation hilarious.

Inside the apartment there were further instructions. Face-to-face with Da. Teresa, to whom we finally submitted by calling her Mamá, it was easier to pick out a few of the details she was giving us. There was much nodding of heads and insistent "*sí, sí, sí.*" Words of which we were certain were repeated to assure everyone that at least that much information had been imparted. As she left us in our small, twin-bedded room, lit by a 40-watt lamp bulb on a round table intended as a shared study desk, she admonished us to speak Spanish as much as we could.

"I speak no English," I understood her to be saying. "The only English word I know is 'fucky-fucky'." She was clearly amused at our shock.

The large window in the room's exterior wall looked directly down onto roof tiles of the Ruzafa Market, a block-long, covered but open-stall market that stirred noisily to life six days a week starting at 4 a.m. We had a heavy Persian blind that was unspooled nightly from its rolled-up resting place just under the ceiling. Its armature of wooden slats fit tightly together and managed to keep out the early sun but did little to muffle the rumbling delivery trucks and haggling of the market vendors. The booth sellers were quite audible by 6 a.m., picking through fresh produce, eager to find fault with every piece on offer, and barter down the wholesalers' asking price. The blinds were useless, too, against the full advance of spoiling fish and poultry still not sold by mid-day.

On the other side of the market, the street was lined with rubble from abandoned houses awaiting final demolition. A few middle-aged men, moving about with hobbled gaits or missing limbs, carried out menial tasks – guarding parked cars or holding keys to apartment buildings – earning a few pesetas through their services. Their income was supplemented by proceeds from lottery drawings hawked in the city's public places. "*Jornada para hoy*" was the chant, offering easy cash winnings to the lucky few. The mission statement on the ticket stubs spoke of feeding, housing, and caring for these wounded soldiers from a civil war no one wanted to talk about anymore.

Valencia is a busy, complex, and self-contained city, the third-largest in Spain. Monuments from its medieval past or its days as a Roman garrison jut out in a few places, as do architectural remnants attesting to other eras. Broad avenues boast palm-trees and exotic flora planted in beds along median walkways, the buildings lining them finished in beaux-arts, art nouveau, or a sleekly modern style. It is also a city of small-time merchants and mechanics, and old women sweeping streets and disappearing up stairwells behind partially closed doors. Bookstores, tobacco shops, and bakeries alternate between upscale clothing and furniture emporia. I learned to navigate all this by studying and memorizing billboards and window advertisements. Language instruction was everywhere. Shop doors bore instructions on their handles: *empuje* (*push*: imperative, third-person singular, formal*)*, *tirad* (*pull*: imperative, second-person, plural, informal) – little flashcards reinforcing a new grammar. On the narrow sidewalks people pressed on in a constant hurry – women clacking in heels and men shuffling in leather-soled shoes at a brisk gait. Pedestrian crosswalks were timed to maintain the pace, urging everyone to move on, move on. It was impossible not to internalize the tempo. I found myself hurrying around corners, entering shops abruptly, and being greeted at once with a similarly brisk "*Buenas.*" I needed my wits about me. No quarter was given for foreignness.

The university was a mile away from Ruzafa. Successfully reaching it without getting lost in the fan-patterned avenues and winding medieval streets required always taking the same route. I walked up the core shopping street of Ruzafa with its shoe stores, butchers, and cinema, toward the bull ring. Two long streets beyond that was the Plaza del Caudillo from which I exited onto Colón, a broad avenue anchored at the far end by the ornate spire of the Banco de Vizcaya. From there, I turned left for one block, then angled off to the right for another two until I came to the university plaza where the bus from Madrid delivered us that first night. The old university where our classes were held was built in 1497. It was, in essence, a sixteenth-century, two-story quadrangle of large *aulas*, or lecture halls. Their tall double doors and transoms opened out to an inner atrium from which dust, scuffled up from bare soil by students moving between classes, rose to the second floor. The men's room lacked flushable toilets. We bewildered foreign students had to learn on our own how to relieve ourselves using its rudimentary openings, too embarrassed to ask for instructions.

Our classes were separate from those of the Spanish students. A kind of apartheid existed between the two groups. I met and befriended a few native students, but always off-campus and usually one-on-one or in small groups. They often mentioned the war in Vietnam as justification for not mixing with Americans, although it was clear the roots were far more parochial. Some of the Spanish guys made exceptions for the more attractive American girls, the same girls who always seemed to disappear when the US navy was in port.

Fonéticas – Phonetics – was a mandatory course that met in a dark-paneled lecture hall with steeply banked wooden seats. Our professor was young and charismatic, well-traveled, and confident enough within himself to comfortably interact with foreign students. He challenged us individually to mimic the sound he wanted us to hear, then to reproduce it by issuing it from a specific part of our throat, mouth, or nasal passage, shaded by the placement of tongue or lips, just so. He wrote the phonetic spelling on the chalkboard behind him and slapped it with his flat palm as he coaxed the sound out of us, calling for it, slapping, repeating it, calling for it again.

The Spanish school- and business-day fell into two distinct parts: mornings went on until the mid-day meal, and afternoons until 7 pm. These were separated by three listless, purposeless hours set aside for a meal and siesta. My room and board were prepaid, so getting home for the mid-day meal was imperative.

It was at the dining table in Ruzafa where I learned Spanish. Its tiny, glazed-tile dining nook was just large enough for a table and four chairs. Beaded curtains separated the eating area from the meager kitchen where Mamá ruled and where Tim and I were reluctant to enter when she was in the house. The door to the hallway was closed in winter to hold in the kitchen's heat. It was paneled with frosted glass to admit natural light coming in from the windows on the flat's south side. The overhead light was from a bare neon tube. The floor was terrazzo, clean and cool in the summer, cold in winter. The sound and light reflected off all of these hard surfaces mixed with the low din rising from the inner courtyard and other apartments beyond the kitchen balcony – a far cry from the acoustics of the language lab at Ball State.

The four kitchen chairs were usually occupied by Tim, me, Don Manuel – a middle-aged lodger who worked as an engineer for the national railway – and Mamá when she finished serving all of us. She would sit down to chat while picking at the little food she ate. On a few weekends, Mamá's son, Pedro, sat in the fourth chair. On those days, she stood over all of us, showering equal attention on the three younger men while rolling her eyes and pooh-poohing most of what Don Manuel asserted as he regaled us with his political opinions and exaggerated childhood memories.

I was learning *Castellano* – continental Spanish – but the language spoken between Mamá and her son was *Valenciá*, the local variation of *Catalán*. Pedro spoke *Valenciá* with his best friend, Juan, a frequent visitor. Pedro and Juan slid into it when they were mocking Tim and me. We eventually understood enough to call them on it. Unnerved that we could follow them, they turned more discreet, ending a prolonged unpleasantness, limiting themselves to whispers in other rooms. I don't blame Pedro for his resentment toward Tim and me. We were sleeping in his former room, forcing him onto a roll-away cot in the living room when he was home. Moreover, his mother doted on Tim and me as she must have doted on him before he went off to his provincial teaching post.

Don Manuel, whose "home country" was Galicia in the northwest of Spain, would have spoken *Gallego*, had he anyone with whom to speak it. He spent most of his evenings listening to a short-wave radio in his room. Most of what he listened to was in English, but I never managed to understand much of his muttering in my own tongue. *Castellano* ruled the house. The talk was engaging, humorous, opinionated, and sometimes agitated. The only way to join in was to lean forward and assert the right to be heard. At first, expressing myself felt awkward, like singing in public using a voice that did not come naturally. When absorbed in trying to make a point, but lacking the vocabulary, my frustration was akin to speeding into a traffic jam and having to elicit the word I wanted from the very person whose obstinacy frustrated me. I soon learned the value of circumlocutions, roundabout ways of saying things for which I hadn't the proper word. *"The tool with which you hit a nail." "That feeling of yes but no."* Progress toward fluency was measured by the number of words I could hold in my head simultaneously as I forged out their combined meaning. I plowed through that initial phase of speaking in another tongue that feels fraudulent, while the urgency of my message and the affirming signs of comprehension in my interlocutor carried me across.

I also learned how addictive siestas can become, and I scheduled afternoon classes as late as possible. Afternoon coursework was more academic. There was "Golden Age of Poetry," "Cervantes," and "The Generation of 1898." The professor who taught Cervantes was a Basque woman who made her assessment of our under-educated state aggressively apparent. She failed to allow that things we knew in English had different names in Spanish. She once blew-up over our ignorance of Erasmo. Someone finally said, "Oh, Erasmus of Rotterdam," but she was unappeased.

On the other hand, her love of Cervantes was infectious. She kept us enrapt with Don Quixote, quoting sly ironies and feigned befuddlements to his faithful Sancho for an entire semester. The Generation of 1898 was an influential group of Spanish philosophers who wrote for the rational, post-religious everyman struggling to find meaning in a world with no guarantee of salvation. They endorsed a kind of pragmatic existentialism. Jose Ortega y Gasset and Miguel de Unamuno were its leading voices.

On many afternoons I passed by two *gitanas,* gypsy women, standing at the university portal, mumbling, their hands out and palms upward. Their faces were soiled, and they were wrapped in sour, coarsely-woven cloth. They held silent, sullen babies while pleading for alms. I have since lived in cities where open begging, panhandling, and even vaguely concealed threats were commonplace. I became inured to those in time and developed little tricks to show deference without acceding to the demands. But these women were my first stark experience of an alien tradition, and I found them deeply unnerving, human testimony to want with which I never made peace.

Inside the building's inner courtyard was a beer-vending machine, lit and refrigerated just like a soda-vending machine, glowing and beaded with condensation. A small bottle of Stark Turia cost five *pesetas*. The beer, always welcome after the long walk and the gauntlet of begging women, did little to aid my appreciation – or comprehension – of 16th and 17th-century Spanish poetry.

I wrote Jackie to send her my new address. Letters between us soon came and went, to and fro. Mamá took a keen interest in their existence while keeping a discreet silence as to their possible content at great cost to her curiosity. Within the first month, I decided to fly to France to visit. The notion of taking a plane instead of a train was as much naiveté as an extravagance, but it fortified my sense that I was now a traveler on the world stage. It cost more than I could reasonably afford. I flew through Barcelona to Paris. Jackie met me at Orly with Chantal in tow, and we stayed in the capital for a couple of days. The two sisters booked a room in a *pension* separate from mine, no questions asked. This arrangement would have been the compromise she struck out of her parents' concern for propriety. It suited me. What enthralled me at the time was Paris. I wanted to see the Louvre, the old Les Halles and Montmartre. I was in love with Paris, intoxicated with being there.

We drove to Jackie's village of Epoye, in the Marne, northeast of Paris. Its flat landscape traced by long, straight, tree-lined roads seemed exotically far removed from the sunny Mediterranean. It was simultaneously stony grey and verdant. The flat, open, and fenceless fields of sugar beets had been the scene of bloody battles in several wars. Epoye's small stone church and City Hall still stood among them, asserting their precarious timelessness. Jackie's family lived in a cut-stone, two-story farmhouse on the edge of the village, with a productive walled garden and several outbuildings. The house was often chilly but always comfortable, full of country smells, some familiar and some quite novel. It was roomy, with a little-used parlor, a large eat-in kitchen where we spent most of the day, a walk-in larder with home-canned fruits and vegetables, and a cellar for wine, champagne, and cheese. Upstairs, the four huge bedrooms had tall, single-pane windows with shutters and metal latches.

Mme. T., Jackie's mother, was a generous, attentive hostess. From the beginning, she was quite reserved in her manner toward me. The family treated each other with relaxed but observant deference, including the use of *vous* when the girls spoke to either parent. I had only a smattering of French but could sometimes follow what was being said through close observation and inference. When addressed on a topic that didn't flow directly from what was going on in front of me, I often stared in puzzlement, repeating the last word of the question put to me. This never failed to amuse everyone. Jackie's father, M. T., spoke a rough English acquired after the war through contact with American GIs, ensuring a positive disposition in the house toward Americans in general.

Chantal was not warming to me, a state that certainly didn't improve on that visit. Jackie and I made a practice of sitting at the kitchen table while she drilled me in French grammar and vocabulary as her mother prepared dinner. One lesson began, "*Marie Duval fait de la soupe*" – Marie Duval makes soup. After the third review of that same lesson, Mme T. turned around from her place at the stove and, in what seemed a moment of pique, said, "Marie Duval is always making soup!"

Jackie had her own car, a Citroën *deux chevaux,* which she named Petronille after a street urchin in a novel set locally. Petronille was perhaps the most basic form an automobile could take. The roof was canvas and could be rolled back like the top of a sardine tin. The interior was so stripped down that most people simply hosed it out to clean it. The doors were removable to facilitate this. The manual transmission was controlled by a lever pulled out from the flat dashboard, turned clockwise or counter-clockwise to the correct angle, and pushed back into the dashboard while engaging the clutch. It was in Petronille that I truly learned to drive a manual shift. The tractors I drove in Indiana were manual, too, but I drove them in otherwise empty fields at slow speeds. I learned how to drive Petronille in the center of Rheims and along the narrow country roads of Bois de Chalmet.

Jackie went to great lengths to show me the sites she most treasured. We would stop in small, grey, unremembered villages to buy baguettes, tubes of anchovy paste, tangy mayonnaise, or a jar of paté. Farther up the road, out in the countryside, we would pull the car over onto a scenic spot to eat and take in the views. We went to Compiegne, Luxembourg, and the Ardennes, and she relayed the local geography and history. French food and French names were on my lips, throat, teeth, and tongue. We would sit on a blanket on the ground, Jackie's long legs pressed together and tucked beneath her just to one side while she read aloud chapters from *Le Petit Prince*, like Scheherazade, prolonging the hour.

Two

FEW FAMILIES IN VALENCIA ENTERTAINED FRIENDS IN THEIR homes as a result, in part, of the Civil War. It had been particularly protracted and violent in Valencia, and economic repercussions still afflicted almost everyone. I arrived nearly thirty years after that war, and this domestic insularity still ruled. Those letting out rooms to students would have been among the less well off whose homes went largely unheated. There was pressure enough to feed one's own family, so the idea of a family permitting their boarders to entertain friends was out of the question. Further, a household with single young females did not, under any circumstances, invite single males. Nor would such an invitation be expected. This was as much societal custom as moral rectitude. Mamá made exceptions to both rules; no other host family that I knew did.

The venue for socializing was the café – any of the myriad eateries and bars across the city. They were enclosed, heated in the cold winter months, and spilled tables and chairs out onto sidewalks from early spring, throughout the summer, and into the long autumn season. The pricier venues were near the main plazas and on the toniest avenues. We foreign students congregated near the university or the Plaza del Caudillo in the city center. After morning classes, a handful of us often looked for a place to have a coffee or yogurt, which we learned to call by its commercial name, Danone. The end of afternoon classes was an excuse to gather over a beer or orange *Fanta*. We sat on tiny chairs, our legs clumsily shoved under tiny tables, as small plates of *kikos* – a kind of fermented, dried corn kernel – were set out courtesy of the house, a gesture to encourage us to return. Even the most comfortable among us was strapped for cash, stretching things out until the next allowance wired from the States, and free *tapas* seemed quite generous.

Our night-spot was Whiskey-a-Go-Go, a small underground discotheque accessed through a nondescript door on a side street. Downstairs the lighting was designed for intimacy, a mood-inducing, alternating red-and-blue glow. The music was American pop, Motown, and the several English hits in frequent radio play at the time, amplified enough to make conversation difficult. The most popular drink was called *Explosivo*. It was served in a tall, slim glass with two ice cubes, American-cocktail-style. It bore simultaneous flavor notes of non-compatible spirits. When seen without the prismatic interference of black-light or strobe, it appeared to have a greenish hue. Most nights, the majority of us left the club benumbed by it.

Ricky and I shared few classes, but from the beginning we sought out places where we could be together. We often went to

Mass at the Cathedral, an imposing 12th-century gothic landmark built on the site of a former mosque, which was itself built over a Visigoth Cathedral. That Cathedral was, in its turn, built over a Roman temple to Diana. A dank, smoke-encrusted side chapel inside displayed what purported to be the original Holy Grail, the actual chalice from the Last Supper. I was naturally skeptical about the small, two-handled bowl sitting in its sanctuary niche, but given the Cathedral's age and size, complex architecture, and phoenix-like history, I suspended disbelief. Awe seemed to accrue to everything in the place, and I imbibed that awe.

Alongside the Cathedral was a tall, spiral-stepped stone tower, El Miguelete. Ricky and I climbed it several times to stand together and look down on the city. A Basilica dedicated to *La Virgen de los Desamparados* – Our Lady of the Forsaken – was part of the same compound. Above a tabernacle, the Virgin's small porcelain statue held a white lily in one hand and cradled the Infant Jesus on the other arm. Jesus, in turn, held a miniature of the cross on which he would be nailed. Mary's small frame was draped in intricate and frequently rotated wardrobes of splendid, over-sized capes, crowns, and haloes. The wig on top of her tiny-featured face was raven-colored, the same tint older Mediterranean women used to hide their greying hair. She slumped forward just slightly, earning her the nickname of Little Hunchback. Nowadays, a barely audible, tinny audio track of Gregorian chants plays softly in the background, but in those earlier days, there was no sound system, only the susurration of prayers from the cohort of older men and women – *los desamparados* – the abandoned. I was impressed by the gothic majesty of the Cathedral, but the Basilica and its supplicants resonated much more deeply.

Ricky had a local church he liked to go to near where he lived, across town from me. When we went to Mass there, we went for coffee afterward at Bar Texas nearby. A cartoon of a cowboy, with Stetson and lariat, hung over its entrance. The thin, non-absorbent paper in the napkin holders bore the same image, imprinted with ink that rubbed off on your fingers. Salted and roasted almonds were sold in little trays to accompany the *café con leche*. The salt and slightly burnt snap of the oily almonds never failed to please me. But then, Ricky's presence cast everything in a pleasing light. Going to Mass with him was my way of acknowledging his path as a novice, honoring it while still pursuing his company. It was obvious we shared a physical attraction to each other. We didn't give voice to it, but neither of us feigned otherwise. He knew I had a girlfriend. I told him I was going to propose to her. I knew he had taken initial vows of chastity, and we kept circling, both drawn to and off-limits to each other.

Jackie came down to Valencia about a month after I visited her in France. Mamá agreed to let her stay with us, giving up her own bedroom for the sofa where Pepe slept when he was home. I can't imagine her lodging was gratis; Mamá was operating a boarding house. Jackie must have made room and board arrangements on her own. She never shared the details with me. Nor did she ask me to meet her at the train station on her arrival. Jackie organized travel details and located my street address on her own. She simply showed up the afternoon she said she would.

I proposed marriage, just as I told my mother I would. Jackie and I wandered the streets for a long time the afternoon that I proposed. I produced a ring. I don't remember where I bought it, how I managed to pay for it, or how it was that it should fit well enough for me to slip it on her finger. I remember its tiny stone – an industrial diamond? paste? – set in a silver band I understood to be white gold. I must have brought it with me from America, which would affirm my determination to do this. I suggested we sit on the stone rim of a fountain along Avenida Jose Antonio. As if blurting it out before I could be interrupted, I asked, with no proper lead-in, if she would marry me. She appeared nonplussed and squinted a moment before responding, perhaps quelling her concern that this had come too soon, that there were preliminaries to be addressed first. And then she said yes. I lifted her hand and put the ring on her finger. It was all negotiated in a few moments. I leaned in for a kiss, at which point a small woman dressed in widow's black, scuffling by in house slippers on the dusty gravel of the park, stuck her face in close to ours and said, "*Por las calles, no, no, no,*" – a sort of tut-tut-tut, not-in-public.

Jackie came to my classes with me and took notes in French while listening to Spanish lectures. There was nothing she couldn't do. I let it be known among my classmates that she was now my fiancée. Several of them, recently wrenched from what had been their own interesting lives heretofore, took in the minor news as a welcome diversion. Congratulations and best wishes were extended. Ricky expressed particular pleasure and was particularly solicitous. For some callous, mindless reason, I was reassured by how the two of them seemed to take to each other so well.

So reassured, in fact, that when I made plans to travel north again to Epoye for Christmas, I asked Ricky to come along. His plan had been to go to Switzerland with friends from school. "Come to France for a few days," I said. "I'll put you back on the train to Paris, and you can leave from there for St. Moritz." I gave no thought to Jackie or her parents' reaction to my dragging a classmate along. I invited Jackie to Mama's apartment. I then asked Ricky to Jackie's parents' home, further blundering through the constraints of propriety.

We booked second-class rail to France. The train pulled out of Valencia's RENFE station at 11:00 PM, slipping out of the grimy steel-and-glass Art Deco building and rolling its way up the Mediterranean coast toward Barcelona in darkness. We took seats in a compartment whose sliding door opened to a passageway along one side of the car. Three seats, with luggage racks overhead, faced three other seats, all of them reeking of sustained human use. Tim was traveling with us as far as Paris. We pulled into Barcelona at about 5 o'clock the following morning, our necks stiff and sore from bobbing up and down while we dozed off throughout the night, waking at the local stops and the random document checks by Guardia Civil. These were grim, knee-booted men in plastic tri-cornered hats who prided themselves on maintaining order and discipline. Their remit seemed boundless. In Barcelona, we took more holiday travelers on board. As a result, people had to sit in the passageway and, later, between the cars in the coupling spaces, unable to find seats. At the French border in Hendaye, we were forced to change trains because the gage of railroad tracks in Spain differed from French tracks. The bulk of the day was spent traveling up through France, past Narbonne, Toulouse, Limoges, Chateauroux, and Orleans. It was a flat, verdant country with open fields much like America's Midwest. But they were alien, too, studded here and there with dun-colored villages, each with a needled spire above a lone church. In Paris, we took the metro from Gare d'Austerlitz to Gare du Nord and found a room in a *pension* where the three of us shared a double bed. In the morning, Ricky and I took the train to Rheims, and Jackie collected us there.

A stiff *politesse* governed the two days of Ricky's visit to the farmhouse. For his part, he seemed to understand the visit was a mistake. The fact that he saw this and came along anyway cemented our closeness for me. A question that Jackie's parents seemed to have, but never asked, was what, exactly, was the purpose of his visit? I was engaged to their daughter and on this, my first official visit as her fiancé, I brought along a classmate from Spain, someone I'd known for only a few months? Was this my gratitude for the hospitality of my soon-to-be in-laws?

A few nights after Ricky left, I was rousted from bed at 3 am. Mom and Dad were on the phone downstairs in the parlor. I had sent them Jackie's phone number, but that didn't occur to me in the shock announcement of an overseas call. When I came downstairs, Jackie's father was doing his best to field my parents' expressions of excitement at the engagement. I had not heard M. T. speak much English, and I was embarrassed to listen to him having to attempt it at this hour. My godparents got on the line, too. No doubt a few drinks had been taken, the gravity of the engagement was sinking in, and someone prodded someone into placing an overseas phone call, failing to calculate the time difference. It was assuring to hear their voices on that first holiday away from home, and they were excited to hear Jackie's voice. Her parents, in half-dazed interrupted slumber, struggled with the few words Jackie fed them by way of saying thank you, Merry Christmas, yes, isn't it all wonderful news, and we look forward to meeting you, too. Now the nuptials were put out in the open, made real, a given thing, something that would require decisions and planning. All was in play. I ended the call with, "I'll write and fill you in on everything. Merry Christmas."

The train back to Spain was even more crowded. Boarding in Paris at the same time as everyone else meant I could not find a seat. For the first several hours, until we reached Toulouse, I squatted in the unheated coupling space, alone, ruminating in the cold. My holidays had been taken up largely with *fiancelles*, celebrations of the upcoming wedding, opportunities to meet cousins, aunts, and uncles. I kissed many cheeks and sat many hours on the periphery of surprisingly formal conversations struggling to catch a phrase – even a word – that I could affirm with a nod or a meager "*oui*." Meals were presented to the American-in-law-to-be that featured the best of the region – saccharine aperitifs, sweet-meats, platters of kidney or beef tongue that slid around as if licking its own gravy, endless plates of cheese, and pastry. Impromptu visits to even more relatives were proposed, including seeing a great aunt in her apartment in Rheims near the little red schoolhouse where Germany signed its unconditional surrender after WWII. She delighted in recounting how happy everyone had been to see the GIs marching through in the liberation. "So tall," she'd say, laughing. "And so big." She smiled at my then-thin form as if imagining me filling out one day to those heroic proportions. Sitting at those *fiancelles* as Jackie's escort, I saw her navigate them with a cool reserve. She would recount the intervention of the woman on Avenida Jose Antonio. "*Por las calles, no, no, no,*" she'd chime with her punch line, while her relatives pretended to admire the underwhelming stone on her finger and struggled to absorb the fact that she had said yes. This marriage appeared as if it were really going to happen. The proposal story became less and less amusing with each telling.

Back in Valencia my spirits revived. In the cafes and in Whiskey-a-Go-Go, everyone had tales from their holiday travels. Most important, Ricky was back. The moment I saw him, I realized I had no more resistance left in me. I wanted to be with him, to hold him, to have my fill of him: the scent of Florida Water he wore, the sound of his voice, the feel of his skin. Everything else crumbled in the face of that.

I told him after Mass the first Sunday how I felt. I said I did so because I knew he felt the same way. And he didn't – couldn't – deny it, but he couldn't move forward. He was stuck in place, rigid, unable to make a move. We spent many evenings with that impasse sitting between us in that dark post-Christmas period. In a cold, candle-lit church, or the far corner of a bar where no one would know us, I softly urged him to let me hold him, to relent. He sat next to me, mute and unmoving. I gambled that patience was the right course. That demonstrating respect for the struggle with his vows would assure him I could be trusted, that mutual prayer and discernment would finally bring us together.

What he never voiced – what he should have since I was pressuring him, he the pursued and I the pursuer – were his doubts about what I intended. If he was struggling with his vows, where was my struggle with my betrothal? How could he picture us as lovers if I was already engaged? I surmised he didn't ask because it would cede too much ground, imply that he cared too much. In fact, I would have had no answer to such a question. He remained troubled and quiet, and I continued imploring.

And so, when words failed, as they always did, one cold, clear night as we walked the street leading from Ruzafa, I pulled him into the roofless, abandoned housing on the market's far side, where hidden on a nearly empty street by half-tossed, half-standing walls, up a half-flight of stairs that led to nowhere but open sky, I put my arms around him and kissed him. He yielded. And we crossed that Rubicon as if there were no going back. There is an old trope that a gay man's first kiss with another man makes the world change from black-and-white to color. It did. Even at night, downwind from a fish market, in the cold, in the roofless dark under the stars.

By now, I was deep into compartmentalization. Disassociation. Detachment from reality. By day I read Don Quijote, the history of the Golden Age, and the writers of the Generation of '98. Evenings I spent plotting reasons to be with Ricky. I allotted no time in that fevered interval for any thought of Jackie or the impending wedding.

Ricky and I were desperate to be alone. He often came up to our flat. Mamá was charmed by him, prompted to sing a popular tune from a 1950's Mexican film. "*Ojos negros, piel canela.*" She warbled in appreciation of his black eyes and cinnamon skin. But Tim sat with us in the cramped quarters of the bedroom on those evenings, chatting and strumming his guitar, working out the fingerings to flamenco runs. We were never really alone. And I was not welcome in Ricky's apartment.

We found occasional escape through visits to Sra. Alfaro, a poetry professor from the university. I'm not certain what class I had with her, but I can hear her reciting from *Platero y Yo* by the Nobel poet Juan Ramon Jiménez. I don't remember what led to the three of us becoming so familiar. We called it our enchantment. She urged us to call her by her given name, Isolda. We never met her profligate husband, Andrés. According to her telling, he was either suffering from tuberculosis or somewhere in Andalucía with a mistress. She never complained about the desertion, although her sadness was palpable. She had two small daughters who seemed to enjoy our company. She would feed the girls early and send them off to bed after a few silly games. Then we settled onto her sofa and talked at length. She quoted lines of poetry and sang medieval *jotas*, a plaintive musical form which Ricky and I developed a knack for intoning. One in particular that we all loved spoke of the singer's desire to turn into ivy and crawl up his beloved's wall to better look into the chamber to see how she sleeps at night. I treasured the interest she showed and felt affirmed that Ricky and I were adults with gifts worth sharing. In retrospect, Isolda asked little about where we came from or what we hoped to accomplish. Our conversations focused on impromptu reactions to songs and readings. I gave her a hand-written, framed copy of my first poem in Spanish, a reflection on Dalí's *Cristo de San Juan de la Cruz*. It began with a trope about the crucifixion: "... Pinned out there like last week's laundry."

As the semester break approached, I mentioned nothing to Jackie about my plans. I had determined that, rather than trekking back up to Epoye, I would go away with Ricky to Portugal for the week. We would be together, and alone. We planned the trip in secret, and in my mind, it took on the aura of a honeymoon. I was surprised when Ricky suggested we invite our friend Jessica to come along. The three of us had become close and shared a natural comfort in each other's company. We spent hours together in cafes and in my room in Ruzafa, where Mama risked scandal by allowing her up. I knew she would add to the adventure of the trip. There was also the advantage of traveling as a party of three, rather than two. Guilt had us seeking cover. She would love to come along, she said. Of course, I said, she'd need her own room.

We took a day-train to Madrid, then a night train on to Lisbon. We found a *pension* there in an area called Thieves' Market. In the course of several days we walked the city and toured other parts of the country by bus. We went to coastal villages and university towns. In faithful response to our Catholic upbringing, we felt obliged to visit Fatima, where Our Lady appeared to three peasant children during World War I asking for prayers for the conversion of Russia. We walked tirelessly, ate what we could afford, laughed at everything, and grew even closer. One afternoon we booked a tour that turned out to be filled with Americans. We decided to avoid them entirely, pretending – fooling no one, I'm sure – that we spoke no English, thus obliging the guide to give his commentary in both English for those in the front seats and in Spanish to the three of us in the back, smirking and aloof.

And at night, Ricky and I had each other, entirely and completely to ourselves, away from everyone, even Jessica. We held nothing back. We bathed each other, made love to each other, clung in our sleep to each other. Unfettered, unhesitant, I launched myself out into what I saw as our common future, as if Ricky were my personal flotation device.

Three

EVERY YEAR IN MID-MARCH, VALENCIA IS CONSUMED BY *LAS Fallas*, a five-day celebration of St. Joseph the Carpenter, a brief easement from Lenten fasting rooted in medieval traditions. Participants, including children, historically costumed as *falleros*, parade in neighborhood syndicates. The men wear white tops with puffy sleeves and colorful sashes at the waist. The women wear an elaborate costume, tightly bound across the breast, and wind their braided hair into donut shapes at their temples. At two o'clock in the afternoon, firecrackers strung above the streets running the length of a city block – *mazcletás* – explode in rhythmic patterns, building to a boom like live cannon fire.

Jackie came down from France for *Las Fallas*. Mamá had long insisted that she plan on doing so. My fiancé and I toured the streets, admired the decorations, and watched the festivities. The crowds were huge; people came from across Europe and farther afield. The *fallas* themselves are complex, slightly grotesque, and bitingly satirical Papier-Mache statuary. They are built up with *ninots*, cartoonish mannequins that address an annual theme under which they are judged competitively. The largest *fallas* were downtown, and that year's theme was "Sin." Ruzafa was too poor to have a decent *falla*, but an intricate one near the bull ring offered commentary on the Ten Commandments. The ninth commandment – *Thou shalt not covet thy neighbor's wife* – depicted *ninots* of newlyweds Jacqueline Kennedy and Aristotle Onassis. She held out a siren-red, over-sized apple and stood voluptuous in a white shift pulled tightly across large breasts and a fulsome derriere while he gaped at her, a paunchy old man ogling and panting. All the *fallas* are set on fire on St. Joseph's Night, a scene amplified by the fireworks simultaneously rising from the dry river-bed circling the city.

Climbing out onto the roof of my apartment building in Ruzafa seemed the perfect place to watch the entire display. I took Jackie and Ricky up there, the three of us looking down on a hundred thousand revelers cheering in the streets and looking up at the rockets bursting above us.

When Easter break came, it was my turn to visit Jackie. On the north-bound train to Paris, looking over the shoulder of a man seated in front of me, I saw the headline in his newspaper: *Eisenhower est mort.* President Eisenhower is dead. I hadn't thought about Eisenhower since Kennedy was elected. He was once a larger-than-life presence hovering over my childhood, ranked somewhere near the Pope. The headline reminded me of an earlier moment that autumn when I walked past a hardware store in Ruzafa with its televisions broadcasting in the window, tuned to the news. I learned that Nixon had just won the election. Both announcements left me feeling a discontinuity of place, a queasy sense that time was out of joint. I was unsettled, troubled as if stumbling through a script that didn't flow. Each president's news was like waking from a dream slowly, coming toward consciousness but not yet fully there.

On the second day in Epoye, Jackie and I walked to the town hall. We stood outside the locked building while she explained what a French wedding entails. A religious ceremony was optional; signing a registry with witnesses was all that was actually required. There would be a meal, she said. There would be pots and pans clanging outside the house on our wedding night. Chamber pots would be left at the front door, partially filled with champagne with small chocolates floating in them. The image struck me as more vulgar than quaint.

We drove Petronille into Rheims, calling on the lovely aunt who had such expectations for me and meeting up with some of Jackie's university friends. The absence of any talk about wedding plans passed without comment. They didn't have much English – the norm then, the exception now. I knew Jackie expected me to hold up my end of the conversation. She translated when needed, and I contributed my small bit. The topic drifted to Mao's *Little Red Book*, which everyone was reading, and Americans' barbarity in Vietnam, which everyone was talking about. I held my irritation in check, not wanting to discomfit Jackie but unconvinced of their capacity to judge the situation in what was, after all, their former colony. One that had been so poorly managed.

On the way back to Epoye, while she was driving, I told Jackie that I had sex with Ricky. I knew I was throwing a bomb and was prepared to absorb her shock. But she was once again nonplussed, just as she had been when I proposed. She kept her eyes forward, looking at the road in front of us.

"Chantal was right, then. She told me she thought you two were too close." Moody Chantal, brooding under the poster of James Dean looming over her bed, whispering to her sister late at night. Jackie then launched into a dissertation that she seemed to have prepared whenever this moment arrived:

"Life as a homosexual would bring you nothing but shame and pain. You have to think about your future, about your happiness. Put Ricky out of your mind. That is your only rational choice. It is your only hope." She explained how my feelings were a natural phase in human development, how I would get over them, how she understood these things, and how everything would work out just fine. I offered no counterargument. She was playing to my deepest fears. I promised her I would think about everything she said.

On my last night in France, after everyone else had turned in, Jackie crept into my room and sat on the edge of my bed. She said she wanted to lie next to me. The moment had come – incredibly late in the course of events – when none of this could make sense anymore. I understood she wanted to lie with me, but I didn't want her to. As strange as it seems, I had never pictured this impasse. Yet it was to this moment that events had been leading for their denouement. The dream state in which I had been moving about finally evaporated. I was face-to-face with the impossibility of what I had set in motion. She sat in her nightgown on the edge of the bed, and I lay on my side, my head propped up on one arm. I told her it was best that she went back to her own bed. All I could think to say was, *"il n'y a rien à faire." There's nothing to be done.* It was a moment of complete clarity. I was unmanned and shamed. If she felt any bitterness, it was not discernible. She stood up, crossed the room, and closed the door behind her. Its closing felt like an amputation, a sundering.

She saw me off on the train in Rheims the next morning, standing over my seat, solicitous, pleading with me to write, to let her know everything would be alright between us. Once again, she said that the only thing that would ultimately make me happy was for us to proceed with the wedding. Chimes sounded for the non-passengers to leave the train. As she walked toward the exit, I gave her a wan smile and mouthed, "Don't worry." While the train pulled away, looking at her through the window as she stood on the platform, I continued mouthing it. It was pure cowardice. I hated hurting her, and I offered the false consolation of a lie.

The guilt I felt reminded me of a passage I read in the Generation of '98 class from Miguel de Unamuno: "Man, by being man, by having a conscience, is, in comparison to an ass or a crab, a sick animal. Conscience is a sickness."

On the seemingly endless trip back to Spain, I played everything over and over again in my head and could see no clear way forward. I knew that I would not marry. I could not marry. It was not a matter of will. Nor was it a question of outgrowing a phase. I could not will myself to be what I was not! I had blithely plodded toward marriage, counting on my capacity for hard work, on accommodating myself to any given task I set myself to. Sitting on the edge of my bed in her nightgown, Jackie showed me I had deceived myself. And I had deceived her. Sexual aberration is alienating; deceit is immoral.

I kept nurturing my aggrievedness, the loss of I what I could not have. Unamuno also wrote, "I'm convinced that we could resolve so many things if, running out into the streets and laying out in full daylight all of our pains, which amount to no more than one common pain, we would become one in crying over them, and shouting to the heavens and calling on God."

I understood Unamuno's argument, on a visceral level, to say there are four kinds of people: 1) the suicidal - *ellos que quieren no ser* - those who want to not be, who don't want to go on living; 2) the miserable – *ellos que no quieren ser* – those who don't want to be who they are; 3) the cowardly – *ellos que no quieren no ser* – those who don't want to not be, who are simply afraid to perish; and, lastly, 4) the brave – *ellos que quieren ser* – those who want to truly be, the only ones who find salvation, which lies within themselves.

I determined I would truly be. I would claim myself.

It was after 10 PM when we rolled into Valencia RENFE, the scene of so many comings and goings that year. This time, instead of the sense of novelty and adventure that usually met my stepping out under its glass canopy, I felt dread. I was caught in a mess that I had created for myself. I would have to call off the wedding. I would have to tell my parents it was off. I would have to tell Mamá, Don Manuel, Tim and everyone at school. And I could never let on why.

First, I would tell Ricky. That was the one conversation I looked forward to. I took a cab directly from the station. I found the *portero* and asked him to ring Ricky's apartment. He was home, but confused that I should show up at such a late hour. He came downstairs, and we went to Bar Texas. I told him that I couldn't get married, that I loved him, and that I wanted us to be together. I'm sure I was overbearing, frantic I might lose my chance with him. He demurred and said the only thing that would bring me happiness was for me to proceed with the marriage.

"That sounds like what Jackie said!"

"She's right. Listen to her. Our being together would never be right. We'd always have this secret between us."

He admitted, soon enough, that he got a letter from Jackie warning him to stay away from me for my benefit. Jackie urged him to end our affair so that she and I could proceed as planned. She alone could help me find happiness, she argued. I was astounded by her determination to disregard our unsuitability, to want to wed anyway, to carry on in spite of what she knew. Her letter persuaded Ricky, convinced him that the only choice for us was to ignore our feelings and stick to our original plans – he to the monastery, me to married life. I was confused that he should be so easily persuaded. What about our intimacy, our love, these last months?

The next morning I crossed the Plaza del Caudillo. Instead of heading to the university, I continued toward the Basilica of Our Lady of the Abandoned. The Forlorn. Another line from Unamuno came to me, "*The holiest thing about a temple is that it is where we all go to mourn.*" I prayed with infinitely more fervor than conviction. I stooped to abject supplication, to spiritual prostration. Casting all doubt and free will down before a small idol bent forward under a dark wig, I wept for the man I would not be. He was already fading to a ghost. I wept for the forlorn boy I was, doomed to a marginal, shadow-filled life, someplace far removed from happiness. I wept, and I prayed for a miracle I could not have described, one in which I had no belief.

Back home in Ruzafa I wept too, off and on, for two days. Mamá seemed intrigued by the drama and asked several times if, maybe, Jackie and I couldn't put things right. Tim and Don Manuel found my reaction to events out of proportion. They knew only that the wedding was called off. Don Manuel finally pronounced, "*Hombre, no llores*" – Man, stop crying. There was the cut of disapproval in his voice, a tone I had never heard him use. It told me he, too, knew disappointment, knew self-judgment and resignation. And weeping was not the manly response, I heard it say. I stopped crying.

I dutifully wrote my parents announcing another failed courtship, conceding another dead-end. I elided its cause, simply claiming - rightly so - that I didn't love Jackie enough to marry her. Later, I learned they had already secured passports, booked tickets, and bought new wardrobes for a wedding and holiday in France. I had given no thought to that. What I thought about was how I dreaded facing them, how relieved I was that setting out the news by post, from a distance, lessened the initial sting.

I had to definitively end the engagement. Doing that remotely was cowardice, too. I wrote Jackie, laying the situation out honestly, asking her to forgive me, to not hate me, to move on with her life. I told her I knew that I embarrassed her in front of family and friends, who must have wondered how an American boy she met while abroad, unemployed, not yet finished with university studies, could blithely talk about marriage. Chantal was right, I said, and her mother's reticence was merited. I hoped she saw that my self-deception brought me misery as well, which might somehow be mitigating.

I did not mention that I knew about her letter to Ricky. I did not ask her what kind of marriage she was prepared to accept. I was miserable with my own guilt. I opted not to point out the part she played in what proved to be our failure.

Even as I wallowed in self-pity, I wondered how the news would be received among my peers. In the following days and weeks, a few people had questions. Most had their own lives to live, dealing with the end of a year abroad and a return to the constraints of the lives they had left behind.

I pled my case to Ricky whenever I could. At length he relented, showing himself, once more, oddly pliable. He had resisted my initial overtures, then succumbed to them, only to be persuaded by Jackie's arguments. Now he relented again. Still, the darkness lifted. We returned to plotting how to slip away from our separate lodgings at night, booking cheap rooms in *pensiones* around town. We posed as tourists passing through, careful not to frequent the same place twice for fear of being discovered and sent by the Guardia Civil to prison for perversion. A cleaning maid unlocking a pension room door sent us flying up out of bed, naked, grabbing our clothing in terror. We twice slept over at Isolda's, who gallantly refrained from questioning why. On such furtive, thrilling nights, whispering in each other's ear, we plotted our future. We would go back to the States. Ricky would leave St. Leo's and come to Indiana. We would get work somewhere, and we would graduate, then come back to Valencia, back to where we knew such happiness.

The days grew warmer and brighter, never more so than there on the coast of the Mediterranean. Ricky recruited other students for outings to El Saler, a local beach a short bus-ride away. The beach was his place to shine. He was fit and brown, and he looked terrific in his white swimsuit. I felt pale, skinny, awkward, and wore a pair of long trunks in blue and red stripes. I took pride in how everyone admired him, how easily they followed his lead. For my part I sometimes wished it were just the two of us there on the sand. It put me in mind of my 21st birthday when he said he wanted to take me to a romantic dinner. In truth, he had organized a surprise party. I was to meet him in front of the imposing Central Post Office on the Plaza del Caudillo. I spotted him, keen to spend a night together. As I climbed the steps to greet him, he gave a signal, and 20 or more of our fellow classmates descended from behind the columns of the building singing Happy Birthday in unison. I saw my fantasy night fading away. Sure enough, we all went to Whiskey-a-Go-Go, where as always, the evening got away from us.

The administrators of our exchange program announced an end-of-term concert. Da. Laura, still den mother to our cohort, organized rehearsals. We would perform a program of American songs at a gathering for the Spanish students and faculty, our way of saying thanks and goodbye. I saw the concert for what it was, a public relations gesture toward the locals who had endured us for two semesters as we moved among them, with our loud voices and coercive friendliness. The night of the concert, as Tim strummed his guitar and we sang *Leaving on a Jet Plane*, I watched tears glide down Jessica's cheek. Ricky and I had confided in her about our relationship. She accepted it with natural grace, as unaffected as the sorrow she now displayed, a sadness that was my sadness, too. Our intimacy was bound up in part with our feelings for the city we were bidding farewell. I reached deep down inside myself for whatever grit I could muster, determined Ricky and I would be back to pick up where we were leaving off.

A week before we were to fly back to the States, I got two separate deliveries from Jackie. There was no note inside the first, a small box containing the engagement ring I had given her and a key next to it, which proved to open a trunk that arrived a few days later. I had sent the trunk to her before Easter. She shipped both the small box and the trunk C.O.D. Among other things, the trunk held the ceramic dinner plates Ricky had given us as an early wedding present.

Very early on the morning I left Ruzafa to return to the States, I stole into Mamá's room to awaken her and say goodbye. She woke up startled and immediately began to weep. She reached out and touched my cheek, whispering, "*Ay, mi hijo, no llores,*" Oh, my son, don't cry. But it was she who was crying. It was she who started it.

The Music Student

Spain

Contemplation

El Saler Beach

Four

ALL I KNEW OF NEW YORK CITY WAS MY TWENTY-FOUR HOURS
at the Idlewild Inn and the marshlands skirting JFK. Ricky knew
his way around, and he arranged for us to stay with an aunt, a
diminutive Cuban woman who spoke almost no English. She
lived in a one-bedroom apartment near 98th and Broadway. She
was surrounded by a sizeable community of her compatriots,
which offered a Spanish-speaking environment's decompressive
comfort. The evening we arrived, we walked down Broadway to
the Lincoln Center on the upper west side. We climbed up its
broad plaza under aggressively yellow security lights bathing the
anxious neighborhood. Cooling ourselves in the fountain that
stood among the performance halls, we looked downtown to where
the spotlights detailed the Chrysler and Empire State buildings'

tops. In Times Square, as if at their feet, the neon lights of theater marquees lit the buildings with an alluring under-glow.

Ricky belonged to the Benedictine Order, a world-wide-web that predated the internet. By day three, we had a visit from Father Jude. Jude was in his mid-thirties, tall, relaxed, slump-shouldered, and self-deprecating. He and Ricky exchanged the patter of friends who knew each other well. Jude drove us in his Volkswagen to his dormitory downtown at Fordham, where he was spending the summer. His car was filled with food wrappers and soda cans. He made an exaggerated show of locking it after parking on the street, as if concerned someone might steal some of its debris. He showed us around Chelsea and the Village, then, with virtually no segue, proffered tickets he had booked for an Off-Broadway matinee that afternoon. In fact, it was two one-act plays – a drama and a comedy – both with gay protagonists struggling with coming out. Afterward, in a basement bar off Washington Square, he asked me what I thought of the plays. I gave a measured commentary on the staging and performances, avoiding any mention of the gay themes. I was hesitant to talk about my relationship with Ricky, even as it squatted coyly in the background, just off-limits to what was said aloud. I sensed Ricky leaning in a bit.

Jude simply nodded. I knew his choosing those plays couldn't be coincidental. I knew I was being vetted. Ricky planned to extricate himself from his Benedictine commitment; Jude's scrutiny was surely connected to that move. I hoped for a sign from Ricky that would affirm my reticence. But he was silent, watching the conversation as if following a slow-motion tennis match. It occurred to me, incongruously, that Jude might be physically attracted to Ricky, that there might be some jealousy in the air. For the first time, I was curious about Ricky's past before our time together in Spain. But I was no more inclined to ask than I was to share my own thoughts.

The most pressing need was an income. I had talked to Tim before we left Valencia and told him I hadn't married Jackie because I wouldn't leave Ricky. He looked confused by that idea and stared at me oddly for some time, trying to re-order his understanding of the many hours he, Ricky, and I had spent together. He sat there in our shared bedroom, connecting the dots in his head. What about that night in Paris, the three of us in the same bed? In the end, he proved tolerant enough. In the spirit of pressing on with things he said we might think about joining him on his summer job. He was going to work with a mobile crew doing track maintenance for the B&O Railway. He gave me a name and contact number in Ft. Wayne for the man who made the hiring decisions and said he'd put in a word and assured me they needed workers.

With Tim's lead in hand, I was eager to push on to Indiana. At the end of the first week in New York, I bought a ticket for the night bus from Port Authority to Indianapolis. Ricky came with me to see me off at the crowded and chaotic upstairs gates. He was leaving for Florida the next day. Everything was moving fast. I turned to queue for boarding in near panic as Ricky was ready to turn away and leave the gate. I put one hand on each side of his head and planted a very public forced kiss on his lips. He looked both embarrassed and pleased.

I took a seat in the rear of the bus. I was alone, on the road, and could still taste the intensity of the kiss, the look of shock on Ricky's face, and the thrill of violating a taboo so overtly. I slept off and on, slipping between confused dreams and memories of so many recent leave-takings. In New Jersey, Pennsylvania, and Ohio, the bus stopped frequently, late-night and early-morning. The trip began at sea level but rose as we traveled westward into increasingly higher foothills, down into valleys, and back up again across taller mountain ranges, constantly gaining elevation. By the time the next day dawned, I was back in the deceivingly uncomplicated geometry of the midwest, a thousand feet above sea level. The linearity of its freeways appeared, in some new and odd way, unyielding. While ordering coffee in the bus stop cafes, I could see the bright faces that greeted me were as steely as they were friendly, eager to welcome and equally disposed to disapprove. I was an outlaw, moving around among a moral citizenry unaware of my fallen state; a native returned to find things were never what they once seemed. I was prepared for culture shock when I went to Spain and alert for signs of it. But coming back to what should be familiar country – a place changed only by my absence – was unexpectedly disorienting. I found myself thinking about footage I had seen of astronauts falling from the heavens and splashing with their capsule into the ocean. When they emerged, everyone wanted to talk about outer space. No one, not even the astronauts themselves, ever spoke of the bobbing waves or the enfeebling gravity of re-entry.

Dad was waiting for me at the bus depot in Indianapolis. We rode home in intermittent silence along the very highway that led home from the stockyard terminal years earlier. Now, we sat a bit stiffer in the front seat, alert for the right thing to ask, cautious of the wrong thing to say. There was no longer the quiet, mutual comfort, no more Dinah Washington on the radio. The reception at home went according to protocol – "how was the trip? Are you hungry? I imagine you'll want to put your things away." Days followed in which I caught up with everyone's news, offered some stories, slept a lot, and checked the mailbox daily. Then, one evening after dinner, Dad called me into their bedroom where he and Mom sat side-saddle on the flower-patterned bedspread. I had barely enough room to half-stand or half-sit at the foot of the bed, in front of the double dresser. Dad's tone was measured.

"Jackie wrote us a very kind letter. Your mother and I are disappointed that things turned out as they did. Is there anything you want to tell us?"

They had more information than they were divulging. As did I, of course. Dad was signaling an upper hand. Holding his cards back betrayed his reluctance to play it out. We had played this game many times.

"I hurt her, and I know I let you down. I'm sorry. I didn't love her enough to marry her. Sorry isn't enough to marry someone."

"All right, then."

I can't say that was that. A storm had passed with no overt damage; climactic conditions had not altered. Dad left a few days later for the Upper Peninsula, and Mom was scheduled to follow him with Maureen and David the week after. She was going to close up the house for the summer and knew I was moving on. By then, I had a letter from Ricky confirming he had squared away everything at St. Leo's. He would fly up to Indianapolis in a few days. Mercifully, things were falling in place.

Maybe because Dad was away when Ricky arrived, or because of the promise of Ft. Wayne, or because I had cast the die and felt emboldened – whatever the reason – I felt an unexpected pride when I introduced Ricky to my mother, saw him treated as a guest in our home, and told Maureen stories about the exciting times we had. A line from Unamuno seemed to capture the fullness of the moment: "*Some people think with their whole body, with their blood, and with their marrow, with their heart and with their lungs, with their gut, with their life.*" For those few early summer days in Springwood, we paddled the canoe around the lake and made love in my boyhood bedroom. I had a brief idyll between what had been and what would come. I had never imagined such contentment, such rightness with the world. I saw Mom eye us, obviously at moments, appraising whether his presence was scandal or routine, and if either, to what degree. But there was a midwestern courtesy for everyone to fall back on. It blurred things sufficiently, made things tolerable. I had no illusion that what played on the surface was what she was thinking. I knew she was anxious over the implications of the course I was set on. But I also knew she wasn't going to confront her worst fears.

Everyone left Springwood on the same day, Ricky and I to Ft. Wayne, Mom and the others to Michigan. Mom dropped us off early, just north of the Frankfort courthouse. Who knew there was a bus to Ft. Wayne? I had always traveled by car. Buses were for people who had no car. When our bus pulled up, Mom grabbed my arm by the wrist, turned my palm upward, and placed a $20 bill in it, a last, silent reaching out. I had given little thought to money, assuming our expenses would be covered by the railway company. I took the $20, having no idea how much Ricky had on him.

We presented ourselves at the B&O Railway office in Ft. Wayne and were given a scrutinizing once-over. A ledger was briefly scanned. Yes, Tim had sent word we were coming, but, well, there would have to be a physical exam. We both submitted to it separately. Then, well, we'd probably need to take X-rays. We both did. Then there would be a consultation, once the X-rays were back, after someone had read them. Maybe later that afternoon.

We killed several hours in a public park nearby, breaking the $20-bill for something to eat, and returned at the appointed hour of 4PM. I was offered a job. Ricky was not. Something about his back. But what, exactly, about his back? Ricky was a gymnast and a strong swimmer. What exactly was wrong? There were some questions. Ricky wasn't completely clear what he had been told. Obviously, I wouldn't go on to Ohio working the tracks if Ricky wasn't coming with me. He'd have no place to go.

There are moments when, regardless of any concrete evidence, you just know something is not right. Something was not right here. There had been too much ambiguity all day. Getting hired might not be an automatic process, but Ricky's failing a physical? It didn't add up. We went back to the hiring agent to say there must be some mistake. "No, sorry." Then a quick aversion of his gaze.

I see now what he saw then: two animated young men who shared an obvious comfortable intimacy, who lacked the ritual stiff-armed apartness that might have assured him of our core manliness. This would be enough evidence of "something funny," he would no doubt say, once we were out of ear-shot. He would probably repeat this observation several times after that. Heads would shake. "Can't have that."

I had not considered that we wouldn't get hired. I was used to things going well, merited or not. They had thus far, but this changed everything. We walked back to the park where we had idled away the afternoon. I found a pay-phone and tried to reach my sister Lee Ann in Muncie, two hours' drive away. No answer, and there was no such thing as answering machines. Dad was in the UP, and Mom was on her way there. I had been away for a year and had no idea where anyone else was for the summer. We had less than $15 between us now, not enough money for food and lodging.

A police-car rolled slowly past the playground across the park from our bench. In a moment of giddiness more than desperation – as if our predicament were some laughable mistake in the script – and with no other plausible alternative, I approached the policeman who sat on the passenger side. I told him we were stranded. We had no money and no idea where to spend the night. Could we stay in the city jail? It was apparent he didn't take me seriously. But if we were arrested for vagrancy, wouldn't they have to put us in jail?

"What would we have to do to get arrested?"

I was ignorant of the forces I was toying with. I only knew everything was screwed up, and I had to buy time until I could figure out what came next. There was a local solution for cases like ours, the policeman explained, for people adrift and seeking refuge. It wasn't the city jail; it was the Rescue Mission House. He made it clear that it was our only option. We got in the squad car, and they took us to a nondescript one-story building in a strip-mall off a busy, four-lane highway on the edge of Ft. Wayne. A large red neon cross fixed over the door cast a barely discernible glow across the afternoon's hot asphalt. We stepped out of the car and were told to explain our situation to whoever answered the doorbell.

This proved to be a pink-faced, middle-aged man who stared slightly off to one side of my face as we spoke. He had a large stomach straining the belt threaded through the loops of his slacks and wore a white, short-sleeved shirt with a dark tie. We were ushered inside to where 15 or 20 other men sat in a receiving area, men with rough complexions, unkempt hair, and wearing more than one layer of clothing as if dressed for much cooler weather. Many were at or nearing middle age, leaving me with the bitter thought that it had taken them much longer to reach their nadir than it had taken us. We took a seat in one of the empty folding chairs and sat silent and still.

At 6 o'clock, the greeter emerged again and announced we were all to follow him. He led us into a large room with windows fitted with Venetian blinds. There were more folding chairs. Against a far wall, a small woman at a piano, her back to us, sat as if incurious about who was streaming in on this, yet another evening of shelter-less men. The greeter passed out hymnals. He stood next to the piano, facing us and offering a few words on behalf of the Risen Savior. He called out a hymn, referring to it by its page number, suggesting it would be an appropriate response.

I was unfamiliar with the hymn and made no effort to join in singing it, like most of my companions. If ever a biblical metaphor obtained, it was a "flock of sheep" in that time and place. What struck me most about the unfolding events was the lack of personal engagement. No one recorded our names or personal data. No one offered encouragement. Resignation permeated everything that was said and done. Many in that room were obviously familiar with the routine, but that didn't seem to engender any camaraderie. Ricky and I were clearly first-timers, but no such acknowledgment was made. Our hosts were Pentecostal fishers-of-men determined to lead us through their program, insisting we keep pace and follow instructions. We were all simply the evening's catch.

After a few mirthless hymns and a plea to surrender all to Jesus, we moved to a dining hall where we shuffled through, cafeteria-style. The food was already plated and simply dropped onto our trays as we passed by. Back in the reception area, we heard that if we needed a smoke, now was the opportunity. I was out of cigarettes.

At 9 o'clock, a prolonged bell sounded, the kind once rung between classes in high school. The pink-faced man led us toward the back of the building through a short hallway. I was told to strip to my undershorts in a locker room, put my clothes and personal belongings into a paper bag, and mark it with my name. It would be held for safekeeping. I worried about my not-quite-empty wallet. Ricky stood in a different line, and I momentarily lost track of him. I entered a shower room where I was more hosed down than allowed to shower. The pink-faced man, still fully dressed, followed us in and inspected us for signs of disease before we were allowed to put our undershorts back on. I kept my eyes fixed downward.

Inside the large, darkened dormitory, I sought out Ricky, who assured me he was fine. I promised I'd keep calling Lee Ann. We'd get things worked out. The exchange was brief and whispered while everyone else moved silently to an empty cot. I claimed one of perhaps forty cots lined up in rows and listened to the subdued snorting, coughing, and throat-clearing from men who were accustomed to being alone, men now rendered submissive in exchange for a place to sleep.

I woke the next morning, newly startled by the bizarre surroundings. As details from the prior evening came back to me, I grew frantic to reclaim my clothing and, especially, my wallet. After a cup of coffee, a small yellow mass of something standing in for scrambled eggs, and a slice of toast, we were abruptly turned out of the night's sanctuary.

I found the nearest telephone booth and placed a long-distance, collect call to Lee Ann. She was home this time. She accepted charges and, when we were connected, sounded surprised but pleased to hear my voice. She made no comment about my predicament, though she twice asked, "Who's Ricky?" Yes, of course, she'd come to collect us. It'd be at least a couple of hours, so I gave her the address of the mission. Ricky and I sat near the edge of the busy highway, resigned to the wait. Neither of us spoke of last night's events. We talked, instead, about the options in front of us. We'd try our luck in Muncie. The sun was already warming things up, and commuters were on their way to work. Other drivers passed by as if out for a pleasure ride. I glared at people who I felt sure would have given little thought to someone like me, reduced to charity for a meal and a roof overhead. How eye-opening it was to see their comfort with privilege. Such heartlessness in the world, so little compassion. One woman passed by in a late-model convertible with her car-top down. She wore sunglasses and a sleeveless sundress, and a scarf tied under her chin protected her hair from the warm wind. She obviously had her own home, a place to go, business to attend to. What did she know of my predicament? What would she care?

I bristled at how people could be so blind to their own good fortune.

Five

LEE ANN PULLED INTO THE RESCUE MISSION HOUSE PARKING lot just after twelve noon, appearing *deus ex machina*, the *machina*, in this case, being what was once my mother's Mustang, now her car. We embraced, and I introduced her to Ricky while smiling fixedly to mask how close I had come to yielding to despair. I wondered, too, how close Ricky had perceived disaster to be. But never mind all that. Somewhere, along the two-hour drive back, catching up on Muncie news, filling Lee Ann in on our predicament, working up a litany of plausible next moves and short-term solutions, my dread started to dissolve. The sense of having nearly hit bottom lingered nevertheless, despite this new evidence that my fear was never really justified.

If Muncie hadn't changed, I had. I no longer aspired to a middle-class life. I was preparing for life on the fringes. All I dared ask was that Ricky and I have our own place where we could quietly retreat, where we could present ourselves as merely two roommates looking for work.

A few friends I knew at the International House welcomed me back. They had stayed on looking for more permanent legal footing than a student visa. Vera was still there, mysteriously "working out of her apartment" in an age when no one did. We teased her about spying for the Russians. In retrospect, she may well have been. She had a car by now, which made friendship with her even more desirable. Linda from Morocco was still there. I last saw her when she came back from California with Jackie and Chantal, glowing with an enviable tan and her marvelous head of light-brown hair that hung heavy, silky, and straight. Linda still had her classic Roman nose, flawless complexion, and fashion model's poised, fluid moves. But she had gained a serious amount of weight attributed to her love of Burger King Whoppers, which she pronounced *hoopers*. I would soon learn she was bulimic, struggling to slim down, and ready herself for reuniting with her boyfriend Michel, an auto mechanic in Paris. Linda said she wasn't prepared for him to see her "like this." It was clear she no longer knew where she belonged, where she was going, or why she was there.

Jurgen was still in Muncie, too, dating a tall, pale, stocky girl from Chile named Regina, who played guitar and laughed as musically as she sang. Her favorite song was *Gracias a la vida*, and it was a guaranteed crowd-pleaser. Most of us never learned the lyrics beyond "Thanks to a life that's given me so much." Jurgen knew all the words. The rest of us invented our own, and we sang them with gusto.

260

Dr. Taylor was still in the English Department. Before classes resumed in the fall, I decided to stop by his office for a visit, encouraged by the interest he had once shown in my well-being. I sought a standard against which to gauge the changes I'd since undergone. Waiting in his office I ran into Barbara, a fellow student from our sophomore Humanities class. I remarked on the coincidence that we should both be there at the same time, which made her laugh. Barbara was now Dr. Taylor's wife. He had divorced his former wife and married her in the last year. Barbara received my news – that I had ended my engagement with a woman and was now living with a man – with remarkable aplomb.

"Harry and I would love to meet him." Just like that, a routine pleasantry, sincerely proffered, as if it were unremarkable news. I was unsure of how to respond. Of course, the proper response was to accept her invitation to dinner, reciprocate, and grow in friendship. Which we did.

Joyce and Faiz had been a couple from the early International House days. Joyce talked about marrying Faiz and moving with him to Afghanistan, but Faiz went home without her. She and I, two local kids who once conspired about living abroad, had more in common with each other than she had with Faiz, or I with Jackie. Joyce was living with John now, a graduate student. When we reconnected, she seemed happy to have me back in her orbit and invited Ricky and me for dinner, aware we were sharing a cramped apartment with my sister. John saw the bond between Joyce and me, and let me know of his mistrust. Joyce explained Ricky and I were a couple and there was nothing between her and me. I wanted to allay John's worries and was working toward some self-assurance, but not yet arrived at root-and-branch transformation. Part of me resented that all this had to be spelled out, that I should be deemed out of play, neutered, as if non-competitive for a woman's affection.

Those reunions played out in a larger context. President Nixon had determined not to abandon Lyndon Johnson's policy of "guns and butter," Great Society short-hand for a commitment to fund both a strong military and a war on poverty. Industry was humming. Work was easy to find. Ricky and I got hired at Muncie Gear, a former auto-parts factory converted to manufacturing tail assemblies for rockets as part of the war effort. Union wages were good, and we had student deferments. Working the second shift allowed us to schedule classes during the day.

The war was always on television that summer and on everyone's mind. In spite of Nixon's election campaign promise, it was intensifying. There were more than a half-million GIs in Vietnam – a few of my high school friends among them – and more than 33,000 of them had already died, as had hundreds of thousands of Vietnamese. I stood against the war, in part because I feared being drafted and sent to fight it and in part because I never understood the argument that it was a necessary battle against world communism. I knew full well that working in a factory making arms to sustain the war made me complicit. I told myself that I couldn't stop it, and I needed the work. Like so many, I took cover in ambiguity.

The war was only one of several gripping stories playing out on television. In July, Apollo 11 landed on the moon's surface, and Neil Armstrong took his *one small step for man, one great leap for mankind.* In August, in the Catskills north of New York City, more than 400,000 people – mostly from my age cohort – gathered at a three-day musical performance and love-in near Woodstock. Peace, love, drugs, and lots of mud.

Peace, love, and drugs had come to Ball State, too. I never heard anyone speak of marijuana before I left for Spain. Now it seemed everyone had some, everyone had tried some, and everybody was offering some. There appeared to open a small, safe niche in the emerging counter-culture where homosexuals were tentatively tolerated. *It was cool,* some assured me, offering lip service if not outright acceptance, making clear *it wasn't their thing, but cool, if that was your thing, on campus, anyway, at least among some people, as long as, you know, you don't gross me out or confront me with it.* Ricky and I spoke more openly among a small circle of trusted people. We came out to them judiciously, incrementally, hoping that doing so with minimum confrontation would ease the awkwardness we saw in them and felt ourselves.

Muncie Gear offered none of the tolerance for what some were now calling "the gays." The labor pool included men and women, black and white, with a few Hispanics and no Asians. Tensions were kept in check through tacit arrangements in which some machinery jobs were kept open for whites to bid on and some for blacks. Shipping and delivery were mostly handled by blacks. Women were usually assigned to assembly lines, although tough women also sometimes bid on the broaches and punches that paid well for high-output piece-work. Inspection work and management positions were largely staffed by white men. The lowliest position, where I began, was emptying the metal shavings out of those broaches and punches, staying ahead of the operators to avoid any downtime.

Talk on the shop floor was routinely studded with words that today are held much closer. Non-politically-correct language that was blurted out then, but now is shared solely among the like-minded or elided by using initials. The frequent intermingling of blacks and whites kept racial slurs to a guarded level. I heard the N-word often enough, even though it was known college students like me didn't like it. Black employees must have had antipathetic language for whites, but being on the wrong side of that divide, I was in no position to know what it might be. References to queers fell easily from almost everyone's lips. The inference was that queers were an invisible, ubiquitous menace. Men of both races spoke the word with no effort to hide disgust. The women who most often spoke it were like Jody, a tall, stylish middle-aged woman from Kentucky. She wore tight slacks and gloves to protect her long fingernails and kept her complicated hair-dos sprayed, pinned in place, and covered with a disposable plastic scarf. Jody spoke it more in mockery than disgust and implied that she knew a good bit about the subject. I worried my presence, or some queer vibe I was giving off, would betray me. I maintained vigilance and let the comments slide by, aware that my half-dimmed smiles gave all of them permission to perpetuate the insolence.

I marvel at the stamina we had in those days. Ricky and I found a one-bedroom rental apartment in a cheaply constructed shotgun house, split length-wise, only a few blocks from campus. We painted, carpet-tiled, and built countertops, all of which I carefully matched in tan, gold, and yellow tones. I pored over curtain fabrics, looking for the right shade of blue to contrast with poppy orange. We built bookcases and put two twin beds in the bedroom, lest anyone wander in there and wonder what arrangements were in play. On weekdays, we rose early and went to class, and alternated cooking healthy meals. Ricky had a talent for learning new dishes, and I learned from him through observation. Mid-afternoon, we went to Muncie Gear and put in an eight-hour shift five days a week and an extra shift on Saturday when we could get it, when the pay was time-and-a-half. By midnight we were home listening to *Blood, Sweat, and Tears, The Beatles,* and *Emerson, Lake, and Palmer* on the stereo using headphones to avoid disturbing the neighbors. On weekends and holidays, we invited people to dinner and threw parties. The crowd at our Halloween party was so large the neighbors called the campus police, who ignored the marijuana smoke rife in the air.

I saw completing my senior year as a necessary step toward our return to Valencia. I valued the experience for what it offered – good times and new friends – but it was a waiting period, nevertheless. I enjoyed my Latin-American Literature classes. There were a couple of provocative Latino profs whose lectures on social history and poetry supplied me with plenty of rumination. In the evenings, I sat at my new job on a conveyor belt testing tail assemblies coming down the line. My task was to lift two of these at a time, each about the size of a short highball glass, insert them into a pressure tester, and remove my hands while I stepped on a pedal to clamp down and force air through their newly-sealed bases. Air bubbles in the tester indicated a bad seal. It was hypnotic, repetitive work. One evening, after a poetry class left me thinking about Vicente Huidobro's "*la vida es una caída en paracaídas*" – life is a fall in a parachute – I failed to get my hands out of the way. The pressure tester clamped down on them and I wailed in pain. The assembly line had to be stopped, the single worst transgression imaginable. I was sent to the medic, then home without pay for the next several days until the swelling went down, and a more natural color returned to my fingers.

Ricky enrolled in a combination of art, music, and dance classes in pursuit of a degree in Fine Arts. He undertook projects that required a lot of his time – building collages, dance performances, and some theater work. I watched him struggle with the first severe winter weather he'd ever experienced. He was initially intrigued by the beauty of snow and ice, then almost overwhelmed by the effort it took to move around in it, given our busy schedule. He pined for a Cuban Christmas with his family in Florida, but that wasn't possible since we'd earned no vacation time at the factory. We invited his sister Alice and her husband Jonas to spend the holidays with us. I don't remember how we made room for everything in the small apartment, but we had a tree, Christmas dinner, and one morning, freshly fallen snow, a novelty that seemed to delight them no end. They were ebullient people, highly voluble about every detail of every encounter: Ricky's new apartment, the campus, the food we ate, and the latest movie they had seen. This evoked an intensity in Ricky, too, that I hadn't seen before. He was animated and attentive to each of their questions and suggestions. Childhood stories were told and retold. A picture emerged of a patriarchal household in which the slightest provocation brought chaos. Their late father once grabbed the turkey off the holiday table just as people were sitting down to dinner, tucked it under his arm, and stomped off to his brother's house, feeling slighted by something someone said. In our cramped apartment, removed by time and distance from that original scene, the story was recast for the humor it now safely offered.

Jessica came soon after they left to spend a few days leading up to the New Year. I had virtually begged her to come, wanting to re-create the special intimacy the three of us shared on our trip to Portugal, to invoke the aura of Valencia. But we were no longer exchange students sitting in cafes or riding a night train across the Iberian Peninsula. We were, each of us, struggling to support ourselves and build new lives. We were confronting re-entry, bobbing in the sea. Things went wrong from the beginning. Jessica claimed the wrong luggage at the airport, and we had to go back to Indianapolis the next day to exchange it. She then announced she wanted to go back to New Jersey to spend New Year's Eve with her boyfriend, Jack. Vera drove us back to the airport for the flight. Along the route, we slid across the icy freeway, seriously damaging the car. State Troopers took Jessica on to the airport while Vera, shaken and near tears, arranged a tow back to Muncie for us. Jessica's fleeting visit failed to evoke the re-incarnation of times past that I'd hoped for.

Late that winter, on a weekday afternoon, just as we were ready to go into Muncie Gear, I got a phone call from my father. It was startlingly rare to hear from him and even more confusing listening to the practiced tone with which he delivered his news. "Dan, your grandfather has passed away." I couldn't quite digest it, in part because it was spoken with such *sangfroid*.

"Oh, Dad. I'm so sorry."

"Your Grandfather Boyle."

He repeated the phrase twice before it dawned on me that it wasn't his father, Grandpa Juday, who had died. Grandpa Boyle was a name never spoken throughout my childhood. I was never daring enough to ask why. Now that he was irretrievably off the planet, permanently out of reach, it appeared it was all right to speak of him. Years after that call, I visited Mom and Dad as they resettled into the farmhouse where Dad was raised. In the dining room I saw a double-frame photo display in a bookcase, hinged in the middle like an open book. There were two sepia-toned photos in it, the one in the right frame a young, handsome woman who looked vaguely like Mom, and the one in the left a dapper young man with his hair combed back with Makassar oil.

"Who's that?" I asked, ready to move on to inventory the other things on display.

"Don't you know who that is?" Mom sounded surprised. Maybe, with more time, I could have made out that the woman was a much younger, thinner version of my Grandma Boyle than I had ever known. She paused a few moments, so I turned to her for a clue. I finally said no.

"That's your Grandma and Grandpa Boyle."

She seemed flummoxed that I hadn't recognized the man about whom she had been silent my entire life. It was strange, hearing her say – for the first time – Grampa and Boyle joined together, two words finally allowed to emerge from the shadows where they had been joined all the time.

In late April, news broke that Nixon ordered an invasion into Cambodia that was unauthorized by Congress. Tensions spiked. In December of the previous year, a new selective service system had been introduced. Lotteries were now drawn based on month and date of birth; if your birthdate drew slot number one, you were among the first to be called into service, regardless of any deferments. The lottery draw for my birthday was 300 out of 365, well above the expected annual quota, beyond the risk of being called up. But now, other privileged sons of America were in the line of fire. Expanding the war into Cambodia was the last straw. Protests and demonstrations broke out on campuses across the country. In Kent, Ohio, demonstrators threatened the downtown business district, putting the Ohio National Guard on alert. Students crossing the Commons of Kent State College campus lined up in protest against the deployed guards. The opposing lines approached each other, shots fired out, and four students were killed.

Four dead in Ohio. It became an anthem. No one was safe. At Ball State, largely un-politicized, a student group called for a university-wide boycott, demanding we join in solidarity with those killed. It was early May, nearly my last week of undergraduate study. I was living in a self-imposed tunnel, working full-time, and studying late nights and early mornings to complete full-time coursework, focused on getting through. On the day of the boycott

I decided to attend classes, as did a few others. It was a warm day as I sat in European History at one in the afternoon. The windows were open and an early summer breeze wafted in. The professor, seated on her desktop, left off talking about Barbara Ward Tuchman to ask those of us in attendance, those who weren't boycotting, why we were there. The conversation wandered and not everyone had a chance to speak. I never did. I had nothing rehearsed, anyway, in the event she had asked me.

My graduation ceremony was scheduled for a Thursday afternoon, which would require my taking a day off work, unpaid, to attend. I decided not to, and my decision had the added advantage of snubbing convention. It was what was done in those days – challenging convention. My sights were fixed far beyond celebrating graduation. I was absorbed in the struggle to get back to Spain. I thought little more about it. My father phoned a few weeks before the event asking the date of the ceremony. I told him I had no plans to attend and explained I would have my diploma sent to me in the mail, and that was good enough for me.

"Well, fine,' he said after a pause. "I was just making plans to go to Michigan, so I guess I can go ahead and travel when it suits me, then. I'll not have to work around your schedule."

My father had never asked about graduation before that phone call. It never occurred to me he'd be interested. A college degree was something whose merit I had decided on my own, something I pulled off on my own, something I earned absent any overt encouragement from either parent. On the other hand, I was the first of the family to graduate with a college degree, a fact whose significance did not escape me. There must have been some part of me pleased to withhold my parents' celebrating it by watching me graduate. On graduation day, I worked the second shift. Everyone let it pass without comment, without so much as a greeting card.

Six

AT SOME CORPORATE LEVEL WELL ABOVE MY STATION – NO DOUBT well above the brass at Muncie Gear – someone decided to bring second-shift work to a halt that summer. By then, I had been promoted to an inspector's post: final inspection of tail assemblies. This included overseeing their packing, separated by cardboard spacers, into cardboard cartons and staging for shipment. Corrugated supplies were stacked on the far side of the large shipping floor, a good distance from where the tail assemblies emerged on their conveyor belt. Two forklifts were needed for the process at all times. I reported this as an inefficiency. Inefficiencies, we were told, lead to factory closings. I doubt this was a contributing factor. I am certain the shiftwork's ending was not due to the war's winding down. The war would remain on strong footing for several more years.

My place at the end of the manufacturing process meant that I was one of the last to be let go as my shift shut down. Warner Gear out on Kilgore Avenue was hiring. Warner made auto water pumps for Detroit, and they were still running shift work. Ricky and I both applied. Because he got laid off before I did, and could apply earlier, he got a day-shift slot. In the avalanche of late applications, I got relegated to night shift, 11 PM to 7 AM. I was back to scraping out the small, tightly curled metal shavings that broaches and punches generated as they rough-cut parts from blocks of aluminum and steel. I shoveled the scrap into a wheelbarrow and dumped it behind the plant onto a holding pile heaped over a slatted pit. I often wondered where it was trucked off to, where it turned to rust. I stopped for a smoke out back every-so-many trips, out of sight of the shop steward, puffing on unfiltered Pall Malls and watching the varied shades of night sky slowly dissolve into pale dawn.

Affluent in a two-wage, low-budget household with overtime checks coming in, we bought a new car, an Opel. It enhanced Ricky's and my standing among our friends, except for Vera, of course, who already had her own car. Now freed of study and classes, we took camping trips on the weekends. Within the first few forays, we acquired a full inventory of gear. We learned the art of car-camping, that pale imitation of the real thing, which is hiking into deep woods carrying everything you need to survive, leaving all amenities behind. But car-camping was easy, and it required less time. We set up at campsites beside fresh-water lakes, or wide river bends with the comforts of a portable gas-burning stove, warm sleeping bags, and a nylon, nearly rain-impervious pole tent. In dire weather, there was a public shelter at hand. A variety of friends came camping with us. Jurgen was supremely efficient, as if he'd been a scoutmaster in another life. Linda from

Morocco came a few times, amusing herself by complaining about the crude, candle-lit environment in which she found herself.

Ricky's drama training led to his volunteering at Muncie Civic Theater after graduation. The relationship between the civic theater and the theater-arts school at Ball State went back several decades, and its history of productions was impressive. Ricky thrived on stage, happy to be part of a troupe. Before my night-shift job started, he cajoled me into taking a small role in a production of *Tea House of the August Moon*. I only had one scene, with two lines, playing a Korean village elder. I found rehearsals tedious. I don't remember what my two lines were, but I well remember the makeup slathered over parts of my body exposed through a costume shredded to depict ragged poverty. The makeup was called Pancake Number Two. I submitted to the basting every night from dress rehearsal through the final performance and remember even more keenly the breath-sapping terror when the curtain went up opening night. I had an out-of-body experience watching myself standing on my mark while also looking down on myself from above the stage where the sets are hoisted. I promised myself in that moment that once this short run was over, I would never submit to such terror again.

The summer days got warmer, and I came home from Warner Gear at daybreak to a still quiet, dewy, and softly lit neighborhood. Ricky was already gone to his shift. I slipped into my twin bed and tried to fall asleep. There was no air-conditioning, and by mid-day or early afternoon, the heat was stultifying. Someone was always mowing a lawn nearby. Sanitation crews worked the alleyway, tossing around metal bins and revving compressor bars to crunch refuse into the truck. My sleep was interrupted several times a day. When startled awake, I tried to relax back into sleep, but it felt like abandoning a world I was missing out on. I needed to restore my energy for the night-world I now inhabited, a different world, peopled by men whose interests didn't intersect with mine. Janis Joplin died during those days, as did Jimmie Hendrix, and no one at the plant seemed to care. Instead, they wanted to tell me strange tales, whispered to me out back, about whores they'd known in Vietnam and about certain women they hoped would grant odd and very specific sexual favors.

Ricky and I ate our main meal in the evenings now after he got home. It fell to me to prepare it, on the theory that I was home during the day. My view was that I was <u>not</u> home all night, <u>not</u> getting enough sleep, and I deserved compensatory treatment. After dinner and dishes, I had only a couple of hours before I had to get ready for work, not enough time to get involved in anything complicated or outside the apartment. Ricky was increasingly busy with the theater. He landed a role in the musical *Gypsy* that autumn, and he became friendly with several cast members. They struck me as being much like the cliché one expects: a theater crowd – brash and self-confident, speaking loudly, as if always projecting from a proscenium. What passed among them as humor was the incongruous insertion of heavily-rehearsed lyrics from *Gypsy* into random conversations as if that showed some remarkable wit. Instead of a simple goodnight when leaving the apartment someone would bellow out:

"All the places I gotta play, all the things that I gotta be at..."

Under the pretense of good-natured ribbing about our twin-bedded arrangement, someone once intoned, "Oh Mama, get married today."

Mannered jokes from an in-group I wasn't a part of, self-referencing performances brought off-stage and enacted wherever they chose. I didn't warm to those people or to what I saw as their demands on Ricky's attention. I tolerated them. I laughed along with them, even as I sensed that things were shifting with Ricky. I told myself Ricky had every right to pursue what interested him. He worked hard. He met his share of the expenses, and he was paying down his student loan. If our schedules didn't coincide, what was he supposed to do while I was away?

Or was that what he asked me?

We were busy, and we lived in separate diurnal cycles. If there was less crossing back and forth between our twin beds on the weekends, at least he was there, breathing audibly. To hear him and to see him shift in his sleep was enough to stoke my affection. I contented myself that better times were coming when we would be in Spain, when we would be on the same schedule, when we would rekindle that rush of magic I felt when I kissed him goodbye at Port Authority.

Then Dean started showing up. Constantly. Dean was in *Tea House*. That's how I met him. Now he was in *Gypsy*. Ricky asked him to dinner in the evenings because Dean was driving him to rehearsal. He was good-looking in a boyish way, taller than Ricky, shorter than me. He had medium-length, mousy brown hair parted to one side, often tossed there with a shake of his head. His complexion was pale, and I thought his skin was often dry and flaky. He was given to sweeping hand gestures and forceful put-downs, dismissive about so many people, places, and things. I didn't much care for Dean.

Before *Gypsy* finished its run, Dean lost his apartment lease and needed a place to stay. Would I mind if he slept on the sofa for a few nights until he got things sorted out?

Why should I mind? Hadn't people helped us out when we needed it?

Who was asking what of whom?

Then letters addressed to Ricky in a florid handwriting started arriving. Some former girlfriend in Vero Beach, Florida. I asked Ricky who she was. His first response was "an old friend." By the third or fourth letter, he told me she was someone he still had feelings for. That was odd, the notion that he was ambivalent about his sexual orientation. I certainly never saw signs of that. But who knew? Unfinished business, perhaps, something that must be laid to rest. He thought maybe he should go down to visit her, confront his feelings. I was fairly certain such feelings would not have survived what we went through in Spain, what he went through as a novice at St. Leo, what we were going through at present.

Several weeks before Christmas, Dean proposed we all drive down to Florida to spend Christmas with Ricky's family. He wanted to meet Alice and Jonas, and Ricky could go to Vero Beach. I had little interest in Tampa at Christmas, but if Dean and Ricky talked about it before raising the idea with me, if Dean knew all about Miss Vero Beach, then I sure as hell wasn't going to let them go without me.

It took 19 hours, nonstop, to get to Tampa. We left after my night shift ended and spelled each other, taking turns driving Dean's small red Toyota. It was limited-access, freeway driving all the way, swept up inside the monotonous flow of holiday traffic, red taillights, and dimmed headlights through dull grey skies and night-driving all across the Southeast: Lexington, Knoxville, and Atlanta. When we hit the Florida border and stopped for something to eat, the air was warm, the sky was blue, and my glass was filled with fresh-squeezed orange juice as if I were back in Valencia. I shook off the funk that had settled over me the last several weeks and I determined to enjoy myself.

As they had before, Alice and Jonas oohed and aahed over

everything Ricky had to tell them. A cousin showed up the first afternoon. She had just seen *A Love Story*, a two-hanky movie starring Ali MacGraw and Ryan O'Neal. Their performances had all the depth of the cinema screen on which they were projected. The cousin couldn't stop weeping as she laid out the plot – boy meets girl, girl dies. I was the only one in the room not moved to tears. I kept my skepticism to myself. Throughout the several days we spent with Alice and Jonas, they answered in English whenever I spoke Spanish. They nodded cursorily at what I thought were my brilliant insights, and laughed heartily at everything Dean had to say. We exchanged gifts on Christmas morning, and Jonas roasted a pig in the front yard. I met Ricky's mother, as did Dean. We went to Ybor City, a neighborhood I had heard Ricky talk about often and fondly. It was the heart of Cuban Tampa and the setting for so many of his earliest, happiest memories. Even there, over festive, wine-fueled dinner conversations, everything was kept to English in deference to Dean.

Ricky disappeared on an overnight visit to Vero Beach. When he returned to Tampa, I asked, as casually as I could, how things had gone. Ricky was non-committal and said he wanted to keep seeing the girl. He might come back down to Florida again soon. I knew then that I was locked out. I did not create a scene. We were guests under someone else's roof, far from home. A scene would do no one any good.

A month or so after we returned to Muncie, I came home early one Saturday morning and found Ricky and Dean had fallen asleep together in his narrow bed. I backed out of the room, walked to the sofa in the front room, numbed and distraught, and lay there pretending to sleep until I heard them leave the apartment. That afternoon I went to see Barb and Harry. I don't know what I thought to do or say. Perhaps somehow, if we talked this through, they could provide some wisdom. I burst into tears when I told them what I had seen, what I now knew to be true.

Harry fixed me a stiff drink, and they both listened attentively. It was the first time I felt empathy extended to me in ages. Before the evening was over, my head was hanging over their toilet bowl. I retched and sobbed. Everything I had risked, everything I had forfeited, had come to naught. I moved heaven and earth to build a life together, one that Ricky was now ready to shrug off. I had no way of understanding what happened. I understood love as a child understands—binary, something either present or absent. Love either existed and burned pure and true, or it didn't exist. I could not process Ricky's duplicity. I was incredulous that I could not have him, but I saw it was not a matter of will. It simply wasn't going to be.

"Why couldn't he love me?" I moaned. Harry, sitting next to me on the bathroom floor, stroked my hair and comforted me, wise enough not to attempt an answer.

There was no way I would forgive Ricky. I had sensed a growing distance and had failed to do whatever impossible thing was required to fix it. How can one reclaim love already trothed, ardent but unrequited love? I had never felt the despair of those first days after seeing Dean lying next to Ricky. I have since known deeper, longer-lasting, more life-shattering grief. I have accompanied lovers through their final days of wrenching illness, and I have crawled back from their graves, shaken and a stranger to myself. But the evening I hung my head over Barb and Harry's toilet bowl bemoaning my loss, I got my first, clear look at disillusion. I once thought that, with Ricky, I had solved the problem of myself. In losing him, I permanently lost the naive faith that any moral justice was due me.

I woke up on Barb and Harry's sofa late the next afternoon, miserably hungover. I knew I wouldn't go back to the apartment. Barb and Harry seemed to understand and, in a gesture of splendid kindness and manifest grace, offered to let me sleep on their sofa until I got myself organized. I still had my apartment key and knew Ricky's schedule. I could slip in and out when he wasn't there. I did just that, gathering my things out of the bathroom, the closet, the chest of drawers, and the bookshelf. He could have the car and the car payments, the furniture, the kitchenware, the tangerine-and-blue curtains, and the gold-colored carpet squares. I took what was unequivocally mine – a strange concept after two years of sharing everything. I stored it in the steamer trunk in the dark, oily garage facing the alleyway behind the house – the very trunk Jackie had returned to me with Ricky's wedding dishes. Weeks later, Harry drove me down that same alley after dark. Brandishing a flashlight, we dragged out the trunk and put it into his car, retrieving my possessions like a thief in the night.

The day I first saw Barbara in Harry's office, when she told me she was now his wife, the day she said they'd love to meet Ricky, she and I both recognized that we stood apart from the norm; we defied convention. Her dinner invitation was, in a way, conspiratorial. Yes, she implied, you have a gay lover. I am married to an older man, my former college professor. So what? At one of those early dinners among the four of us, Harry told me that he said he was old enough to be her father early on in their courtship. He chuckled to recall that Barbara answered, "No, my father's a year older than you." Such was the camaraderie in our friendship. We were all excitedly at the beginning of something. I now no longer was. But they still were, still forging a life together. They had made a down payment on a comfortable, three-bedroom ranch house in a leafy neighborhood at the edge of campus. When the deal closed, I was still sleeping on their sofa. The sofa and I moved into that house with them.

I switched to working the second shift. I did not get home until nearly midnight, and they were usually asleep when I did. This afforded them some personal space during the week, at least in the afternoons and evenings. When summer vacation came, Harry had his two daughters come to stay with him. I watched Barbara, still so young, learn to be an attentive stepmother. Before the summer was out, she was pregnant. With all this going on in their lives, I was one more thing to contend with, the wounded friend trying to pull himself together who slipped in late every evening and quietly opened up the sofa bed. I look back on their patience and generosity with astonishment.

They provided me with a place where I was spoken to as a peer by intelligent, caring people. I haltingly learned to respond with the same intentionality. I was treated like family and encouraged to share in the excitement of the new house, and later, the excitement over Barbara's pregnancy. One Saturday morning, on an outing with them to a flea market, I bought a framed picture of Barbara Stanwyck and a pair of black, high-strapped, open-toed platform heels. I kept these on a bookshelf near the sofa bed. It was a slightly camp display, but I remember it now as an homage to some missing feminine presence. On Sunday mornings, we often went to Communion Service at Grace Episcopal Church. Its rich liturgical language, novel in its beauty yet rooted in the Roman Mass, washed over me in a vocabulary redolent of the English enlightenment. On Sunday evenings, we strolled the lush, quiet streets of the neighborhood and returned to the house to watch PBS broadcasts of *The Six Wives of Henry the 8th*.

I was healing. I was being loved and cared for. I was working my way back to Spain.

That same summer, Grandma Boyle suffered a series of strokes. She was living in an apartment in Munising, Michigan, twenty miles from my parents' new home. By the time I could drive up to see her, she had been moved to a nursing home, paralyzed and confused as to where she was and who I was. I was emotionally unprepared to see her in that state and had to momentarily leave her room to compose myself. When I re-entered, she asked me to come closer. Both her arms were immobile, resting beside her on the bed, but her mouth continued to make the sucking and blowing motions of someone smoking a cigarette.

"Bernard," she said to me, confusing me with my dead grandfather, "the keys are on the dresser." It was the last thing she said to me.

She died a few weeks later. Mom and Dad brought her body down to Elwood for burial. I skipped the viewing held the night before the funeral, fanatically choosing to work instead. When I arrived the day of the funeral, emotional on greeting my mother, impossibly wanting to console her, impossibly wanting consolation, she simply said, "We missed you last night."

Within six months, what once seemed fixed showed itself again to be transient. Grandma Boyle was laid to rest in the Catholic cemetery just outside Elwood city limits. My brother Glenn married Marybeth, walking her down the aisle of St. Thomas Aquinas Center near the Purdue campus. My sister Maureen married Ron in their parish church in Munising, Michigan, an increasingly familiar 600-mile drive north. Two weeks later, in a Muncie church next to the Ball State campus, my sister Lee Ann married her own Ron. At each wedding, I shared contagious joy for the couple giving themselves to each other in front of their nearest and dearest gathered to approve and support. I also intensely felt my otherness on each occasion.

Standing in the parking lot on the afternoon that I knew was to be his last day at Warner Gear, I confronted Ricky as he left the plant for the last time. It was important to me that I tell him how much I loved him still, that he would never be loved like that again. He looked annoyed at my assertion but listened calmly, a bit back on his heels for having done me wrong. He challenged the idea he would never be so loved again. "You can't say that," he said, shaking his head vigorously at the thought. I have no idea if he ever was. He and Dean moved to Florida that weekend.

Two weeks after the last wedding, I boarded a plane to Valencia. I had to buy a round-trip ticket – airlines didn't sell one-way tickets in those days – and I invented a meaningless return date, knowing I would never use it. Barbara and Harry drove me to the airport and said goodbye at the ticket counter. I checked in my suitcase and the trunk Harry and I retrieved from the garage that spring. It held some clothes, a few personal items, and a complete collection of all the Barbara Streisand LPs released to date, meager stakes with which to rebuild a life.

PART IV

Reckoning

Most merciful God,
we confess that we have sinned against thee
in thought, word, and deed,
by what we have done,
and by what we have left undone…
Have mercy on us and forgive us;
that we may delight in thy will,
and walk in thy ways…

Confession of Sin, Rite I
The Book of Common Prayer

One

JURGEN HAD GONE BACK TO WEST GERMANY EARLIER THAT summer. We wrote to each other on occasion. He told me he went down to Valencia frequently on behalf of Peter, a friend of his who owned a Spanish restaurant in Heidelberg. Jurgen was earning a decent livelihood sourcing plates and saucers, wall décor, and in avoidance of border customs, hundreds of kilos of Spanish wine and rice. He drove these up to the Heidelberg restaurant. Before open EU borders, if undiscovered and untaxed, a trunkful of such merchandise, bought and sold at the old exchange rates, made the long drive profitable. He also recruited Spanish waiters, young men willing to contend with West German winters in exchange for West German wages. When he learned I planned to return to Valencia, he wrote that he knew two Swiss guys there, friends who would be happy to take in a third roommate to help with the rent. *Just get here*, he said, *and I'll meet you at the airport*. Leave it to Jurgen to get things organized.

The Swiss friends were renting a three-bedroom flat near the Port of Valencia, in the El Grao section, across the river from the old city. It was on the ninth floor of a modern, nondescript apartment building set among row upon row of similar buildings spreading from the River Turia east toward the sea. Many of the street-level storefronts around the base of the building stood empty. Electrical power was intermittent, which made the elevator ride a calculated risk. In European fashion, the lobby was designated ground-floor rather than first-floor. If electricity was off when you came in, you had to climb nine flights of stairs – actually, 18 half-flights. If the electricity cut off while you were in the elevator, you were likely stopped between floors. Because the doors could be forced open, you had three choices: climb out and pull yourself up to the higher floor; slip out and hop down to the lower floor; or decide to wait until the electricity came back on so you weren't sliced in two by a suddenly re-engaged car while you were half in, half out. I chose among the three options, depending on circumstances.

My new roommates were not adjusting well to Spain. They were financial industry apprentices gaining early-career foreign experience, theoretically acquiring language skills, and grooming their resumes for a climb up the Swiss corporate ladder. I spoke no German, Jurgen said their "low-German" was nearly unintelligible anyway, and they made little effort to speak Spanish. They were usually out on the town in the evenings. I had no money for restaurants or bars, so I settled into a domestic routine and carried on without them. I fixed my mid-day and evening meals, then cleaned the kitchen, including clearing their breakfast mess. I took in a cat one of the neighbors fobbed off on me. The Swiss had what we now call Type A personalities. My homebody approach and low macho affect irritated them – indeed, it earned their derision. They were particularly unhappy about the cat. I didn't know what they were talking about most of the time, but it did not escape me that I was sometimes the topic of conversation. Within less than a month, it would be fair to say we weren't getting along. Arguments broke out over what was on the television and over the claw marks the cat made on the back of the faux-leather sofa. Their impatience boiled over soon enough. In a rupture of our protracted standoff, they burst through the door one evening, well intoxicated, and charged at me. Fists were flung, but in their inebriation and stubborn, slow-witted way, they mostly charged at me head first, like butting rams. This was easy enough to deflect initially. When I started receiving direct hits, I panicked and put up a wall of blind, aggressive resistance that involved knees and elbows, which paused the mindless charging. As they backed away, I told them I was going to lock my bedroom door, pack my things, and would be leaving within the week. I said it with sufficient finality to stop the aggression.

Jurgen knew some people at the Mangold Language Institute in the old city. It was my good fortune to be in Spain in an era when people were deciding English was the language of the future, a must-have skill. I taught ESL classes at the Institute in the evenings. The managers there gave me leads for private tutoring and translation work on contract, mostly from businessmen. I plied those in the afternoons. I had to learn business terminology – *invoicing, shipping, tariff duties,* and the like. The businessmen were serious and spoke at a level basic enough that I could stay abreast of their need for specific vocabulary. The students at the Institute were less focused. Deep down, as Spaniards, they saw themselves atop a colonial empire. The parallel structure in the English-speaking world, to their minds, put England at the apex. They wanted to speak like Englishmen, not like Americans. So broadly held was this prejudice, Mangold Institute advertised that all its English professors were authentically English. It's true; most of the other instructors were, although there was a girl from Scotland whose brogue I could never penetrate. If I wanted to get employed there, I was admonished to tell everyone I was from somewhere in England – the details were left to my own invention. This required, beyond an otherwise clear and moderately paced diction, that I answer, and teach my students to answer, "How are you?" with nothing less than "I'm well." Anything like "fine" or "good," I was informed, would give away my true identity. I went along with the ruse, easy enough to maintain with first and second-level students. No one seemed interested in where I came from anyway. I don't remember ever being pressed on it.

Money was chronically short, even with six-day workweeks. I learned the major bus routes threading across the large, sprawling city and took them to far-flung tutoring and translation assignments. I usually stood as the tallest passenger on board, and with my higher center of gravity, I was prone to losing my balance. I became skilled at towering over everyone without falling on top of anyone. I never got used to the pushing and jostling. When a bus pulled up to a stop and opened its doors, serious shoving began. People entered and exited in an aggressive cross-flow. To maintain dignity, I learned to stand close to the curb and let the people behind prod me up the steps and inside while I kept my hands to myself as much as I could. The shoving was administered impersonally. Once, waiting in the rain while wiping my eyeglasses, one of the lenses popped out. As I leaned over to retrieve it from the gutter, the bus arrived. A very tiny old woman dressed in widow's black standing just behind me put one hand on each of my buttocks and shoved with surprising strength, forcing me into the legs of a passenger descending the bus. I recovered as best I could, turned around, and in barely restrained anger lifted her by her upper arms and shook her, gritting "No, no, no" through clenched teeth.

I would like to think I helped some people learn some English in the course of my efforts. There was little direct feedback, little evidence of progress; acquiring a language is a slow process. I translated court documents and provided simultaneous translation with mixed success. I relied heavily on the well-thumbed *Pequeño Larousse Ilustrado* that still sits on my bookshelf today, with its dried-out pages yellowed and fragile. I experienced some unqualified failures. The Canon camera company once hired me as a simultaneous interpreter at an exhibition center's small auditorium to demonstrate a new product line. Attendees, mostly Spanish commercial buyers, sat in chairs equipped with headphones plugged into the armrests' channel and volume controls. I sat in the back in an elevated booth, listening through my own headphones while looking down through soundproof glass. I was to listen to the presenter's English sales pitch and translate it into Spanish. Questions from the audience, spoken into boom microphones provided by ushers, would go from Spanish to English for the presenters.

Management undertook no quality check of the setup before the presentation, nor any run-through for key participants. I was untrained in simultaneous translation, a high art form. The promoters who emerged on stage were Japanese, and they began speaking in what was for me, nearly indecipherable English. In my panic, I translated what I could understand of what they were saying into clear English. I looked down to see the audience adjusting their dials, looking for the Spanish channel. The moment struck me as hilarious, and I was torn between laughter and panic. The Japanese continued their sales pitch, unaware that no one was taking it in. Once I got control of myself, I tried again, stammering intermittently. Eventually I had to give up, explaining a few times into my microphone that I couldn't understand what was being said. The event soon ended and I slipped out of the sound booth surreptitiously, left the building with my head down, and hoped no one would recognize me.

My limitations were more often due to a lack of life experience than a lack of Spanish-language skills. In the earliest, most desperate days, I had two interviews with an encyclopedia publisher looking for door-to-door salesmen. The initial session went well. I enjoyed the conversation with the man who initially screened me. He seemed interested in me, impressed with my motivation and with my pluck, I surmised, that I should be across the desk from him in this small, struggling publishing house in a Mediterranean city so far removed from my native soil. I was determined to convince him I could handle the job. That first interview ended in a non-committal offer of a follow-up interview. When I returned, I was met by a more seasoned bottom-line manager who, after less than 15 minutes of rapid-fire role-playing at a pace that was patently beyond me, turned to me and said, "Daniel, do you really think you could make any money selling encyclopedias?" I was relieved to admit to him that I probably could not. We parted amicably.

I soon found another apartment after my fall-out with the Swiss. It was also in El Grao, in a newer cluster of apartment buildings. A family in the next building, pinning their hopes on the rising middle class, had bought it on speculation and they were having trouble finding a tenant. I got a good deal on the rent. It was a few blocks off the main avenue to the city, along which buses ran frequently. It was a quiet neighborhood, so new that my building, the last one built, stood facing out over an onion field. An irrigation ditch ran along its edge and in two channels through its middle. Its foul, muddied water seemed to neither rise nor fall, regardless of season or weather. I found a bleak beauty in it, even with its fetid odor. I was content to be looking out across a small patch of farmland once more. Back on the avenue there was a race track used mostly for dog-racing, a popular sport. I went there occasionally in the evenings. A few *pesetas* gained me admission to a brightly-lit place filled with people having a good time. I enjoyed standing among them, a stranger eavesdropping on their banter, cheered by their good humor. I was never all that interested in the actual races, which were in effect, tight-knit packs of dogs following a mechanical "rabbit" on a pole extending from an inner rail whizzing around the track. The dogs themselves were beautiful, shiny, well-groomed, and impossibly thin. They were kenneled nearby. Often, walking my neighborhood during the day, I would see the dog-walkers exercising their sleek, super-alert charges. They held the reins of more than a dozen greyhounds in each hand, walker and dogs moving as if of one mind. When they came to a corner they all turned in unison, silently sure which way to go and how fast to walk.

I warmed myself by the thin blue flame of a portable butane heater in the grey winter light. Like most apartments in that era, mine was designed to be a family home. There were few, if any, one-bedroom apartments. People didn't opt to live alone. A few pieces of second-hand furniture sat in each of three bedrooms, a sitting area, and separate dining room, with a tiny kitchen and balcony in the rear. My memory of the place is associated with struggle, weariness, and a gritty determination to remain hopeful, to keep looking for a better situation. With no radio or television, I spent my evenings poring over English-language paperbacks I found in bookstores. George Orwell and Aldous Huxley were two favorites, the former for his bravura in the face of struggle, the latter for his ability to transcend struggle. I took delight in what I could buy at the end of the month – biscuits, coffee, fruit, rice, tins of fish and meat, and especially English marmalade. I made an arrangement for mid-day meals – *la comida* – with Rosa, who ran a small working-man's diner near the docks. She and her husband were from Andalucía, and she spoke in her regional accent nearly void of consonants. She was quite pale with a very thick head of black hair and fine, dark fuzz on her arms and legs. She posed as gruff and someone put upon, but she always asked what happened to me whenever I skipped a day or two. At Rosa's, I was served whatever simple meal was the special that day – rice with eggs and tomato sauce, or liver and fried potatoes – washed down with a glass of *vino tinto* thinned with water. I settled my account with her at the end of the month. I treasured the feeling that I belonged there in that diner amid the workmen's clatter, however intermittent and temporary the connection.

I functioned by dint of determination. I was back in the beloved city where I had first tasted independence and urban life. The city whose familiar scale, seductive aromas, and soft, round-cornered contours comforted me in its disinterested embrace. I had expected to come back with Ricky, but I had to press on without him. I was sorry I wasn't building a life with someone, but I told myself no good comes of bemoaning what is not possible. Living alone requires interior balance. I was in my own blind way struggling to achieve that.

Jurgen was courting a Valencian woman, MariCarmen, with whom he was clearly head-over-heels in love, so he found reasons to come down from West Germany on a regular basis. His other ongoing local interest was an antique automobile, a lovely 1940s pale yellow roadster convertible. It needed sand-blasting, extensive bodywork, a new coat of paint, reupholstering, and a complete engine overhaul. Jurgen liked to take me to the garage during siesta hours to show me how the mechanics were bringing it back to vintage condition. He was proud of this venture, bought with – and repaired with – Pesetas. Once fully restored, he planned to drive it to West Germany where it would bring a good price in *deutschmarks*.

Mamá was still in Ruzafa. She and Don Manuel were happy that I was back in town. With no mention of what she must have understood to be my precarious financial state, she invited me every few weeks for an evening dinner – *la cena*. Sitting at the same table that had been my private language school a few years earlier, I listened to the lone new American border, my doppelganger, as he struggled rather listlessly to learn *Castellano*. I don't remember his name. I avoided speaking to him in English. He seemed out of touch with his surroundings, uninterested in them, and seldom stayed at the table after finishing his food. Mamá dismissed him with a shrug as a mamma's boy. She had seen so many of us come and go; she seemed to say, *you win some, and you lose some*. Don Manuel, happy to have someone to talk to – someone with whom he could disparage the new lodger – insisted that I call him Manuel, that I drop the honorific *Don*, and that I speak to him in the informal *tú*, instead of the formal *Usted*. In short, I was to think of myself as his peer. I struggled to make the adjustment, even as I was heartened by the fondness he showed me.

I met MariCarmen. Soon, through Jurgen's urgings, I became an occasional guest at evening meals at her family's apartment as well, situated in a sector of the old city I didn't know well, near another old market. Her parents were kind, and her brothers were very good-looking, talkative, and ready with a joke. Her little sister, Vicky, was a glamorously beautiful, raven-haired teenage girl. It was usually a Wednesday when they invited me, and I would look forward to time spent with them as a high point of the week. The talk was of local news, of what we were up to, and of family reminiscences. The paterfamilias was old enough to have fought in the Civil War on the losing, republican side. He discouraged any political talk. One evening I said something against Franco that I didn't think too provocative. He dropped his spoon loudly into his empty soup bowl and said in a low, firm voice, "*las paredes oyen*" – the walls can hear. Silence fell on the room. I suddenly realized I had never fully appreciated what Valencia suffered over those years. I was indebted to these people for their kindness, and I valued their company. I never made another political remark while communing at their table.

I came across a newspaper ad for a job I thought myself well suited for. It was from an import-export company called Excofe. The owner interviewed me. He was a short, early-middle-aged man with thinning, jet-black hair named Don Pepe. He had about him the air of the March Hare in *Alice in Wonderland*, always late, checking his watch, only half-completing his thought, then running off again. He seemed delighted when I appeared for the interview. He took my word about the interpreting and translation skills I possessed, assessed my general sense of business decorum, and offered me permanent, part-time work six mornings a week. I would be handling international correspondence, catalog preparation, and occasional business dinners with English-speaking clients, remunerated over and above base salary for those evening hours. I would have shown up just for the food, but I always accepted the extra money.

The other employees at Excofe were three young women. They were thought of – thought of themselves – as girls. Certainly Don Pepe thought of them as such, calling them *las niñas*. They were no doubt underpaid, as was I. We all worked in one cavernous room with an enormous, south-facing window. We were seated at small metal desks, huddled around a space heater in the cold weather where we stopped at times to warm our hands. There was plenty of time, with Don Pepe so often out of the office, for idle conversation. The girls trained me on the Spanish typewriter keyboard and offered their own language tutoring – a useful supply of colloquialisms which by now would be entirely out of date. I regaled them with semi-accurate stories of life in America, of hippies and rock-and-roll. They didn't appear interested in hippies or even rock-and-roll, except what was finding its way onto the Spanish radio airwaves, dominated then by Joan Manuel Serat, Camilo Sesto, and the Beatles. They were young, modern Spaniards of their time with their own contemporary interests. But I was an exotic and offered an unexpected distraction. Luci was the leader. She was about my age and had long auburn hair, freckles, and a markedly focused presence. It was she who doled out the work, who knew the comings and goings of Don Pepe. It was her to whom I submitted my translations and from whom I received correspondence and sales literature to be translated.

I was precariously insolvent even with my mornings filled with steady employment, afternoons with tutoring and translation contracts, and a couple of evenings a week at Mangold Institute. The office routine included a break at ten a.m. for a mid-morning snack – *la merienda*. When Luci saw I brought nothing to eat she had her mother prepare something extra for me, usually a Spanish omelet sandwich or a piece of chocolate in a baguette. I knew her generosity stemmed from and affirmed her moral vision. It was not alms-giving but a recognition of the primacy of solidarity. It was consistent with her conviction that everyone be treated equally.

Luci lived in El Carmen, one of the oldest sections of the city. In the evenings, she was involved in the preparation of the El Carmen *casal faller*. In the weeks leading up to *Las Fallas,* she invited me to their gatherings. Neighbors met in a large warehouse entered through what I would have taken to be an abandoned section of the *barrio*. Inside were benches set along the walls with a few tables and chairs here and there, over which loomed a tall wooden frame – that year's *falla*, not yet covered in Papier-Mache. No one seemed concerned by the slow progress. People were drinking wine and chatting in small groups, occasionally breaking out in drinking songs. I was introduced all around, thrilled to be part of the real thing. I met Luci's parents there. I came often enough that, by the time *Las Fallas* began in earnest, I felt invested in El Carmen's entry, its parades, and *mazcletás*, and fireworks displays. The festivities played out in fine fashion, and seasonally warm weather came with it.

Jurgen and Mari invited me to their wedding. I was fond of both and happy for them. Jurgen asked me to his bachelor party, along with two German friends and Mari's oldest brother. The celebration started with dinner at the Ateneo on the Plaza del Caudillo, a posh club in the heart of town through whose windows I had enviously peered on many evenings. The meal included filet mignon, at Jurgen's insistence, with lots and lots of cognac, some served aflame in small snifters, downed with increasing abandon by the five of us intent on helping Jurgen sow his obligatory wild oats. The party moved on to a basement club in the *Barrio Chino*, the Chinese quarter, much whispered about for its reputation for ladies of the evening. We soon had five such ladies seated at our table, and someone ordered champagne. The tacit arrangement was that the lady ordered champagne with no intention of drinking it. The gentleman paid the management a fortune for the bottle and maybe for another one. The couple drifted off for some intimate coupling, and because no money actually changed hands between them, there was no *quid pro quo*. When the champagne arrived, I saw what was lining up and was dismayed to think Jurgen might prove disloyal to his intended, especially when her brother might witness. More urgently, I was alarmed at where things were headed for me. The small, dark-haired woman who led me onto the dance floor was many years older than I. She may have been well skilled in the pleasuring arts, but she was dancing with the disinterested. I felt cornered. It was my recurring bad dream: prowess is expected while I remain frozen in shame. In the dream, I manage to wake up and shake off the terror. In the case of Jurgen's bachelor party, I excused myself to go to the gents, then continued on up the stairs, out of the club, and down the street to the nearest bus stop. I do not know if there were any infidelities committed that evening or not.

Soon after the honeymoon, Jurgen came by to ask if I would be interested in sharing my apartment with Mari and himself. They were newlyweds and eager to move out from under her parents' gaze. I was more than happy to agree, if for nothing other than relief with the rent. A few pleasant months followed, in which I came home in the evenings to the aroma of chicken and rice or hake and *fideo* noodles. Other rooms in the apartment were lit, there was a radio playing, and there was life in the kitchen. I had someone to whom I could relate the events of the day. I was not alone. The idyll lasted until the pale yellow roadster was fully restored. Jurgen was then pleased to tell me Mari had agreed to move to West Germany and give life there a try.

I came home one evening to find a letter in my usually empty mailbox. It was a rare thing to see my name in my mother's thin, careful cursive on the outside of an aerogram. She did not write often. The last word I had from home was a Christmas card. Slitting it open and unfolding it carefully, I read how she, Dad, and my godparents had, on a whim, gone on a low-cost tour of Spain. How cheap the price had been, how the weather had been inclement, how tiring she found all the travel, and how much my godfather disliked the food and disparaged the locals. She was writing an after-the-fact confession. She kept quiet about the trip until it was over, until they were back home. She then felt compelled to tell me how they had fared.

I was indignant; *they should have contacted me*, I said to the empty apartment. I would have gone to Madrid to meet them. I didn't have a telephone, however; they couldn't have phoned me. They were on a package tour, moving from what would have been place-to-mysterious-place alongside who knows how many others on a bus. They would have been up very early every day, their luggage sitting outside the hotel room door, eating what Dad and Louie would grumble was not proper breakfast food, clinging to each other's company in the face of all the strangeness. Nevertheless, I was hurt. They had been so close and had not let me know.

I had a dream soon after the letter arrived that left me deeply rattled. I remember it still, although it never returned as a dream. I am speaking to my parents in Spanish. They cannot understand me, and they are telling me so in English. I can't understand their English and insist on speaking louder and louder, trying to get them to understand me. I speak so loudly and with such effort that I wake myself up. When I woke, I sat upright in bed for some time while the dream played, repeatedly, in my mind.

When I was young, I would seek out Grandma Boyle to tell her what I dreamt, hoping she could give me the kind of oracular interpretation she sometimes furtively did when "reading my cards," a dark art she kept hidden from my mother. She tried her best at divining my dreams, offering, for example, that dreaming about snakes meant I had been drinking heavily, even though I was ten years old at the time. I was simply grateful that she listened to my dreams. Recounting them cemented them in my memory and instilled the habit of thinking about them. Later, when I discovered Jung's *Memories, Dreams, Reflections*, I hoped it would lead to a code-breaking methodology. To this day I dream in rich detail and remember most dreams on waking. I no longer believe in oracles or code-breaking. But I still think about that dream in which I couldn't understand my parents' English, and they couldn't understand my Spanish. I once thought it was telling me that I had reached total immersion in Spanish, that I could see my "mother" tongue from the outside. I now believe it was simpler than that, that it was rooted in all those things we didn't tell each other.

Two

ONE MORNING, JUST BEFORE I LEFT DON PEPE'S OFFICE WHERE I had been taking dictation for correspondence, I carefully pointed out he was late with my paycheck. I explained to him that things were difficult for me. I had lost my roommates. My rent was past due, and I had a mounting meal tab at Rosa's. Don Pepe muttered a few truncated, elliptical responses to the problems as I listed, then assured me that things would sort themselves out soon.

"*Paciencia, Daniel.*" Be patient.

Patience might be in sufficient supply for someone who maintains his sense of trust. My trust in Don Pepe and my supply of *pesetas* were waning. As the *pesetas* ebbed, so ebbed my patience. I stomped back to my desk, and Luci read my mood. She appeared, indeed, to have some knowledge of its cause. No surprise; she knew so many things.

"*I can't pay my rent if I don't get paid,*" I sighed as if she and I had just been talking about that very thing. She was quiet the rest of the morning and limited herself to task-specific instructions. She was solicitous when she handed me a baguette-and-chocolate-bar for the *merienda,* her voice modulating to a "there-there" tone. We all knew what it meant that I was working without a permit. I was a foreign national. It was an illegal arrangement for me and for Don Pepe as well. But he was Spanish and an established member of the business community, a gad-about-towner whom everyone knew. I was a skinny, long-legged *yanqui,* a hippie to all outward appearances, an impression reinforced by my flared jeans slung low at the waist and bold-print shirts. In cold weather I wore a second-hand, loose-fitting overcoat of nubby, dark wool tied around my waist with a woolen sash. My landlady often teased me about it, calling it my bathrobe. To most of those around me, I must have appeared mildly amusing, a passing sign of the times. I certainly did not cut the commanding figure Don Pepe did. That was a liability in any potential demand for justice.

Standing amid the shelved tins in the *supermercado* that night, winnowing from my shopping list every last non-essential, it came to me that I was in an untenable position. I was the cartoon character who suddenly looks down to find he has run off the cliff some while back and is simply treading air. I was accumulating debt just to cover rent and food. My existence was marginal and precarious. I was battling the odds, and I was tired. My revelation was that I didn't need to keep doing this. I could stop trying to stay afloat, stop the dog-paddling. I could go somewhere that held out more promise. All this came to me in one complete, unpremeditated thought.

A few days later, I went back into Don Pepe's office, this time with a focus. I would tell him I needed my back pay or else. My plan lacked any clarity about how to effect the "or else," but I knew mine was a righteous cause. I wanted what was due me. I would show some gumption and demand it.

"Sí, sí sí, Daniel. Paciencia."

When I sat back down at my desk, Luci dropped any pretense of ignorance this time and asked me to come home with her to dinner with her family. They had been talking about me. They remembered meeting me during Las Fallas and thought I was a nice young man.

"Come home with me. See where I live."

Luci had, indeed, been talking to her family. She told them I was in dire straits. She told them there was no reason I couldn't sleep out on the balcony behind their kitchen until I got myself together. She argued that Don Pepe was having a temporary problem and that it was not my fault. If I could just hang on, things would improve, business would pick up, everything would be fine. She pitched it as the logical short-term solution.

The generosity of the offer, which her family extended that very afternoon, has to be seen in light of those two strongly mitigating facts: Spanish families did not open their homes to strangers, and households with young, marriageable girls did not permit young, unattached men inside. Aware of that, I was slow to understand their offer was genuine. But it was. Her mother, a direct, take-charge woman, had learned how to make do ever since she moved from her village to the capital as a young girl. She put it to me simply: *You stay on the balcony, you take your meals here, you accept what we offer, and when you get on your feet, we sort things out. Luci says it's important.*

Luci's father was a happy, easy-going, and completely uxorious man. He nodded a smile and chuckled to himself, amused that anyone would try to struggle against any plan his wife and

301

oldest daughter had already settled on. I could only respond with gratitude, quickly adding that I was planning to leave Valencia. I wouldn't impose on them for long. Indeed, I had already written Farmer's Bank, reminding them of my excellent credit history with student loans and asking for a signature loan to clear my debts. I wrote Jurgen, too, asking him if he thought I could get work in Heidelberg. I wrote Jessica in New Jersey to ask her what she thought the possibilities would be for me there.

I dragged the trunk with me one more time, this time from the apartment in *El Grao* to Luci's family flat in *El Carmen*. I assured my landlady I would settle with her as soon as my loan came through. Rosa didn't hide her disappointment when I said the same to her at the diner. She gamely wished me the best and said she trusted me. I saw resignation on both their faces. They had heard such assurances before, in what had been decades of Spain's hand-to-mouth economy. Perhaps they had even given similar assurances to others. They would have had few illusions about how contagious indebtedness can be.

Those weeks I spent in *El Carmen* were like a return to the cocoon of family. Luci had a little sister, about ten years old, whom I dubbed *Doña Mariposa* – Madame Butterfly. She bounced around the small flat in a clumsy version of ballet moves, her pirouettes and jetés too grand for the small rooms stuffed with bulky furniture. We ate at a table in a small dining room, as in the days with Mamá, talking, talking, talking. I had a coffee cup with MAXWELL HOUSE silk-screened on its side. Luci's mother set it where she wanted me to sit, and her father called me Mr. Maxwell. They regaled me with family lore. Luci's mother collapsed in laughter every time she tried to tell the story of the night she woke up from a dream in which everyone was running down the street. She jumped up from bed, roused the entire family, and forcefully ushered them downstairs in their nightclothes, yelling, "*Corre, corre, que todos corren*" – Run, run, everybody's running. They unbolted the lobby door onto the quiet, empty, lamp-lit street just as she fully awoke. Everyone laughed so hard each time she told the story that sometimes her husband had to finish it.

On Sundays, we boarded a regional bus for the village where Luci's maternal grandparents still lived. The bus was marked REQUENA, but we disembarked in a mountain village before ever reaching Requena. It stopped in a small central plaza in front of her grandparents' house. The façade was a fresh white stucco whose wooden door had a small, frosted-glass window set at eye level for someone shorter than I. The interior was old and sparsely furnished, a combination of stone walls and wooden beams. It was two stories deep. A rear door led from the kitchen to one level below the entrance, a basement with an open fireplace and slate floor. Luci's *abuelo* – her grandfather – spoke *Valenciá* in a deep, guttural voice. When he wanted to tell me things about the village or his garden, which lay just outside the back door, Luci translated his commentary and I answered in *Castellano*. She treated him with a deference that moves me to recall it, myself now an old man who has never known such solicitude. There was a black-and-white television on the pantry shelf in the kitchen, which was turned on after dinner. *Marcus Welby, MD* finished airing just about the time we had to catch the return bus to the capital. We sat together watching Robert Young doling out wisdom to his patients in dubbed-over *Castellano* while we ate stuffed artichokes from *abuelo's* garden. I assured him there was nothing quite as exquisite as those artichokes anywhere else in the world. As indeed, there never has been since.

On one of those Sunday visits, several women in black skirts and rope-soled slippers set out large paella pans in the plaza, propped up on cobblestones, and stuffed bundles of twigs and branches under them. Rice, vegetables, chicken, and rabbit were put into the pans, and the women squatted in front of them, stoking the twigs into flames, stirring and seasoning the dishes until they bubbled into perfection, each part of a village-wide meal celebrating the feast day of the village patron saint. It was the Virgin Mary herself, who in an apparition one miraculous morning saved an ass that had fallen into the communal well. The disaster had occurred in those distant days of even more hard-scrabble poverty. Losing a beast who helped to shoulder the burden of so much want would have brought on endless woe. Its rescue still merited a communal thanksgiving.

I have no idea what fed the deep well of kindness from which those people drew. The novelty of my company? Enlightened gratitude? A state of grace? Whatever it was, it nourished genuine, replete, and widespread happiness.

Jurgen wrote back to say that, yes, he could get me a job at the Spanish restaurant in Heidelberg. I went one more time to Don Pepe's office. This time I came in well-stoked righteousness. I was leaving town, and he now owed me more than two months' wages. I stood across from his desk, leaning over it slightly. I had more than eight inches' height on the man, and given his seated position, I also had the kinetic edge.

"Insisto." I mean it.

He rolled back in his chair a bit and tried his first gambit. "What are you going to do, Daniel? Go to the *Guardia Civil?* What do you think they'll say when you tell them you have been working without a permit? Do you think they will be of any help to you?"

"Don Pepe, this is between you and me, not the *Guardia Civil.* I need my money."

Don Pepe then produced what he hoped was his winning card. He opened a lower desk drawer and pulled out sales samples from one of the clothing manufacturers we represented. He laid three pairs of gabardine slacks on top of his desk, one black, one navy-blue, and one a deep-maroon. It was no coincidence he had them on hand. He had prepared for this moment. In truth, I was not inclined toward physical violence; it held no promise of satisfaction. I knew this was the best I could hope for and tried on a pair huffily while making him look the other way. They fit perfectly. They were very well-tailored. That settled our affairs.

The loan from the Farmer's Bank came through. I went back out to *El Grao* one last time, happy to acquit myself of my indebtedness to my landlady and Rosa. I could see that I surprised both of them. The money meant less to any of us than did the honoring of our agreements, the honoring of our relationship. It brought a rush of goodwill to our farewells. I booked an inter-city bus to Paris, from where I planned to take another to Germany. My well-traveled trunk, with what I once held to be irreducible contents – including the Streisand LPs – was too much to travel with, so I left it with Luci. She was free to keep its contents or do with them as she saw fit. I pared down my holdings to the clothes I was wearing and those I could stuff into my tall, cumbersome backpack. I managed to also fit the Maxwell House cup, the gabardine pants, and a Neil Young album, *Crazy Horse*. Luci and her mother came with me to the bus station, boarded with me, and walked me to my seat. We each shared a quick, diffident embrace. They walked back down the aisle and out the door, the bus pulled out of the station, and Valencia slipped away from me once again.

I had leaned on their kindness, their cheeriness, their sustaining warmth, and I was overwhelmed when bidding them goodbye.

I was too callow to wonder how they might have viewed my departure. One in a series of life's random ruptures? It occurs to me that perhaps the two of them – for they were always thinking and acting in tandem – had seen potential in me as a suitor and a son-in-law. We shared a love of language and laughter, and I had the advantages of a university degree and an American passport. Was I blind to such aspirations on their part? I don't think so. I think they had a clear understanding of who I was, how lost I was, how very much still in motion I was. I certainly never signaled any interest in Luci in that way. She and I liked each other's company. We had long, rambling discussions about how we saw things, about current events and what made people do the weird things they did. But I never sensed the silent awkwardness that comes of someone waiting for the other to make a move, to express that *other kind* of interest.

I am often blind to these things. I don't know. Maybe Luci's mother always wanted a son, and perhaps she took to me because she saw a chance to mother a well-mannered young man who liked to talk, who laughed a lot, and who had enough grit to land where I had. Perhaps she saw in me a kindred spirit. I don't know. I kept in touch with Luci for almost two years, writing off and on. Her letters trailed off after she started writing about a young man she was seeing, a local boy studying at the university. I hope they found happiness with each other. I hope her mother liked him, too.

Three

THE BUS HEADED OUT OF THE PROVINCE OF VALENCIA, NORTH into Aragón, across Navarra and Guipúzcua, then up into the Pyrenees with their heavy forests and dim twilights. Terra incognita. I had returned to Valencia to mend a broken narrative and pick up the trail again. But we don't go back to any place as the same person we once were. I would now roll the dice and lean into the new. I drifted off after we cleared customs at the French border in Irún and woke up the next morning in a large plaza in Paris where inter-city buses collected and deposited passengers.

I had only a handful of francs, but I did have an address in Saint-Cloud, a well-heeled suburb where Philippe lived. I met Philippe earlier that spring on a night boat from Ibiza sailing back to Valencia. I was returning from a get-away weekend, courtesy of one of my business students who managed a shipping company and could comp free passage. Philippe had traveled far and wide. He was worldly-wise from years living in London, Singapore, and Paris as his father relocated for business. He spoke English with a posh, plummy accent. We formed an instant affinity sitting in the dark on our cheap, top-deck seats. I met a group of Mexican students that night, too, who were traveling around Europe post-graduation. Like Phillipe, they had put off sorting out where they would stay in Valencia until the boat docked, so I invited them all to stay with me. The Mexicans slept in the living room on the sofa and floor in sleeping bags while Phillipe and I got caught up in our nerdy enthusiasm for books we had read and authors we valued. We sat up most of the night talking and began a correspondence after he left. He wrote that he would be happy to have me visit him in Paris on my way north.

I took the *metro* to Saint-Cloud. Just outside the exit on a hill overlooking the Seine, downriver from Paris, the Eiffel Tower stood out against the distant skyline. The address led me to a roomy townhouse on a large, open square. Phillipe's mother answered the door. *Yes, Phillipe was in his room, and he was expecting me.* The house was astir. She was packing everything in preparation for their move back to Singapore, where her husband had accepted a new post. She wore a cotton dress fitted at the waist, low heels, and earrings, a kind of French June Cleaver receiving a house guest while closing down the house for the next few years. *That's all right*, she assured me. There was time for an evening drive into the city, a fine meal at a white-table-cloth restaurant, as well as a tour along the Seine. We passed through a tunnel I would recognize decades later as the place Lady Diana met her demise. The next day we drove to Chartres so that the family, including his little sister, could say goodbye to an elderly aunt. They took me to the Cathedral, undoubtedly the pre-emptive stained-glass marvel of medieval Europe, and we had another splendid meal at a riverside restaurant that lasted much of the afternoon. The aunt, ostensibly the guest of honor, displayed infinite patience with my fumbled French and showed attentive concern for my comfort, couching everything in *monsieur* and *s'il-vous-plait*.

Once back in Saint-Cloud, more packing and boxing went on in the background while Philippe was excused from the task. He and I wandered the neighborhood on foot, talking, happy in each other's company. A giddy moment passed in which we both turned cartwheels and summersaults for each other's amusement. As we lay on the expanse of well-manicured grass, he volunteered that he found me beautiful. I had never heard such a thing before. I determined to keep the moment unblemished and preserved, tucking it away, risking no response.

I was assured the best way to get to Heidelberg was by train. I spent precious, dwindling cash on a ticket at Gare de l'Est and boarded my train. Many hours later, I emerged from the Heidelberg *hauptbahnhof*, the central train station. It stood at one end of a thoroughfare leading into the old town, to the Spanish restaurant, to Jurgen and Mari's apartment. I had their address from Jurgen's letter and was relieved that, on showing it to passersby, people could decipher his cramped handwriting and point me onward. I was enchanted by the human scale of things, the absence of automobile traffic, the shops, and public-house doors opening directly onto cobbled streets. The cinema posted black-and-white promotional stills for coming attractions under glass panels, something I hadn't seen since childhood days in the early 1950s. I passed the *Heiliggeistkirche*, the Holy Ghost Church, looming up from a large, open market plaza. Its northern gothic stonework was flanked along both sides by hinged and shuttered wooden stalls that ran its length. Set apart from the rest of the town by the medieval square, it floated in front of me like a centuries-old collective memory.

Jurgen and Mari were home and seemed happy to see me. Mari, especially, was eager to have someone to talk to, someone to complain about how impossible German was to learn. Mari didn't want to talk about Valencia. She seemed keen that I get up to speed on their new life. Jurgen took me to the restaurant that very afternoon. *No time like the present*, he told both the kitchen staff and me. I was to work in the bistro upstairs, above the formal restaurant on the ground floor. I actually never entered the restaurant. I remember seeing it through the open doorway on my way upstairs, its low, warm lighting glowing over formally set tables in the evenings. At night, we sometimes heard a guitarist performing for the diners beneath us. The bistro had a long bar running more than half its length and several café tables set at small windows in the front and along the side. A menu offered sandwiches and salads. A constantly replenished complimentary supply of dark bread smeared in grey pork lard sat on the bar. Jurgen said it helped absorb the lagers, bocks, and pilsners available from the row of beer taps against the back wall. The conversational level was usually low when I first arrived in the afternoon. As the evening wore on and as the faces at the bar and tables reddened, it grew in volume.

The bistro kitchen was separate from the restaurant kitchen below. I was shown where to scrape off the uneaten food into rubbish bins, and where to wash and dry them and the tableware. I helped the cook by rinsing heads of lettuce or slicing round loaves of bread. I arranged empty plates for the cook's orders and brought the plated food to the bartender to serve. I collected empty glasses and returned them to the bar, and dunked them in soapy water, swiveling them upside down on a brush fixed upright in the center of the sink, then rinsing them in another sink of continuously running water. It was hot, sweaty work and required maintaining a constant pace. A thin film of grease covered everything. It even hung in the air we breathed. The cook, a surly Catalán, seemed to always be annoyed with me. He barked at everyone in the kitchen in Spanish but raised his voice a few decibels when he grunted or spoke to me, as if my being American required it.

I had the mornings free to wander the town. After long breakfast chats with Mari, who wondered what she was going to do with herself, I headed out in unexplored directions, determined to see as much as possible. A large castle loomed over the town and the Neckar River below. It required an entry fee, for which I splurged only once. I was often drawn to the Holy Ghost Church, which was almost always closed, and was disappointed when I finally gained entrance. It was stripped of much of its original ornamentation and statuary and bore no signs of regular devotional use. The Reformation rendered many similar time-worn places of worship into empty museums.

Mainstreet shops displayed stylish clothing in novel ways; others offered tourist trinkets. There were a few "head shops" tricked out in marijuana-leaf décor with an array of pipes, bongs, and rolling papers – the kind of place that boasted of selling "everything you need except the weed." At first, I was confused by the number of Americans, especially African-Americans, until I discovered there was a US Army base nearby. I came across a bar that was popular with the GIs and would spend an hour or two there before reporting to work, drinking beer and listening to American radio announcers play the current US hits. The guys who came in swaggered a bit in the stiff way young soldiers do, reassuring each other of their kinship and delineating themselves from civilians in their vital role as defenders of the Berlin Wall. I listened in on conversations, but I didn't talk much with anyone, not wanting to betray my ignorance of military parlance. I also felt strangely out of place as someone living in a Spanish-speaking milieu, reluctant to have that known. I felt if I kept silent, I presented a passable profile, nodding for another pint and sitting in a confident slouch on my barstool, simply orbiting their space. I quietly soaked up American English, R&B, and heavy metal. I was grateful for the respite from all the inscrutable German – written and spoken – that surrounded me the rest of the day, pushing in against me with its impenetrability.

One evening, the bartender failed to show up at the bistro, and Jurgen was called to fill in for the night. After the kitchen closed, he asked me to take over for him because he wanted to go home. I protested. I didn't speak German, so how could I serve drinks to people whose language I didn't know? He laughed and handed me a wine and cocktail menu.

"Just point. They all have some English. And don't forget to keep the bread-and-lard tray filled."

It was, in its own minor way, a bit of excitement. The bistro was small, and most of the customers were regulars. I'd been there long enough to have been observed. I'd spoken to almost none of them but was assumed to be part of the Spanish help. I gamely took my place behind the bar, feeling a private flush of importance. When someone approached to order a drink, I improvised with hand gestures or by pointing at taps or bottles, often accompanied by a running commentary in English: "I guess you want another of those? Is this what you were drinking?" I learned *eins, zwei,* and *drei.*

A few – there were mostly men in the bistro – responded in English, earning a grateful smile and nod from me. They weren't there to interact with me, but they weren't put off by switching languages, either. It was a mildly pleasant turn, being barman, anticipating everyone's needs, inventing ways to discern those needs, pointing, smiling, pouring, cleaning, rinsing, stacking, drying. I'd been groomed for such utility since childhood: kitchen duty, alertness, helping out. The evenings passed pleasantly enough. Closing hours were early and non-negotiable – well before midnight during the week. Once we'd cleaned everything and readied it for the next morning, the kitchen crew often spent an hour or so shooting pool in a back room, pilfering a beer or two before heading home.

There was a turntable behind the bar, and the barman's tasks included keeping the music going when it seemed appropriate to the mood. Albums were rotated in a quasi-regular pattern. They were slightly dated – American Motown, Charles Aznavour, Jacques Brel, the kind of eclectic assortment popular in that era. On the third or fourth night that I was on duty, I decided to slip in the Neil Young *Crazy Horse* album I had salvaged from my trunk. It was a new sound that most of the customers would not have heard. It proved to be a crowd-pleaser. During his brilliant performance of *Everybody Knows This Is Nowhere*, as the guitar riffs morphed and mounted to anthemic heights, the room fell quiet. I turned up the volume. We all smiled and let the music dominate the bistro and the moment.

I didn't see the small, round table of three men off in the corner and turned to change the record back to the regular playlist. When I turned back to the bar, I saw them well enough. They were leaning forward against the bar, glaring at me. Before I could ask what they wanted to order, one of them grabbed my shirt front and pulled my face up close against his. He was crimson and teary, well inebriated. I seemed to vex him. It wasn't my first time aggravating someone by being me, and I was wise enough to know no logical argument would assuage him.

I started talking in a calm, steady voice, hoping to soothe the situation. His companions looked on, watching as if contemplating which way they thought the encounter might go: de-escalation or violence — as if waiting before placing a bet on their hunch. No one else in the bistro made any move to calm things down. It was clear that I could expect no allegiance in my moment of need. So I simply kept talking. I talked slowly and steadily until the tension eased out of the moment. His companions seemed to sense the storm passing, calmed him down, and got him to back away. They walked down the stairs and out the door. Other customers turned back to their drinks and resumed their interrupted conversations.

When I told Jurgen the next day what happened, he laughed it off. "A lot of people think there are too many Americans here," he shrugged. Mari thought it was just like the West Germans to do something like that. I didn't care to side with either attitude. I tucked in my wings a bit, kept a lower profile, and refused to serve behind the bar again.

Jessica's letter, when it came a few weeks later, couldn't have been more welcome. Yes, she wrote, come to New Jersey. I think I can get you a job where I'm teaching; they need bilingual teachers. I leave for South America in July. I'll be gone until the fall. You can have my apartment while I'm gone. I told Jurgen, and he came home a couple of days later with the news that he'd found a seat on a charter flight from Frankfurt to Hartford, Connecticut, for $85, within my means. It was leaving in six days. I wrote Jessica, telling her I'd find a way to get to East Orange. I was indebted to her, I gushed.

Jurgen borrowed someone's car for the drive to the Frankfurt airport. It was the last time I saw him or Mari. In spite of many attempts, I have lost contact with them.

Four

THE FLIGHT JURGEN FOUND WAS A CHARTER FOR A GROUP OF German clubs from the New York City area. When I asked what a German Club was, my fellow passenger said it wasn't so much a place to learn or practice German. Most people in the club didn't speak the language very well; it was more like a place to be among Germans. I took her literally and asked where most of the Germans had come from. What she meant, she clarified, was a place to be among other German-Americans, her own people. She, for one, lived in Union, New Jersey.

"Is that anywhere near East Orange?"

"Yeah, just down the Parkway."

"Oh, because that's where I need to get to. East Orange."

"We have a bus chartered to Union. You're welcome to ride with us."

Deus ex machina.

We landed in Hartford at 4 AM. No one was there to man the customs booths. We stood, sat, squatted, or lay down in an improvised queue for over an hour before someone finally appeared. I followed my German-American friend to the bus bound for Union, disoriented and staggering under the weight of my backpack. I slept through most of the trip while we hurtled along the greater New York metropolitan area's tangle of freeways, turnpikes, and bridges. We slipped off the Garden State Parkway and onto the Union rest area before nine that morning, pulling up next to a faux log-cabin shelter that offered a men's room, a women's room, and a phone booth.

I had no US coins on me, so I called Jessica collect. "Where, exactly, are you?" I put my new friend on the line, and the two of them sorted out the location. "Just wait there," Jess said.

She showed up soon enough, stepping out from behind the steering wheel as a tall, lanky guy unfolded from the other door. Jess and I hugged, reassuring ourselves and each other through the momentary awkwardness that I was happy to see her, and she was happy to see me. I reaffirmed my delight that things had worked out with another hug. She introduced her companion. John was in his mid-twenties, pale and bearded, with collar-length brown hair clinging close to his scalp and parted down the middle. He was diffident, nodding rather than offering his hand. I sensed instinctively he was there in lieu of Jack, the boyfriend she had spoken of so often in Spain, the boyfriend who called her back from Indiana for New Year's Eve. We got into the car and merged out onto the parkway. New Jersey seemed cemented over by multiple traffic lanes curving off in every direction, on-ramps, off-ramps, and toll booths sprouting up regularly. Eventually, we reached the East Orange off-ramp and rose suddenly up to street level, onto a tree-lined avenue. We parked in front of a three-story brownstone set back on a walkway from Prospect Avenue. I was back in America and sitting on Jessica's sofa.

I was unsure what to ask and what to wait to have explained. It was soon established that Jessica was going to South America with John. Jack was going to South America later, too, but with Neil. I hadn't yet met Neil. Were the four of them going to travel together? "We might meet up somewhere along the line." Jessica's voice trailed off. That was all I needed to hear. I dropped the subject.

Over the next few days several people came by to visit, to wish Jessica and John a bon voyage, and to surreptitiously check me out. A shared history held most of them together, forged through common college experiences. I could piece together that much. It was also clear that the bond was being tested as they moved forward, post-graduation. John was just returned from Vietnam, Neil was working on an advanced degree in Washington, and Jack was working for a speed-reading enterprise and often traveled out of town. He came by that first weekend. His hair tightly curled, his frame tall and wiry, Jack was quick-moving and teasing, as excitable and talkative as John was laconic. I had hoped Neil might provide some backstory to the evolving situation with Jack and John, but he remained vague on the topic when I broached it. He was vague, too, about what he expected to see in South America. In those first few days, I had the sense everyone was improvising his conversation. I waited for conversational openings, searching for something to add. To mention anyone I knew, other than Jessica – anything I had done or any place I had been – would have been a non-sequitur for them. I was simply Jessica's gay friend from her Junior year abroad.

Jessica took me to Summer Avenue Elementary School in Newark's North Ward, where she taught during the school year. She introduced me to Mrs. Dietz, the principal, and Ms. Mellows, the Latina coordinator of the bilingual program, both of whom were working through the summer. Jessica vouched for my character and encouraged me to speak up, to establish my credentials. Both of the women followed up with a few questions, as if conducting an interview on the fly. I had no basis on which to judge if I was making a positive or a negative impression.

Jessica and John went off to South America, leaving her apartment to me for the rest of the summer. It was comfortably roomy in an old, solid building with a large central hallway and a proper lobby. The East Orange business district, only a few blocks away, offered a diner, a pub, and a drug store among other amenities. The Newark *Star Ledger* was the paper of record, and I pored over its classified ads looking for a job, hoping for a chance to settle in. I needed to make some money, clear my loan, get a place on my own, and find my niche. New Jersey seemed pleasant enough. It was time to buckle down.

I got out of the apartment every day to buy the newspaper or simply roam the area to get my bearings. If I turned right when I left the building, I was on the campus of Upsala College, from which Jessica and her friends had graduated. Most of her male friends were members of something called the Camel Drivers. I assumed by its name that it was informal, perhaps an anti-Greek quasi-fraternity. I heard their references to what a Camel Driver would do in certain circumstances. They talked of Camel Driver meetings and Camel Driver history. It came to signify to me something I didn't belong to, something I wasn't meant to understand. It reminded me of my father's affiliation with the Elks, a secretive body that minted meaning through membership, a meaning not intended to be deciphered.

If I went farther up Prospect Avenue, beyond the Upsala campus, the neighborhood became predominantly black. A soft-ice-cream outlet a few blocks up from the campus sat back from the street like a drive-in. I sometimes walked there in the late afternoon for a treat. Many of the customers and employees were members of the Nation of Islam, a Black Muslim sect. They identified themselves by their dress. The women wore long-sleeved, enveloping clothing – floor-length skirts or body-length shifts – often with a hijab. The men wore sandals, loose-fitting, unstructured pants, and button-less pullover shirts that often reached down to the knees. The fabric was light-weight – appropriate for the summer weather – in white, brown, or muted solid colors. Some men were bearded and wore small, brimless caps. Everyone moved about in an un-self-conscious way, all part of something, their clothing said, of which I was not. Few people established eye contact with me, although I was generally treated properly as I queued up for a cone. I remember the humidity, the hot sun, and a sense of being somewhere other than New Jersey, somewhere more exotic.

One evening, as dusk was approaching after another day of intense heat, I sat out on the steps above the sidewalk in front of the apartment building. I was lost in a book that lay open across my knees. I felt a whizzing sensation pass by my left temple. I then heard glass shattering on the walkway behind me. I looked up to see a car pull away; one of its inhabitants, a black teenager, let out a whoop and turned his face away from me as the car drove off. He had tried to hit me with a soda bottle and nearly succeeded. I went back inside. From the moment that I boarded that chartered plane full of German-Americans seeking out each other through club affiliation, it felt to me that I kept getting the message that New Jersey was a tribal place, full of exclusionary zones.

The bus from East Orange to downtown Newark stopped at the intersection of Broad and Market. Bamberger's Department Store had a large clock on Market and Halsey, and if there were one spot that stood as the very center of the city, it seemed to be there. That summer marked five years since the 1967 riots. Broad and Market still offered all the elements of a once shiny and thriving mid-century metropolitan center, but it was now a grittier place. Penn Station, the City Building, and the Robert Treat Hotel, all nearby, were proof that there had been other, more affluent eras. Buses still shunted up and down the major streets, domes and spires still gleamed, and neon signs still shone. Bamberger's was still well-stocked, as was the nearby Kresge's, and streets still teemed with people. But the German immigrants who had built up the city in the late 19th century had moved out as newly immigrated Italians and Jews moved in. Later, African-Americans moved up from the South and started populating the Central Ward and downtown. They were now the largest ethnicity.

Everyone seemed content to go about his or her business. The store windows offered endless displays of ladies' wigs, formal gowns, and complicated dress hats that appealed to the tastes of a black clientele. The men's shirts were cropped by elastic waistbands and over-sized collars, their shiny synthetic textiles printed in intense color combinations and outsized geometric patterns. I marveled at the height of platform shoes, the breadth of the flared trousers, and the angled set of the broad-brimmed, rakish hats on the mannequins.

I liked the intensity and vitality of street life. Its din was layered and dense. I heard whistles and cat-calls that passing women elicited from groups of idle men and saw the insouciance of those same women as they flashed either amusement or annoyance at the attention. Regardless of the improprieties

shouted out – in cheeky admiration or just this side of bel-
ligerence – people seemed to take it all in stride, as if the
raucous, intrusively high volume was now acceptable on the
city's streets, as if windows would now open to air out some
passé formalities. I maintained a fixed gaze and a deliberate
posture. As a Caucasian, I had passed with little notice among
my neighbors in Valencia and rural France. In Newark, I was
indelibly in the minority. All the same, I found the place
compelling. I learned circumspection, and I adjusted.

Within less than three weeks, my job search led me to a
mid-rise building very near the intersection of Broadway and
Market. It housed the attorney offices of D'Agostino, Bretikopf,
& Tous, specialists in immigration law. I interviewed with the
senior partner, Mr. D'Agostino. He was remarkably short and
round, his ovate shape emphasized by his completely bald head.
I sat across from his desk while he pored over my resume, looking
concerned, scrunching his face a bit, sneaking a quick peek at me
from time to time as if to make a connection between what he
was reading and the applicant who was facing him. He chucked
the resume onto his desk.

"Are you going to keep wandering around? Are you one of
those lost souls who can't settle down, who doesn't know what to
do with himself?"

I wasn't sure why he asked me that. I saw little in my resume
that suggested wandering. There was Indiana. There was Spain.
There was Germany. That wasn't so much, was it?

"What are you doing in New Jersey?"

"Getting established," I answered, attempting to assure us both.

I later heard that Mr. D., as everyone called him, said he saw
in me the makings of an apprentice, a clay he could mold. He
offered me a job that same morning. The following Monday, my

first day at work, he introduced me to the staff and told me I was to train under Melba, the office manager. Melba had been with Mr. D. for more than 25 years. She specialized in working with the Greek-speaking clientele, of which there were very few left by then. I would work with Spanish-speaking clients, shepherd them through the immigration application process, and tailor the details of their life experiences in order to fit a few routinely-approved application categories. I would translate birth certificates and corroborating documents, attach affidavits affirming the accuracy of those translations, and have Melba, a notary public, sign and seal them. I would submit it all, along with filing fees, to the Immigration and Naturalization Office on Raymond Boulevard.

The clients were always anxious to explain their personal situation: where they came from, where they were living, what they hoped for, the obstacles they had overcome to get there, the determination they felt to stay, their still unmet needs, and more often than not, the emotional price all this flux and turmoil was costing them. They pleaded with me, offered me bribes, and all but groveled. I was habitually called Doctor, a Latino honorific for a lawyer. The level of deference was unsettling, and I did what I could to discourage it. I tried to put people at ease, to assure them I was doing everything possible to get their paperwork in order.

I was the lone male in the office pool once again. Graciela, from Buenos Aires, and Eti, from Lima, also worked with the Spanish-speaking clients, the vast majority of the firm's caseload. Inés, the Portuguese caseworker, was kept fairly busy, too. We chatted among ourselves in quiet moments, teasing each other about our accents, advising each other on client relations, providing tips on navigating the highly-Balkanized environment in which we lived and worked, offering advice on places to shop and to avoid. Inés told me about a butcher in the city's Ironbound section who had rental apartments on the market.

Mr. D. had frequent afternoon meetings with a State Senator who came to visit him, during which times we were instructed to stay away from his office. I was sometimes called in to Mr. Tous' office to take dictation in Spanish. His spelling and grammar needed focused attention. He was Cuban-born and spoke in that soft, legato accent to which I had become adjusted. He sometimes seemed befuddled about the logical next step in practical, non-legal matters. My process questions about his instructions seemed to help him get focused. This put me in good stead with him.

Mr. D. told me he had an excellent opportunity to offer me. His wife, Mrs. D – who looked at least 20 years younger than he – ran a program called Review Courses in Nursing. She needed an assistant in the evenings. The job, presented as something I was expected to accept, entailed ushering Mrs. D. into and out of rented conference rooms in the venerable Robert Treat Hotel several blocks away. I was to ensure that the students, almost exclusively Filipinas seeking US accreditation as nurses, moved efficiently from room to room as well, and to make certain the instructors, mostly white middle-class women, had the supplies they needed. More importantly, I was to usher Mrs. D. safely back at the end of the evening to her car in the hotel garage where she kept a Mercedes Benz convertible. Review Courses in Nursing was one of two regular clients leasing the hotel's conference rooms. The other was Amiri Baraka, formerly known as LeRoi Jones, a poet, activist, and founder of the Black Arts Movement. Loud, angry voices emanated from his seminar rooms, where a kind of group choreography included screaming and stomping. Everyone in the hotel gave them a very wide berth. They seemed to put Mrs. D. on edge.

I rode the bus back home in the evenings. The route ran up through the Central Ward, wending through a large swathe of land cleared for the New Jersey Medical School, only partly constructed at the time. The general devastation left behind by the riots and an air of abandonment still clung to the neighborhood. The housing stock that remained habitable was startling for its level of neglect and decay. It formed a grim, uninterrupted backdrop out the bus window. The people packed densely inside with me were mostly black, expressionless and passive, tired from a day on the job, icily indifferent to the tall, slim white boy in their midst. As the bus rose uphill along the city streets toward East Orange, the first major suburb, billboards floated by. They promoted Kools or Salems and showed handsome, smiling, dark-skinned models enjoying a game of tennis or a pool-side meal. Lit cigarettes in their hands, with dazzling white teeth, perfectly-coiffed afros, and well-tailored wardrobes glistening in the sunshine, everyone was shown laughing under bright blue skies. Look, the billboards seemed to say, how winning our smiles are, how handsome our features, how varied our skin tones, how hip, how brassy, how desirable we are. They hovered over everything like a public affirmation, a positive cultural iconography re-imagining the neglected state that haunted the many still hoping to struggle their way out of the Central Ward.

I needed to vacate Jessica's apartment before she returned, so I took a trip one Saturday to the Ironbound to find Lo Biondo, the butcher Inés had told me about. The neighborhood was named for the elevated train tracks that cut off its streets and sidewalks from the rest of the city. Once populated by Italian families, now, increasingly, it was an enclave of Portuguese, Spanish, and South American newcomers. Ferry Street was its commercial heart, and that's where I found Lo Biondo, standing behind his glass-fronted counter in a white apron. He posed a series of scrutinizing questions – where I was from, why did I need an apartment, where did I work? I had already passed his initial, *sine qua non* test by simply being white. Sure, Lo Biondo had a few places available. He'd show me some.

I put a deposit down on a ground-floor apartment in a row-house on Jefferson Street. It was on the very edge of the Ironbound. An elevated rail-bed spanned Jefferson Street just next to the buildings, the last ones before Raymond Boulevard and the Passaic River. The only thing between my door and the river was a scrap-metal yard, a large liquor store with off-street parking, and the boulevard's constant traffic. It sat as the last in a row of six identical houses dating from the 1880s or '90s, each converted to three one-bedroom flats, one above the other. They were in serious disrepair. Aluminum siding and single-pane replacement windows had been slapped onto the exteriors to hide their rough state. Inside the front door, a stairway led up to two other apartments. My apartment entry was a door behind that stairway. It opened into the original kitchen, a small corner of which had been roomed off to accommodate a toilet and shower stall. Painted pipes from the water heater rose up through a hole in the ceiling to service the apartments on the second and third floors. The other two rooms were a bedroom – once the house's dining room – and a sitting room, in the center of which sat a gas boiler the size of a large office desk. Its ductwork was vented up the fireplace flue. When the boiler kicked on, a rush of flaming gas across the fire grill made hearing the television difficult. Intense heat filled the living room, even when the kitchen was freezing. I came to discover a severe rodent infestation. At night a few rats scurried around in the dark. When surprised by my suddenly turning on the lights, they clawed up the water heater pipes through the ceiling, turning a beady red eye to glare at me for a moment before leaving.

But it was my own place, and I could walk downtown in twenty minutes. I liked the neighborhood. Most of the shops, cafes, and restaurants were Spanish- or Portuguese-speaking. In the 18 apartment units in my row, I was the only native English speaker. Almost everyone else spoke Portuguese, some with a Brazilian accent. After I had a telephone installed, I sometimes got calls for people in other units who gave out my number because I was so friendly and spoke English so well.

One Friday afternoon in February at D'Agostino, Bretikopf, & Tous, the new coordinator of the bilingual program at Summer Avenue phoned me. She had an immediate position available, newly funded, that required teaching fourth grade through sixth grade in both English and Spanish. I accepted immediately. Within the hour, I walked into Mr. D's office and told him what had transpired. He was furious.

"I treated you like a son," he yelled. "Get out. If you're going to leave, get out now!"

I returned to my desk to clear out a few personal items. Melba motioned me over to her. She said I had to settle petty cash, one of the many niggling responsibilities that fell to me as the last hire. I fumbled through the receipts, and I was $17 short. I couldn't figure out what happened.

Mr. D. came storming out of his office, stalking toward the front door. He saw me still at my desk, hunched over the petty cash box.

"What are you doing here?"

Melba intervened. "He's settling up petty cash."

He turned to her. "I treated him like a son. Like my own son. He could have had a career here. He could have studied law. He's a drifter. I saw that when I hired him."

Melba kept her head down, looking at a distant spot on the floor in that practiced way of hers. Mr. D. waved his arms about for another short while, then stomped out the front door. I ended up having the $17 deduced from my last paycheck before Melba cut it, no small sum for someone earning $6,000 a year. As I took the hand-written check, it occurred to me that Melba probably knew what happened to the petty cash.

Two years later, I read in the Newark *Star Ledger* that Mr. D., Mr. Tous, and Melba were all indicted by a federal grand jury "in a scheme to provide false documents and job offers for aliens in pursuit of permanent residence in the United States."

Like a son, he said he treated me.

Five

IN CONTRADICTION TO MY EARLIER DICTUM – YOU DON'T RETURN to a place as the same person you were before you left – I did experience one exception. The first day I went through the doors of Summer Avenue Elementary I became my twelve-year-old self again. I already knew the building's wide wooden floorboards. I knew its powdery-slate blackboards and large, multi-pane windows letting weak winter sun stream across dusty radiators. I knew the top-hinged desks lined up in fussy-straight rows, the presidential silhouettes, and the American flag thumb-tacked high on the wall. I was back in school in Jefferson, Indiana. Only this time around I was standing at the front of the room, looking out at the students as if searching for myself among them.

Miss Nicastro was introducing me as the new team teacher.

I fumbled for the right place to put my hands as the roomful of children stared at me. All I could think to do was smile. She had received me decently when she learned I was assigned to her classroom, noting that the "team" in my title denoted a subordinate role. She told me she welcomed the help, although she didn't think lessons in Spanish were really necessary. She said she was worried I was too green to handle discipline – her major professional focus. Her technique, which she urged upon me, was to squelch all physical movement in the classroom from time to time. In such moments every activity, even lining up for lunch, should be reviewed aloud, each time in great detail describing how it should be executed. If there were any deviations in the execution, everyone was to return to his or her seat, and the process was to begin again, after a thorough review of what went wrong.

Miss Nicastro was a large Italian-American woman, single and of a certain age. She stood firmly in her pleated skirts and sensible shoes. Her main personal interest was pari-mutuel betting, and she never tired of letting me know how she had most recently fared with the horses. She was steadfast in her dedication to her North Ward Italian neighborhood and her chosen career, even as successive decades brought more and more recent arrivals from the Caribbean, students whose families spoke Spanish at home and whose aunts and uncles had no interest in the horses.

"And when I'm not here, you're going to treat Mr. Juday just the way you treat me. Aren't you?"

"Yes, Miss." The response was choral in its pitch and tempo.

I had signed up for, but did not complete, a course in educational psychology my sophomore year at Ball State. I found the syllabus vague and the theories amorphous, and by mid-term I decided its intent eluded me. I dropped out, taking an incomplete rather than lowering my grade point average, a decision that meant I was not getting a teaching degree. Now, on my first day as a teacher, without proper accreditation, even as I lacked proper standing, I was already sensing things weren't going well. This insistence on authority above all else was not the tone I wanted.

Miss Nicastro had no interest in the Spanish grammar or the Puerto Rican history I taught and excused herself once I began the lessons, at first watching from the back of the room, then from the hallway, in time slowly inching herself toward the teacher's lounge. Rapport between the students and me seemed good. I tried a few jokes, asked a few questions, and made an effort to loosen things up. The kids liked having a "*maestro*" they could talk to in Spanish, liked watching me evolve through this formative period, at the end of which they might even come to accept me as a teacher, if not this year, maybe next.

One afternoon a crisis befell Miss Canowith across the hall. She sat on a pencil that seriously punctured her posterior and needed to go to the emergency room. Could Miss Nicastro have Mr. Juday fill in for her? I entered her classroom with less than a month's experience under my belt and addressed Miss Canowith's students – African American, English-speaking, urban born and reared – with the same posture that was working for me so far across the hall. But the class was half-crazed by the hilarity of what had happened. All hell broke loose. I was immediately challenged by a boy who defied my call for him to return to his seat. The challenge drew loud guffaws, which signaled that everyone was free to do whatever they wanted. I stood to my fullest height and engaged my most stentorian voice, to no avail. The din in the room was so loud Miss Nicastro had to come in to re-establish discipline, something her bearing seemed to pull off all by itself. She smiled the smug smile of vindication. It was my first lesson in authority.

After two months' monitoring by Ms. Nicastro, I was given a schedule that had me moving among several classrooms of fourth, fifth, and sixth graders throughout the day and week. I provided Language Arts and Social Studies in Spanish for Spanish-dominant students. I discovered in some classrooms, only half the students had ever fully understood the English instruction they were exposed to all day. I can't imagine what test scores must have shown, even in an era when test scores were fudged or explained away as immaterial in the face of rapid social upheaval. I found myself becoming more and more pedantic, insisting the children use proper grammar and vocabulary, a nearly impossible challenge so late in their multilingual and often chaotic lives. There were idiomatic differences among them, but after a year or so living in the US, they converged on a patois Spanish heavily skewed by English. I was once told by a sixth-grader, "*Maestro, el roofo está leakiando*" – the roof is leaking. Neither *roofo* or *leakiando* has roots in Spanish, nor does the sentence structure itself.

Where I lacked training and expertise, I tried to compensate with enthusiasm. Moving around the classroom, gesticulating, throwing in asides in a bet-you-didn't-know-that manner, all but singing and dancing, I held their attention. They tolerated me and went along with my shtick. The teachers I relieved for an hour or two a few times a week were grateful for the break it afforded them and demanded little of me beyond that. Occasionally they sat in the back of the room while I taught, taking notes. I supposed that they were writing evaluations, none of which were shared with me, which meant I still wasn't getting training in educational technique.

A core group of us younger teachers, including Jessica, gathered early in the mornings before class. We chatted in the cafeteria over coffee and cigarettes and often lunched together in the teacher's lounge, too. Many of us were single. Our weekends were free. Occasionally someone threw a party. Notes were passed around via students sent from classroom to classroom with invitations and details about time and venue. Diane was a great animator of the group. She lived in the same apartment in Bellevue where John and Jess had moved to. Her mother was the superintendent there. I sometimes spent Saturday afternoons between the two apartments, visiting Jessica, then Diane and her partner Malcolm, who was English. Malcolm had "jumped ship" from the British merchant marines a couple of years earlier, one more among a multitude of illegal residents. He was a ceaseless raconteur, and we became drinking buddies. Paulie was another of the young teachers, as were Torpey and Pat. Pat was a tall, light-skinned, freckled woman with a cotton-candy Afro, half Irish-American and half African American. She had a glamorous bone structure and poise. She was a substitute teacher sent from the Board of Ed to Summer Avenue on a temporary assignment.

I rode with Jess to one of Pat's parties in East Orange. Her small apartment was on the top floor of a converted single-family home. When she opened the door, an LP by a salsa group called *Ocho* was playing. It was top-drawer, genuine, funky *caliente* salsa. We soon threw ourselves into dancing. Pat's style was cool and aloof. At some point later in the evening we sat in front of her television. Martin Luther King, Jr. was delivering his *I've Been to the Mountaintop* speech. This couldn't have been on video; there was no videotape then. It makes me think the party might have been arranged around this re-broadcast. King was five years dead, most of which time I had spent overseas. Now I was living in Newark, a black city, surrounded by black culture, daily navigating racial politics and steeped in the idealism promulgated by an integrated school system. I heard King's speech in a fresh way.

When Bobby Kennedy spoke in Indianapolis the night of King's assassination, he had been the focus of my attention, a leader rising to a crisis. At Pat's party, King was the focus, and I heard for the first time how deep the religious traditions were behind his plaint for dignity and justice. So resonant was his argument, so true and unadulterated was the place from which it sprung, so melodious was its expression, that it tapped into the well each of us has, just below our placid surface, no matter our self-regard. I wept tears in the way humans do, wired as we are with a universal knowledge of justice. I felt deep remorse for not having understood all this before. Pat looked as if she wanted to console me, as if she grasped the enormity of these things, too, and she was watching me awaken to them.

I remained captivated by the infectious music of *Ocho*. I sourced the LP downtown the next week and played it in what DJs call heavy rotation. I told Pat how often I was playing it. One morning she popped her head into my classroom to tell me that *Ocho* was playing at a club that Saturday in the Central Ward. I said, "you're on."

I think I took a cab to the club though I might have walked. It wasn't far from the Medical Center, a handful of blocks beyond my old law office. When I entered the club, a converted storefront, I realized I was, so far, the only white person in the room. I determined to keep a low profile. Pat was already seated and talking to some people at the next table. When I sat down to join her, their conversation trailed off. No other white person came in to what turned out to be a very popular venue. I was relieved when the band finally started the gig. They were brilliant, and for two hours they lifted up the room and took it – and us – to the Caribbean. After an initial reluctance, I joined Pat on the dance floor and let myself drift along with the music. No one looked at me directly, and there was no friendly chat with anyone near our table. I decided the best thing to do was to ride the night out and stay focused on the band members, some of whom smiled at me from time to time.

When *Ocho* left the stage and the lights rose, we slowly stood up in ones and twos, adjusting to the changed ambiance. We pulled on coats and fumbled for gloves and hats. I knew the sooner I left, with minimum fuss, the better. I put on my long, nubby-wool overcoat, the one my landlady in Valencia called my bathrobe. I stepped out the front door, and to the best of my recollection, someone asked if I had seen Oliver. The question made no sense to me. It was in that moment when I turned to ask him to repeat his question that I took the first blow. I heard Pat scream. Blankness after that, no doubt due to the pummeling I sustained from a handful of men. I can remember nothing except finding myself moving away from the front of the building, down the street a short way, and into the gutter as I continued to be hit both in the face and the stomach. It is odd how the body absorbs that kind of thing. I don't remember how the blows felt when they landed. I only remember that they were moving me along this trajectory.

Ultimately, I fell backward into the gutter at the edge of the sidewalk. The beating stopped and I had my first lucid moment since it began. I lay still, taking stock. I wasn't dead. The worst seemed over. That was when a handful of women started screaming, leaning over my prone, woolen-wrapped body, beating at it with their purses, as if in some kind of coda to the men's blows. I bore the purse-slapping for a few minutes. It wasn't violent so much as contemptuous. Then I stood up, tightened the belt around my waist, and declared, "That's enough." The windmill of purses stopped. I walked off down the middle of the deserted street, alert for any sign of someone pursuing me. I moved at a deliberate pace to show I was offended and would tolerate no more of that behavior.

I don't know how many blocks I walked, determined not to collapse. It was very late, and that part of the city was deserted. A fire station lay ahead, only another block now. I knew I needed to get off the street. I approached the side of the building along an alley and peered into a small window from which light shown. There were two firemen inside – one white, one black – sitting at a table, and I tapped on the window. They looked out at me, and I saw alarm on their faces. I felt relief. I had worried about what I would say. I had no plan. Their startled look and the speed with which they brought me in let me know that I no longer had to sort it all out by myself. I was so grateful, so relieved. They eased me onto a gurney and up into an ambulance. I was ready to sleep now.

I spent the night in the hospital, in the emergency room. A loud drunk resisted every effort to attend to him. I remember the splattering sound his nearly naked body made as he rolled out of his gurney and hit the cement flooring after a four-foot drop. For my part, I was grateful for everything – for the lights, for the cessation of blows, for medical attention. I even admired the detachment with which it was administered. Everyone in this room is a saint, I remember thinking. I had a broken nose, sore ribs, a bruised skull, and a severe concussion. Bed rest, they said. Your own doctor can see to the nose. By then it was in a taped-over splint.

Diane and Malcolm appeared in my hospital ward the next day. Diane said Pat had phoned them early in the morning, distraught, telling them what happened. Diane started phoning local area hospitals. I never saw Pat again after stepping out of the club, after someone asked me if I had seen Oliver, after I heard her scream. I phoned her a few times over the following weeks, but she never answered. She was soon reassigned to another school. She told Diane she went up and down the alleyways around the nightclub looking for me. In point of fact, my slow departure down the middle of the street would have been quite visible to everyone. Some people later said that I had got my comeuppance. If so, I had been too clueless to know it was due me. I always wondered if Pat saw that night as her comeuppance. I have to believe she was, in some way, disillusioned.

Diane and Malcolm insisted I spend a week under their care. Diane had deep roots in her Italian community. Like many people who have grown up in crowded, multi-ethnic, contentiously zoned urban neighborhoods, she shared her tribe's reflexes and grievances, essentially borne of territorialism. She had connections to the mafia, she implied, and her first idea was to turn to them to sort out who was to blame, to exact revenge. I insisted I wanted nothing to do with getting even. I was worried about escalation, among other things. It was over. It happened. I'd be alright. My focus was to see a doctor about the nose and concussion, and to rest. Diane said she would tell the school office what happened. I pleaded with her not to tell the children I had been beaten.

"Please, tell the kids I was in a car wreck. I don't want them to know about this."

By midweek Diane brought home hand-drawn get-well cards the kids had made for me. There were several – mostly from the boys – that showed a stick figure flying up from the front of crudely drawn automobiles. The stick figure was labeled "Maestro." Some of the girls drew a stick figure resting in a hospital bed, next to which sat multi-colored flowers in vases. "Get well soon, Maestro." I was grateful Miss Nicastro went along with the ruse.

Although I hadn't anticipated the danger of being in that nightclub with Pat, the more I ruminated on it, the more I started to wonder what was true. Should I have known better? Should I have left earlier in the evening? Could I have? Maybe, just going there was asking for trouble. That was certainly the message intended for me. I had been naive, at the very least. This line of thinking, of course, indicated the onset of post-traumatic stress disorder. Another symptom was the anxiety about retribution and the fear of my assailants' outrage. It was important to preserve a veneer of normality for the kids. If I could be certain they remained ignorant of the cause of my injuries, if all remained hidden, that would be sufficient. For months after the event, I was on edge whenever an unknown black man looked at me in public for too long. I would start to worry he recognized me from the club, that he still wanted revenge. The fear lingered for a long time. I was lucky to overcome it. Fear doesn't always go away.

Just as my mother wrote to me after her trip to Spain, I phoned my parents to tell them I had been mugged. I could have let that news go unreported. I used the word "mugged" because mugging implies a hit-and-run robbery; my beating came of racial animus and outrage at the appearance of miscegenation. The compulsion to tell them stemmed in part from concern they'd find out anyway. It may have also been a play for sympathy. With whom else should a boy seek to share his trauma, if not his mother and father? I think now it was also a response to the aborted boxing match in the kitchen with my brother so many years before, to all the snickering about Ferdinand the Bull, to the countless incidents where my courage had been challenged. I had withstood a major beating as if passing a test, a hazing preliminary to manhood. I described the actual beating and my medical condition, and took pains to assure them it was nothing and that I was fine. Whatever the reason, I told them.

Summer Avenue Elementary was renamed Roberto Clemente Elementary that spring. The rededication honored the Puerto Rican baseball player and humanitarian killed in a plane crash the previous winter. The name-change was recognition that Puerto Ricans now dominated that sector of the North Ward. In an era of rapid political realignment, they wanted that ascendancy recognized. The renaming ceremony was exciting for the kids, but they had less perspective than the adults, who rightly saw their growing influence in a City Hall dominated by African-Americans. Due to tenure rules, the faculty within the school did not reflect those demographic shifts. Some of the teachers, many Italian and Jewish, carried on as if the world outside their classroom door was unchanged. In fairness, some responded to the moment with their best selves.

The young family living in the apartment just above mine on Jefferson Street had recently come from Brazil, although Tony, the husband and father, was Portuguese by birth. Tony never talked much about how he ended up in Brazil, where he met his wife, Isaira, or how they and their three children came to Newark. They moved onto Jefferson Street, as the saying goes, straight off the boat, and I was clued in enough to immigration issues not to push the subject. None of them spoke a word of English when they arrived. The eldest daughter, approaching puberty, was dark-haired and shy. The youngest, the only boy, was doe-eyed and moody. Their timorous nature made me wonder about the heavy-handed discipline I occasionally heard coming from their apartment overhead.

I didn't speak Portuguese but Tony's Iberian (versus Brazilian) version of it, with enunciated consonants and a close kinship to Castilian, allowed me to develop a serviceable form of it. I translated and interpreted for him as best I could, offering advice about public services and community amenities. Tony was a bit like his son, doe-eyed and moody as well. One minute he would be full of braggadocio, crooning about how wonderful this new life was going to be for him and his family. Then, just as precipitously, he'd collapse under new worries and doubts. His mood swings ranged from "O, *rapaz*" – Oh, lad – "it's going to be so fantastic," to "Oh, Daniel, what am I going to do?" I would offer formulaic assurances that things would work out fine. I had my own struggles, too, but I had social advantages that served to buoy my confidence.

Tony and Isaira had Portuguese friends who sometimes came over to barbecue smelts and sardines behind the house, where the ground was strewn with rubble and broken glass. They spoke not about their current lives, but about the *saudade* – the pain of nostalgia – that they held for the old country. By gathering together they reconstructed a few moments of that world in our harsh, brick-and-soot neighborhood, among railroad tracks and scrap-metal yards. I was always welcome to join in and did on a few occasions. Mostly I lived on white rice, black beans, and canned asparagus. My kitchen was ill-equipped for much else. Isaira worried that I had no wife to cook for me. Every Sunday afternoon she invited me up for roasted chicken and pasta in tomato sauce. We shrugged off the strain under which each of us lived most days. We were loud and no doubt repetitive in our Portuguese/Spanish mix. By early evening a fair amount of wine had been consumed, and we would sit in Tony and Isaira's bedroom where they kept the television and watch Sonny and Cher. As the room darkened and the kids sat in the TV glow soaking up their newly adopted culture, we eased back in a tried-and-tested ritual that got us through the week, relishing its reliability.

New York City was a short walk up Ferry Street to Newark Penn Station, where the PATH train went directly to midtown at 33rd Street Station or downtown to the World Trade Center. It was a grim ride across the polluted Passaic River and over the New Jersey Meadowlands, dotted with abandoned factories and spanned by rusted railroad spars, and the even rustier Pulaski Skyway. Once the train entered the tunnel that burrowed under North Bergen, once we were cut off from New Jersey sunlight, the city began, dark and subterranean. Either destination, downtown or midtown, led to an underground complex of train lines I never really understood. I knew how to get uptown because I knew the number-line: 55th Street was uptown from 33rd Street. I knew Central Park began at 59th Street. I knew Times Square was around 42nd. I had no idea which numbered or lettered train to take. I fumbled my way among thousands of strangers in the funk and heat, negotiating turnstiles and multiple platforms.

I went up into the World Trade Center once. I wandered into its main lobby and braved the express elevator up to the Windows on the World Restaurant, as if I were contemplating a bite to eat one hundred floors above the pavement. When I stepped out at the top I saw waiters walk by balancing large trays while adjusting for the building's undeniable sway at that height. I saw them shuttle their trays with the dexterity of seamen swabbing decks in a swell. I immediately took the next elevator car down and regained my composure only after exiting the building.

I found Spanish-language movie theaters on Seventh Avenue. Over time I must have walked the entire length of the Met, the Guggenheim, and the Frick, even if I rushed through many of their galleries only half alert. I developed a fondness for Japanese noodle joints and Jewish delis. I strolled up and down Christopher Street in the Village many an afternoon, nervously browsing its bookstores but not daring to enter any of the dozens of gay bars there. I settled for being in their proximity, fearing whatever there was to fear in everyone's confident posture as they went in and out of them. In warm weather on many Sunday afternoons, I ended up in Central Park near the Umpire Rock, sitting on its granite outcroppings watching dark-skinned young men, shirtless and sweaty, drumming on bongos and congas, putting everyone in a trance.

I took Tony and his family on day-trips to the city, too. We went to Central Park Zoo, the Empire State Building, and onto the Staten Island Ferry. The first time we passed the Statue of Liberty, Tony's eyes glazed and his face reddened.

"*O, rapaz. A Liberdade.*" It was such a moving sigh, prompted by the sight of the universal icon. I heard the sigh tinged with pining. I wondered – as surely he did – whether freedom lay behind him or before him.

Six

AT THE END OF THE SCHOOL YEAR I LEARNED MY CONTRACT would be renewed for the following September, but I needed to get through the summer. Lourdes, the new bilingual coordinator, found a secretarial job for me at a school in the Central Ward that was running a trial program that summer. It was to be administered by a friend of hers, and she thought we would be a good fit. During the school year, its student population was predominantly African American. The program was an acknowledgment that there were unaddressed needs among the Latino minority. Because the courses were limited to Spanish-dominant students, the school wouldn't suffer the usual overcrowding. The teaching staff would be assembled from other schools, precluding the usual cliques of entrenched vs. newcomers. The principal was Cuban, a very affable man, efficient and well-intentioned. Lourdes was right; I had the necessary skills, and we forged a good relationship. Most of the teachers seemed surprised to find an Anglo on staff. They often affected not to see me standing behind the office counter in front of them, notwithstanding my six-foot-one-inch frame. I had to learn to be pro-active, introducing myself, and offering assistance.

One of the teachers who did notice me was Pedro. He was friendly and ready with a quick laugh. He was in those days called *prieto* – perhaps a term not used any more – which my *Pequeño Larousse Ilustrado* defines as "very dark, almost black." He was short, a feature ironically accentuated by the platform shoes everyone wore at the time, and he wore his hair in a close-cut afro. I found him charming. I lived in *de facto* celibacy at a stage in life in which celibacy does not come naturally. I may have been responding to the warm summer weather. Whatever the impetus, I determined to get closer to Pedro. I signaled this in subtle ways, balancing between discretion and forthrightness. My efforts included inventing excuses a few times to visit his classroom *ex officio*. He got my drift soon enough.

Unsure of the best next step, I boldly invited him to dinner, to the apartment where I could cook nothing but beans and rice. It is a measure of how oblivious I was to gay signaling – indeed, to any sexual code – that I didn't immediately see his accepting the invitation as a positive response. Instead, I fretted over the food. I combed the best bodegas up and down Ferry Street to piece together a presentable assortment of meats, cheeses, and breads. I bought both white wine and red. I brought in some beer as well, unsure of his preference, not wanting to ask. I displayed all this on the kitchen table just as my mother would have prepared for one of her afternoon bridge-club parties. When Pedro saw the array of food and drink he looked surprised and asked who else was coming. I assured him no one else was. As it turned out, most of the food and drink went untouched. More pressing issues were in train.

We spent time with each other over the course of that summer. He came to my place, or I went to his. He shared a large two-bedroom apartment on the top floor of a mid-rise near the edge of the North Ward with a friend who was also a teacher. The view from their floor-to-ceiling windows took in the Passaic River and parts of Kearney and Harrison, ethnically demarcated inner suburbs. Pedro and his roommate threw large parties fueled by salsa music, great food, and plenty of alcohol. The guests were almost all Latino, mostly gay men, with a few lesbians coming by from time to time. Over the course of a Saturday evening, the apartment slowly filled with young men more or less my age. My presence signaled I, too, was gay, and I looked for the camaraderie they seemed to extend to each other. But word went around that I was seeing Pedro, and it was as if I blended in with the furniture, sparse as it was.

One night we all gathered at Pedro's and left *en masse* for a popular gay disco in Harlem, up around 150th. We walked to Penn Station, onto the PATH, and then into an uptown subway. The club was on the second floor of an abandoned commercial building, and access was up a long, narrow stairwell. Upstairs, under the shards of light cast by a suspended disco ball, salsa ruled. At least a hundred men were paired off. Each one's arms were raised, one to his partner's waist and one to his shoulder, head held high, back straight and hips in sway: *one, two three*, hold, *five, six seven*, hold, *one, two three*, hold, *five six, seven*, hold. Pedro and I stepped out onto the surface of the music and joined them, sweaty and impervious to Harlem downstairs and outside.

Eventually, the music stop and the lights went up. Most everyone understood what was happening before I did. A general rush started toward the narrow exit, like the Sunday morning bottle-neck trying to get out of church while people in front stopped to talk to the priest. The push from behind grew stronger. Agoraphobia set in. The climb down the stairwell was clumsy, fitful, and physically awkward. Harlem street was badly lit and nearly empty and we clustered together for safety. Once in the subway, most of our party jumped the turnstile. I didn't want to lose the crowd and jumped, too, fearful I would be fined, although nobody on the subway platform at that hour would have dared detain us. Telling myself that didn't allay my qualms. I was moving along with mindless gate jumpers in a heightened state of alarm. When the PATH pulled into Newark I went directly home from Penn Station, grateful to be back there without having been crushed in a crowd, arrested in the subway, or mugged on the streets. I needed to recalibrate. This was not my style.

The last time I saw Pedro was at his apartment. He had been in Puerto Rico for a couple of weeks visiting family, and his roommate threw a welcome-back party. By then, I knew a few of the people there and talked for a while with some of them. Pedro avoided me the entire evening, brushing away my attempts at conversation and insisting on dancing with almost everyone else. With this as a signal, other men began to approach me, hitting on me as if I were on my own that evening. The scene had shifted. I saw the choreography. The tacit truth was that these men were not here for camaraderie. They were in a shared bunker, huddling together in a place where they could turn a few heads and be fetching and sought after, all within the safety of Pedro's place. These were men who had been hiding secrets since boyhood. If they acted provocatively, it was an ironic, partially feigned provocation. It was a performance.

I walked out through the crowd, Pedro still in its midst, took the elevator down to the lobby, and made my way back to the Ironbound, if not wiser, then with fewer illusions. I had been in a strange land where monogamy was something to be mocked, in a land where men, responding to a life-time of public smirks and smutty references to their natural instincts, had turned to acting out ritualized self-denial. In their rudderless state they flaunted the norms under which they had been reared. They elevated physical beauty and thrived on conquest but scorned anyone looking for happy-ever-aftering. They prized the lothario and mocked the naif.

The heavy Hispanic immigration coming to the North Ward was providing me a unique opportunity. My race and gender were, counterintuitively, in my favor. The bilingual program was staffed almost entirely by Latinas, most of them Puerto Rican. To have a Spanish-speaking Anglo male on staff technically countered charges of racial or gender exclusion. If I was a token, I was also an employee in good standing of the Newark Board of Education bilingual program and the National Teacher's Organization, and I had the full support of Roberto Clemente. My Achilles' heel was that incomplete certification. I had to get to work on getting credentialed to keep my contract. I needed several education courses offered at Newark State Teachers College in Union Township. Without a car, this required riding the commuter train from Penn Station, after a long day of teaching, to Elizabeth, then a bus from Elizabeth to the college. I committed to it reluctantly, and soon became inured to a twice-weekly litany at Penn Station, waiting for my train among the men commuting home from New York who clutched small brown-paper bags with the evening's first relief: Elizabeth, Rahway, Metuchen.

When September came around, I was happy to learn that I would have my own classroom. Fourth-grade. We would be housed at the Boy's Club annex. Roberto Clemente itself, two blocks away, was overcrowded. My classroom was fitted to accommodate thirty-five students. As part of the renovations, they had installed chalkboards and desks, and built bookshelves across the back wall. It was all I needed to set up a fiefdom. With a few days' preparation I covered the bulletin with "Language is a Bridge Between People," featuring a bridge modeled on the Brooklyn Bridge, the very essence of bridgedom. It bore lots of little people in various shades of black, brown, and pink, crossing from one side to the other. I wrote out the alphabet across the top of the blackboard in my best cursive – both capital and lower-case. I pinned an American flag above it all, to which we would recite "I pledge allegiance" every morning in English, then "*Prometo andar*" in Spanish.

I was assigned a teacher's aide. Aida was a young woman of 19 or 20, recently arrived from Puerto Rico with no post-secondary education. Her function was to help keep the classroom calm and orderly, a mothering presence I suppose. Aida proved to be of very little use. She sat in a chair against the far wall smiling beatifically at the backs of the children's heads. No one approached her outside of recess, and she seldom interacted with anyone. When the kids were with her, it was as if they were doing the mothering. It took me until Halloween to realize that she came to work stoned most days and went home for lunch to smoke another joint. By Christmas she decided to return to Puerto Rico to stay.

Keeping the calm was mission one. Heretofore I was a roaming teacher, a novice auditioning to become a real one. I had no turf of my own. This year I did. I was determined to establish my authority. There were so many children – the number at one point swelling so that a few had to share a desk. Now I was the one who said nothing would begin until order was established. And established it was, through my persistence, my height, my flair for sudden and startling noises, and my oddness. My Spanish was morphing. I was losing the distinctive Castilian "theta," and I dropped the use of *vosotros* – a form of "you" used only in Spain. At least I tried to make these adjustments. I slipped up often enough that the kids were thrown off, unable to peg exactly what planet I came from. This, too, became useful. It gave me an edge.

In spite of my authoritarian shake-down, the children's best spirits shone through. They were bright and social, grateful not to be dealing with the chaos we heard seeping in from other classrooms. I was diligent in preparing both English and Spanish lesson plans for the week, tying spelling words to reading assignments, and prepping special lessons on topics the kids showed random interest in: moths, ancient Romans, Latin-American Revolutions. On Fridays I covered everyone's desktop with a fresh sheet of butcher-paper and asked them to draw the last dream they could remember, or the nicest place they ever visited, or the smartest person in their family. We had a coffee tin filled with crayons for those who couldn't afford their own. Some talked privately to me about what they were drawing. Some were more than happy to stand up and explicate their work for the entire class. On Friday afternoons, in those last hours when everyone was nearly bursting in anticipation of the weekend, we played multiplication baseball. I assigned different teams every week, and when a child came up to bat, I pitched a formula.

"Three times six."

"Eighteen" would get you to first base; anything else sent you back to your batting order with a "strike" for the error. Bases were designated at the center of each of the four walls, and a base hit allowed a dash across the room to burn up a little energy. Whispered coaching was tolerated when the pressure was on, and a good amount of cheering went up as we approached the ninth inning in a close race. Booing was not allowed. *Rely on your teammates, support each other.*

Monitors from the Board of Ed popped in sometimes. We conspired to present our best selves on those days. It was always a stiff, formal exchange but respectful all around. The kids regaled the *maestro* with their best behavior. There was never a Spanish-speaker in the review group, just as there were no Spanish-language textbooks. The kids knew switching from English to Spanish and back to English presented the best argument for a bilingual program. I was never audited by Mr. Marshall, our beleaguered, warm-hearted principal, the first black principal in the school's history. The Boys Club annex fell into the assistant principal's bailiwick. He was a blond, small-boned, stiff-backed former Army officer with a trace of an Appalachian twang, given his post as a sinecure after his military retirement. He wandered in from time to time, ostensibly taking notes he never shared with me. The only advice he offered was that my cursive capital C should have a larger loop at the top. He told me this one morning after listening to the class analyze a story of family loss we were reading aloud. I had been proud of the kids' comments – varied, genuinely felt, and insightful, I thought. My impatience at the handwriting critique flashed across my face, I'm sure.

As it happened it was his last visit. Over Christmas vacation a classroom opened up in the basement of Roberto Clemente. Mr. Marshall offered it to me, a chance to be in the main building. I knew the kids wanted to be closer to siblings and friends. I accepted the offer and arranged with some of the other teachers for a moving party over the holiday. Mr. Marshall himself showed up to help. We transported all the desks, the "Language is a Bridge" poster, the bookshelves, the American flag, and the tin of crayons to our new place. I was initially concerned about one serious flaw in the arrangement; there was no door to close us off from traffic in the hallway. The open doorway was next to the stairwell that everyone in the basement used to go up for lunch in the cafeteria. The saving grace was that the rest of the students on the floor were first and second graders, small enough to be respectful as they passed by. For some reason, no one ever made an effort to get a door hung to close off the room. We all grew accustomed to the sounds of the lunch-hour scuffling.

I had two Angels and one Jesus in the classroom, their names an indication of their parents' religious piety and love of the precious. There were Lupitas, Harrys, and Lisas, too. The first Angel was, in fact, angelic. He had light-brown hair and fair skin, as smooth as an alabaster cherub over a church altar. His face had that same kind of delicate poignancy. His comportment was that of someone twenty years his senior. He stood erect beside his desk during the pledge of allegiance, after which he sat to it carefully, like a journeyman returning to his craft. He was respected by his peers, but treated as somewhat apart from them, not so much aloof as remotely called to other things. I developed a deep affection for him, touched by his constant desire to please. I was careful not to show it, but I'm sure he sensed it, indeed, fed on it, much as I had fed on the same from Sr. Lilian.

The second Angel was a frequent discipline problem. He was pudgy, raven-haired, usually in need of washing, antsy, and unable to sit still. On occasion he had fits of temper that required me to physically stand next to him and, a few times, to constrain him to avoid harm to others. I was never told the rules of engagement for a teacher viz-a-viz a nine-year-old. Disciplinary decisions were left up to the teacher alone, challengeable on occasion by an angry parent threatening a lawsuit; the administration laid low in such events. I knew force was to be kept to a minimum and that the only defensible force was steady restraint. In fairness, the second Angel seemed to dread his own outbursts. He would almost apologize as the fits set in, throwing himself down on the floor in exasperation, angry at himself as much as anyone else. The class gave him space in those moments. I don't think anyone held him totally responsible. They recognized that something came over him and that it would pass. My standing nearby seemed to calm everyone. He picked quarrels to create a pretext for his fits. The root of most fights lay in the aggrieved party's assertion that Angel "menshed my mother," a Spanglish coinage that was the most powerful weapon in the arsenal of provocations. The root of the phrase was "mentioned my mother," the inference being mentioned in a disparaging way. I never actually heard a mensh-attack in real-time. It may have been a mere "your mother," said in defiance or as a dare. Once one's mother was menshed, however, budding manhood demanded a response. Non-combative by nature, I was always taken aback by the ferocity with which the calmest, most mature of the boys would explode. There was sometimes a more immediate, more closely contingent offense that lay behind the menshing and subsequent bantam fight, but the second Angel was not above menshing the mother of a randomly chosen bystander.

The girls, in large part, ignored the boys' fights. I don't know how they coped with such things outside the classroom, but they knew fights wouldn't be tolerated inside the room. They had a kind of communal way of sitting them out, nodding and chatting among themselves, diagnosing causation, and turning to me with a benign look that said, "we know you're on this."

There were a few frightened girls whose homework illustrated their fears and uncertainties, their very reluctance to fully express themselves, even on butcher-paper. Those girls quickly moved away from the skirmishes, seeking safety at the periphery of the room. They turned to me for a nod, an acknowledgment that things were under control, something the others didn't seem to require.

Over the months, we came to learn all these things about each other the way the young do, alert to signals, eager for predictability, contented by routine. I navigated my way as one of them, learning what was needed, what I could provide, and most achingly, what I could not. I could bring order to a room, make the class laugh, and provoke discussions. I could repeat and rephrase until I found the right simile, the right metaphor to bring everyone along with a new concept, a new skill. I could be trusted to get the joke if something amusing passed through the classroom. I could talk of dreams, of right and wrong, of other ways of looking at things.

I could not cure the second Angel of his fits, or satisfy the first Angel's bottomless need for approval. I was more hindrance than help when a nine-year-old girl sat silently weeping in shame as her first menstrual period came on. I would be cued in by the calmer, wiser girls to recognize the signs and deftly facilitate a dignified exit. Nor could I provide the order some of the children so sorely needed in their home lives or on the streets beyond the walls of Robert Clemente. I could not enkindle the familial love some sorely lacked in their nurturing.

What is required of a teacher is that he (or she) stand his ground and say, "Know this, class," and "Know that, class." After a while, he comes to feel as if he somehow partially represents knowledge itself, as if he were there to assert, "I am the knower, the one who knows things." And he can come to believe that he knows many things. It is a seductive thing, teaching.

The children colluded with me as we solved arithmetic problems and read about the underlying principles that made our world – in which two languages sat side by side – a wonder to contemplate. They beamed their curiosity and sense of trust in my presence. They manifested their happiness in our fourth-grade corner of a school basement there in Newark's North Ward. There was the thin but always impenetrable wall – the taboo – that prevented the exchange of hugs and kisses natural to such feelings. It was a discipline that made our bond all the more precious. Childhood provides a natural courage and resilience necessary to ride out its tumult of rapid, constant change and growth. I watched the innate aplomb with which they navigated those, and I grew steady in my own path by seeing them do so.

Seven

A BODY IS HELD TOGETHER BY FLESH, BONE, AND ROUTINE. On school days I rose out of bed and dressed in the dark. I left the house on Jefferson Street and walked along an empty Ferry Street. I bought an espresso and a roll at the same diner every morning, the only one open at that hour. The waitress was from Uruguay. She sipped yerba maté while Lou Reed, on the jukebox, told us to take a walk on the wild side. At least he told me; the woman behind the counter spoke no English. Rain or wet snow meant some heedless motorist between Penn Station and the bus stop on Broad Street would probably soak me thoroughly by boating through the standing water. I would then sit in soggy pants on the bus to the North Ward. I would get off at Roberto Clemente and wade through the piercing, raucously gleeful wall of sound that rises from an elementary school, a noise that washes over everyone and everything. Even adults time their conversations to be heard above it.

In the evenings, I settled back into a second-hand Barcalounger with its footrest raised, grading essay-question papers, one-pagers piled in my lap, each needing attentive correction and notes of encouragement. The radio was tuned to WNEW as the conspiratorial voice of Johnathan Schwartz purred from it, reading from Joan Didion or riffing on urban life, interspersing those with cuts from LPs of musicians I would never have discovered on my own. Sometimes the black-and-white portable television, volume turned down, mimed war reporting from Hanoi and clips of Watergate hearings from D.C. I was content enough with this routine and found comfort maintaining it.

I had the diversion of friends, too. I visited Jess in her apartment in Bellevue. John sometimes stayed in the back bedroom, not so much avoiding me but collecting himself, pulling himself together after the exposure to war, contending with re-entry and all that entailed. Jess and I visited her parents' house in North Bergen, where her mother fed us exquisite Italian meals and eagerly sought my concurrence on all the things her daughter should be doing. Gabriel García Márquez's *One Hundred Years of Solitude* was sweeping the English-reading world. Jessica enrolled in a course on The Modern Latin-American Novel at Montclair College, and I tagged along to audit the lectures. I discovered the labyrinthine worlds of Julio Cortázar and Luís Borges.

Sometimes Malcolm and I would sit on the train overpass above Jefferson Street next to my row of houses. We'd bring a bottle of Mount Gay rum or a couple of joints, and we would inventory life's absurdities, the inherent contradictions that later in life become demystified, rendered into simple, familiar signposts.

There were seldom any trains on those tracks, and Jefferson Street bore little traffic. One of our amusements after a wasted afternoon was to try to move Malcolm's car from one side of the street and parallel park it on the other side in a single U-turn. The street was always too narrow. The best we ever managed was what we called a K-turn, which required a shift from forward to reverse and back to forward again. We found each failed attempt hilarious. I reveled in the shared laughter, in the repetitive inanities.

There was a Catholic church in the center of the Iron Bound, standing at the upper end of a formal park that covered a few city blocks. I remember it as a classic 19th-Century building, cruciformed and steepled, home to an Italian-American parish. The church doesn't appear on my Google Maps search now. I would occasionally sit in its pews during Mass with a now somewhat blurry sense of where I was, or when. It would have been on Saturday evenings, for the Vigil Mass. The specifics of when or where don't matter, really. They made little difference then. Why I was there at all was a bit unclear as well. I suppose I felt I belonged there, that we all belonged there in that time and place. We belonged with each other, seeking spiritual sustenance, however thin the wafer, however infrequent the meal, however tenuous the belief.

Jack moved to Washington before I moved to Jefferson Street, but he came back regularly to visit his mom in Summit, bringing his dirty laundry with him. He stopped by sometimes and extolled the virtues of life in D.C. "Better weather, for one," he'd say. I had gone down with him on the train a couple of times before he moved there, and Jack urged me to come down again on weekends to see if I didn't agree. He was right, of course, especially when the seasons changed; the weather always seemed better there. For my part, I was struck by how much more relaxed race relations were, at least in the places I frequented. Jack had an efficiency apartment in Glover Park, an almost exclusively white neighborhood then, above Georgetown, across Rock Creek from the city core. Georgetown had the appeal of quirky stores, good restaurants, and open spaces along the canal and the river, but I soon came to feel it was for tourists. DuPont Circle was a much more interesting place, with alternative bookstores, head shops, and gay bars. The gay scene was open, interracial, and unapologetic.

On Easter break, Jessica and I flew to Puerto Rico and drove down to Boquerón, a small village on the Caribbean coast. I had grown my hair long enough that I could tie it back behind my head. The sudden heat, after New Jersey's bracing winter, left me annoyed with its length and with the heat and perspiration it trapped against my head and temples. We spent a few listless evenings watching through the slats in the pier of our motel as garfish fed in the shallow water below us. We read the instructions and contact information printed in small type on our toiletry products aloud to each other. When I returned to Newark, I went to a barber in the Ironbound and had my hair cut short. The gesture felt momentous, but the barber made no comment on it.

I continued with the coursework at Newark State Teachers College. As part of the requirements for one class I was to submit a lesson plan using handmade teaching aids. I brought large, brightly colored wooden beads with holes bored through them and a spool of pliable wire to construct models of simple molecules for a planned science unit. It was a knock-off of a science fair project I once put together in high school. I kept the components in a box in the back of the classroom, tinkering with them now and then. But the course was no more engaging than the Education 101 class I dropped at Ball State. The time and distance required for travel each night became more and more onerous. I finished class at nine PM and had to walk the length of campus, then to the center of Elizabeth to catch a bus home to Penn Station. There was no commuter train at that hour. I was strategic, waiting at a bus stop near White Castle, a hamburger outlet where I could finally get something to eat. I was often the sole passenger on the bus back to Newark. I got to know the driver, who indulgently looked the other way while I ate my burger. He was a short, middle-aged white man whose grandparents had fled Newark, "when, you know, it started turning."

It was on that bus one night, more than halfway through the spring term, that I determined I was going to leave Newark. Just like my road-to-Damascus moment in Valencia, it was abruptly clear that I was running in place, living out a routine that didn't fit me, didn't promise me a better situation if I would just bear down and endure it. I still couldn't make sense of the educational theories highlighted in my textbooks. I still felt fear on the dark streets where I had to transfer. I had found no community that shared my assumptions about the world, whose customs and ethos meshed with the habits of thought that carried me thus far. I decided I would move to Washington. I knew young people there from across the country were carving out professional career paths for themselves, relatively unencumbered by neighborhood turf and territorial taboo. I came to understand that I wanted to work among other adults.

I never went back to the college to collect the loose atomic detritus in that box. I notified Mr. Marshall in the principal's office that I was not returning in the fall. I told Lo Biondo, the butcher, I was vacating the apartment at the end of June. Lourdes approached me shortly after my announcement with an offer to appoint me to a bilingual coordinator position. It meant a good bit more money. I surprised myself by responding that if I were to stay, it would have been to remain in the classroom, not take up an administrative position.

I knew that saying goodbye to my students would be difficult. I wanted to model strength and maintain dignity through our last day together but feared succumbing to tears. I had come to care for them deeply. I devised a plan. I announced I would hand out final report cards one-on-one, in private. I would stand just outside the doorway-without-a-door and call them out, one at a time. They were to have everything ready they needed to take with them. El maestro would hand over their report card, that final, precious paper exchange between us. The privacy mitigated the tears. One by one they exited, smiling, accepting both the card and a quick embrace. I wept as discreetly as I could. I had watched them blossom, and in turn, they had watched me mature. The aplomb with which they embraced their circumstances showed me the strength I had failed to see in myself. I had carried a wounded child within me for years. I was ready to release him.

Eight

I DECIDED TO TAKE THE SUMMER OFF. I WANTED TO VISIT MY
family, mend a few fences, reconnect. I wasn't seeking anything
specific. In the Biblical story the forgiving father, seeing his prodigal
son return, ordered his servants to slay the fatted calf. I didn't
see myself as a prodigal son, but perhaps as a self-forgiven son.
I wanted to go home, not to a fatted calf, but to a reconciliation
that might align with how I had reconciled things within myself.
I was tired, too, and needed to recharge. I phoned Mom and Dad
to tell them I would visit them in Michigan. My plan was to pass
through Indiana on my way and stop in to see Lee Ann.

Jack said I could stay with him in D.C. in the fall until I got
on my feet. I took him up on his offer, and true to his word, he
showed up at my apartment the last weekend of June with his huge

Pontiac sedan, a 1960's model with bench seats, incredibly wide and long. He drove it through city traffic with a slow aggression, like a tank in occupied territory. We crammed into it everything I would be taking with me to Washington. I left Muncie with a trunk and left Valencia with a backpack. It required an over-sized sedan to leave Newark.

I spent a week with Lee Ann. I had come to see her in a different light. Her instinctive generosity when I was stranded in Ft. Wayne, her open anxiety about her engagement, our tearful farewell in the sacristy on the day of her wedding - she still in her gown and me bidding farewell, leaving for Spain – all this had drawn us closer. Teenage angst was behind us. She knew she, too, had not fit the role expected of her. I witnessed this in the same wordless way I saw the world through her eyes in the sandbox, long ago.

Ron and Lee Ann lived outside Indianapolis in an apartment complex just off Route 40, the Lincoln Highway. They were in the blossom stage of a marriage that would ultimately disappoint both of them, one that wouldn't survive. The week before I arrived, they'd gone spelunking. The idea of my sister being lowered on ropes into a dark cave was quite hilarious to me. But she seemed happy, and Ron seemed happy. They had a large, constantly bounding dog kept outside most of the time. I slept on a sofa bed in their living room. One night, while I lay in bed, Ron went out the back door to empty a bin. When he came back in, the dog followed him, sensed my presence on the sofa bed, and jumped on top of me, holding me down with his paws and growling murderously. Ron interceded for my safety.

Dad and Mom were settling into their now-finished house in the Hiawatha National Forest. It, too, had a private lake, this one formed naturally. They were still young; neither of them had yet reached fifty. Dad was as enthusiastic about this new venture as he had been years earlier with his move to Springwood, that earlier Eden. He had thrown himself into clearing land on the north side of the lake and overseeing the house's construction. The modern, wood-paneled split-level sat at the end of a long, gravel lane running in from Forest Highway 13. It boasted fireplaces, balconies, picture windows, and a sunken bathtub off the master bedroom. Mom had all the modern conveniences in her kitchen – double oven, open-flame grill, built-in microwave – and she eagerly displayed them for me. A long row of over-the-counter windows opened to hundreds of acres of deep forest. She had taken up collecting agate stones, which she polished to a high shine in an electric tumbler. She knew all the spots to look for them. She and I drove to them on scenic day-trips.

David was in school in Munising, some 20 miles away. Mom said he was doing well there. He appeared fully outfitted for life in the north woods, with his kayak tethered to a pier at the shoreline and snowshoes hanging on the basement wall. He stored a snowsuit and helmet for snowmobiling in the garage. But he was in the nether regions of adolescence, accustomed to being on his own. David's hand had slipped away from not just mine, but another brother and two sisters over the years, one at a time. He was as terse toward my awkward efforts at re-connecting as he had been on our intermittent phone calls since I left, conversations that were deeply unsatisfying. I knew the age gap and separate paths we walked accounted for the distance, and I felt powerless to dispel it.

Dad was busily engaged in local politics, working on an associate's congressional race. He was also investing in commercial property in Munising with proceeds from the buy-out from his business. He kept a full schedule away from the house but occasionally brought me along for a tour of what he called "his town."

He introduced me to a local banker, who asked how "a country boy" like me could survive the East Coast. I said Midwesterners could survive anywhere. Dad's face suggested he thought my answer harsh, impolitic. Perhaps, but I wasn't to be patronized.

I spent most of the first week of my visit following Mom around, remarking on how nice she had the place looking, how lush the shag carpet looked. She had installed bug screens on a cupola near the lakeshore where the deer flies were voracious. I complimented her on the electric fountain nearby, its whirring pump muffling the sound of falling water.

They kept a small-cabined pleasure boat moored in Munising, on Lake Superior. Dad talked about showing it to me, about giving me a water-borne tour of the Pictured Rocks and Grand Island. The tour remained a several-times-postponed event that had to wait until he got a few more things done for the campaign. When we finally boarded the boat and were preparing to cast off, Mom muttered under her breath that he hadn't take it out in ages.

"I don't know why he bought the damn thing."

I was sure it was for her, I said; Dad knew how she loved being near water. I reminisced about the speedboat he bought for her 33rd birthday. Dad had named it Sweet Thirty-Three. We towed it up to Traverse City on our annual summer vacations, in the days before we moved to Springwood.

"That was before he tired of it."

The weather those few weeks was splendid, not always a guaranteed thing in the Upper Peninsula. David and I paddled a canoe through a chain of lakes connected by rivers. We rolled out of the canoe from time to time to swim in the clean, clear, shallow waters. Some days I wandered the pine and birch woods behind the house, lost in reveries until the morning I came across bear scat. That concerned me enough to curtail further wandering.

I drove into Munising on occasion, eager for something to do, volunteering to pick up what was needed at the store. In the evenings, the cocktail hour – as always – played out against the background of the evening news.

News those days was all about the Watergate investigation. Throughout the previous summer, the country had been riveted by Sam Ervin, Howard Baker, and John Dean in the Senate hearings. In October, public interest peaked again during what would come to be called the Saturday Night Massacre. Details of Nixon's malfeasance and obstruction never faded far into the background and, just as I arrived, the Supreme Court ruled unanimously that audiotapes Nixon had secretly recorded must be released. I felt affirmed. I blamed Nixon for the drawn-out, senseless war in Vietnam, his constantly shifting justifications for it, all the mindless death and destruction. I saw his stonewalling Congress over the break-in at Democratic headquarters as part of the same pattern. The court ruling put him in deep jeopardy, which pleased me. When I heard it on the television, I barked out a loud, "Good!"

Dad growled. "What's so good about it?"

I had never heard my father speak in that tone. It was immediate and full-throated. I was stunned to hear its intensity. I stared at him, blinking a few times, unable to mount a cogent response. He was serious. He wanted an answer. He wanted a fight.

"They've been trying to tear this good man down for years. Why? What has he done? Where is the crime?"

I stammered, recognizing that he expected me to speak, afraid that if I did, he would unleash his pent-up rage – rage at the social upheavals he resented, the cultural shifts he denigrated, the way he saw me as a perfidious, willing partner to those things. There were other layers to his anger, too: his sense of diminished relevance now that he no longer ran a large business; the tedium of boating aimlessly across the same lakes; the cocktails started earlier in the day than was prudent. His face was crimson. His voice cracked. I didn't fear him physically; I feared the boundlessness of his rage.

"He has lied about everything, over and over again," I asserted.

"But what did he do wrong? Where was the crime?"

I was too intimidated to sustain a reasoned counterattack. My father's anger had me off balance. I grappled for coherence. *I have no mouth, and I must scream.*

Everyone sat in silence for a few moments. Mom announced that dinner, still in the oven, was ready. She stood from her chair, crossed the shag carpet, turned off the television, and went into the kitchen.

A tacit truce settled over the next few days, shored up by our avoiding political talk. I was going to Washington soon, so by extension, the topic of my immediate future was also off-limits. We discussed the present with zen-like probity during subsequent cocktail hours. Downstairs, a television was left on for long periods in the den. Dad shut himself in there in the afternoons. When he was not there, I watched it. He and I separately slithering like penitents into and out of a confessional, ensuring we were alone and not overheard. The days took on a deadened, post-hoc quality. Crisis in Washington was imminent. Because of our TV monitoring, we knew a few days later that the President had scheduled an address to the country. We sat upstairs, solemn and silent, as Nixon announced, "Therefore, I shall resign the presidency, effective at noon tomorrow."

Dad sighed. "There you go. I hope you're happy."

The news came both as a shock and an inevitability. I had the fleeting thought that, in some way, I was somehow at fault. I knew, at the same time, that wasn't true. Anyway, it was done now. When I got to Washington, the war would still be going on, but Nixon would no longer be waging it.

On the evening before Dad was to drive me down to Escanaba for the flight to Milwaukee and on to Washington, I found myself outside, alone with him. We stood in the slant of golden light that colors the long summer evenings in northern latitudes. I don't remember what purpose – whether intuited or explicit – prompted us to walk down the drive away from the house. We passed under the white-birch canopy, ferns at our feet, the air pungent with pine resin, and the sound of lapping waves breaking at the lake edge. I sensed that the catharsis of Nixon's resignation had created a moment, a rare moment that I couldn't let pass by.

"There's something I have to say, Dad."

I hadn't rehearsed this and feared it wouldn't come out properly. I didn't have the right language. "Gay" had no currency for Dad in those years. "Queer" was too harsh for me to bear saying, too harsh for him to hear. "Homosexual" sounded clinical and evasive, and I wanted him to know more about me than that.

"Ricky and I were very close, Dad."

Pause.

"I don't mean just as friends. I felt toward him the way you feel about Mom."

It was the best I could do. He knew that Ricky had long since moved back to Florida, that I was talking about a specific situation that was safely behind us. I hoped my phrasing had the grace of being indirect, tactful to the ear. I saw he knew what I intended, even if I failed to name it. A stone lifted off my chest. I was shaking slightly, but I could breathe now. For a few seconds, I waited for him to say that everything was alright, that he had known for years, that he was proud of me anyway, that he understood. He remained silent for another long moment, respectfully so. I will always remember that respectful silence, as if he, too, was searching for the discreet thing.

"Don't tell your mother."

My eyes lost their focus in their sockets.

"Promise me you won't tell her. It will break her heart."

Springwood

Springwood

Jurgen

The Luci Family

Epilogue

WHEN MY PARENTS MOVED TO THE UPPER PENINSULA, THEY sold Springwood to Walter, the man who felled our trees, who helped us build the lake. I went back there only once after that, making the trip with my sister Lee Ann on a rare visit to the States from my home overseas. Fifty years had elapsed since I had seen the place. By then, both Mom and Dad were dead.

Walter had gone on to raise his own family there, becoming a recluse over the years. Eventually, his wife left him, and it was commonly understood that he was largely estranged from his children. But he greeted us warmly on the sweltering September afternoon of our visit, still proud that for decades Springwood had been his. We sat on the frayed webbing of folding aluminum lawn chairs set out on the patio that I helped build, and we talked about the days of clearing the woods for the lake. Looking into the house through the front window, I could see that Walter was a hoarder. He apologized for not being able to invite us in. I said that I understood.

Lee Ann and I, awash in nostalgia, excused ourselves by asking Walter if he minded if we walked down the path leading to the lake's nearest shoreline. When we reached it, we saw that its surface was encrusted with pond scum. I suspected that was due to the run-off from so many years of chemical fertilizer in the neighboring fields. The water level was low, too low to rise to the level of the spill-way, so it sat stagnant and still. Its surface had a strong, unpleasant odor to it. Several feet above the shoreline, set in a grove of beech trees, Walter had built – by hand, no doubt – a classic log cabin. Its door was unlocked, and we stepped inside. It was one large room walled in dark, naked logs chinked with white filler. It stood empty, save for a few nutshells left by rodents and cobwebs no one had disturbed for years.

It was a melancholy place. I felt no connection to it. I did not know this cabin. It wasn't yet there when I moved away from Springwood, when the lake was still fresh. A torpor hovered over it that afternoon, a foreign thing.

I kept the vow of silence that my father extracted from me that evening in Michigan, the day before I went to Washington. I never once spoke to my mother about my sexuality. There were times over the years when I saw her squirm under the silence in which we all conspired. There were times it felt like a foolish sham. Of course, she knew. A mother always knows. But we never spoke of it. In rare moments – of mirth or irony – an oblique reference slipped out, but the truth remained cloaked, unuttered. She conjured half-truths to signal that was how she wanted things, misremembering the number of bedrooms in my old apartment, forgetting the names of past lovers I had obliquely introduced to her. In later life, on my dutiful visits back to Indiana, she and I took great pleasure in our long chats and small-talk. We also struggled over what, actually, we could speak of, what we could pleasantly reminisce. There were so many stories I could not share. I became adept at using the false "I" instead of "we" when remembering events. I kept buried so many enthusiasms, so much loss, and grief.

My father patrolled the borders of that silence as long as he lived. He would set the scene when recounting where I had gone, what I had achieved, by always casting me as a lone agent. In a private conversation with him, the two of us sitting together in the basement where he was permitted to smoke, I sighed once that this secret took so much out of me. He displayed annoyance, punching his cigarette butt into a coffee can kept for that purpose. He asked what being gay had to do with anything. I stayed silent. I did not ask him what his love for my mother had to do with anything. One afternoon, a few years into the AIDS epidemic, he inquired out of what sounded to be mere inquisitiveness, if I had lost many friends to it.

"Several," I replied, then abruptly changed the subject. Silence is a salve, too.

I remembered that moment and the friends and lovers I had lost, those I never spoke to Dad about, as I stood in Walter's log cabin those many years later. And I was suddenly struck with a pang of gratitude. Gratitude for my memories of the beech grove where the path led down to the water. Gratitude for my youth in Springwood. With my sister standing next to me, lifted by the emotion, I thought of all the people who had walked with me on the path that led me out of there, that long path that led to the life I dared live, the men I dared love, and the room I made for